The
Weather
for Poetry

The Weather for Poetry

Essays, Reviews, and
Notes on Poetry, 1977–81

DONALD HALL

Ann Arbor   The University of Michigan Press

Library of Congress Cataloging in Publication Data

Hall, Donald, 1928–
   The weather for poetry.

   (Poets on poetry)
   Includes bibliographical references.
   1. Poetry—Addresses, essays, lectures. 2. American
poetry—20th century—History and criticism—Addresses,
essays, lectures. 3. English poetry—20th century—
History and criticism—Addresses, essays, lectures.
I. Title.   II. Series
PS3515.A3152W4 1982   811'.009   82-8544
ISBN 0-472-06340-5   AACR2

For Sharon Giannotta

Acknowledgments

Grateful acknowledgment is made to the following publishers and journals for permission to reprint copyrighted material written by Donald Hall:

American Poetry Review for "Adding Eden On" which first appeared as a "Knock, Knock" column, *American Poetry Review,* 1976; and for "Russell Edson," *American Poetry Review,* 1977.

Atlantic Monthly for "Edson, Bidart, Broumas, Creeley" which first appeared as "Other Voices, Other Tones," *Atlantic Monthly,* October, 1977; and for "Robert Frost Corrupted," *Atlantic Monthly,* March, 1982.

Aquarius magazine for "John Heath-Stubbs" which first appeared in a special issue of *Aquarius,* no. 9, 1978.

Beacon Press and Poetry East for "Robert Bly" which first appeared as "Poetry Food" in *Of Solitude and Silence: Writings on Robert Bly,* edited by Richard Jones and Kate Daniels. Copyright © 1981 by Poetry East. Reprinted with permission of Poetry East and Beacon Press.

Field for "Robert Francis," *Field,* 1982; and for "Notes on the Image: Body and Soul," *Field,* 1981.

Georgia Review for "Robert Lowell and the Literature Industry," *Georgia Review,* Spring, 1978; and for "Poetry, Pop, and the Golden Age," *Georgia Review,* Winter, 1981.

Kentucky Review for "To Imitate Yeats," *Kentucky Review,* 1980.

Richard Kostelanetz for "Note on Innovation," 1981.

Nation for "Adrienne Rich," *Nation,* 1978; and for "Thom Gunn, Seamus Heaney," *Nation,* 1979. Copyright 1978, 1979 *Nation* magazine, The Nation Associates, Inc.

New England Review for "Richard Eberhart" which first appeared as "The Internal Cape" in *Richard Eberhart: A Celebration,* © 1980 by *New England Review.*

New Republic for "David Wagoner" which first appeared as "In Broken Country," *New Republic,* November 24, 1979.

New Review for "Letter from New Hampshire," *New Review,* 1978.

New York Times for essays on: Kenneth Rexroth, November 30, 1980; Archibald MacLeish, July 9, 1978; Robert Giroux, January 6, 1980; James Laughlin, August 23, 1981; Wendell Berry, September 25, 1977; C. H. Sisson, December 18, 1977; Basil Bunting, July 2, 1978; Robert Penn Warren, November 8, 1981; Ferris's Thomas, November 13, 1977; Tomlinson's House of Memoir, March 1, 1980; Richard Hugo, March 25, 1979.

Ohio Review for "Two Critics," *Ohio Review* 19, no. 25 (Winter, 1981); and for "Two Poets Named Robert," *Ohio Review* 18, no. 3 (Fall, 1977).

Parnassus: Poetry in Review for "The Nation of Poets," *Parnassus,* 1977; and for "Reading the English," *Parnassus,* 1979.

Poetry for "Geoffrey Hill" which first appeared as "Naming

Contents

An Introductory Note

This book collects most of the prose I have written about poetry during the past five years—reviews, articles, profiles, notes, and one interview. Because I support myself by freelance writing, many of these essays were undertaken to boil the pot. In times other than ours, poets have traditionally made a living by literary journalism. I am not sure that such work helps people write poems—neither do office hours and committee meetings—but I remain grateful for many essays that writers of the past wrote to pay the bills. I do not suggest that I belong in his company if I mention T. S. Eliot, whose best essays were written for the *Times Literary Supplement* to supplement a small income when his wife was ill. If Eliot had occupied the Walt Whitman Chair of Creative Writing at the University of America, we might never have heard about tradition and the individual talent. I wish more poets would support themselves by writing prose.

The first section here reprints pieces in which I have tried for generalization. The brief second section collects notes on six poets written for magazines which celebrated them; it is a pleasure to toast old friends. In the third section I gather reviews of poetry and criticism, most of them brief; because editors approach reviewers—rarely does it happen the other way around—the selection of books reviewed reveals little. The final section assembles notes on poetry, many of which hover at poetry's peripheries, looking into fashion, reputation, and the marketplace. I do not find such subjects trivial;

nothing is alien to the writing of poems—neither politics nor society nor economics nor grants nor public attitudes nor private convictions. If I attend to the social weather for poetry, I hope to investigate the conditions under which poetry happens.

I have many people to thank. Harvey Shapiro at the *New York Times Book Review* has commissioned interviews with publishers and another half-dozen of the pieces included here; two articles appeared in the *American Poetry Review*, where my editor is Steve Berg; Herb Leibowitz of *Parnassus* suggested two review-articles; I am grateful to Wayne Dodd of the *Ohio Review*, to John Gross of the *Times Literary Supplement*, to John Frederick Nims of *Poetry*, and to Stanley Lindberg of the *Georgia Review*.

Jane Kenyon regularly shames me out of my most euphuistic constructions. Linda Howe has researched and checked a hundred matters, most invaluably providing me statistics on Lathem's Frost. As well, I wish to thank the friends who have argued with me.

Donald Hall

I
Generalization

Kenneth Rexroth

(1981)

In December of this year, Kenneth Rexroth will turn seventy-five. Among his lesser accomplishments, he has appeared as a character in two famous novels: James T. Farrell put him in *Studs Lonigan*, a kid named Kenny who works in a drug store; with more creative denomination, Jack Kerouac called him Rheinhold Cacoethes in *The Dharma Bums*, that 1958 Beat Generation testament, where he is the figure we recognize: anarchist, leader of San Francisco's literary community, and poet.

For decades he has written lines like these, setting human life in a context of stone:

> Our campfire is a single light
> Amongst a hundred peaks and waterfalls.
> The manifold voices of falling water
> Talk all night.
> Wrapped in your down bag
> Starlight on your cheeks and eyelids
> Your breath comes and goes
> In a tiny cloud in the frosty night.
> Ten thousand birds sing in the sunrise.
> Ten thousand years revolve without change.
> All this will never be again.

One thing that is without change is that everything changes. Like many of the greatest poets—Wordsworth, Keats, Frost, Eliot—Rexroth returns continually to one inescapable perception. Maybe this elegiac vision of permanent stone and vanishing flesh derives from the great private event of his middle years—the death of his first wife Andree in 1940 after thirteen years of marriage. Her name and image return decades after her death.

But Rexroth is not limited to elegy; he is the most erotic of modern American poets, and one of the most political. The great public event of his young life was the execution of Sacco and Vanzetti. Years after the electrocution he wrote "Climbing Milestone Mountain":

> In the morning
> We swam in the cold transparent lake, the blue
> Damsel flies on all the reeds like millions
> Of narrow metallic flowers, and I thought
> Of you behind the grille in Dedham, Vanzetti,
> Saying, "Who would ever have thought we would make this
>   history?"
> Crossing the brilliant mile-square meadow
> Illuminated with asters and cyclamen,
> The pollen of the lodgepole pines drifting
> With the shifting wind over it and the blue
> And sulphur butterflies drifting with the wind,
> I saw you in the sour prison light, saying,
> "Goodbye comrade."

In Rexroth's poems the natural world, unchanged and changing, remains background to history and love, to enormity and bliss.

When a young man, Rexroth was a Wobbly and studied Marxism as a member of a John Reed Club. Later he moved into anarchism and pacifism, ideologies which his mature philosophic poems support with passion and argument. His politics of the individual separates him from the mass of Americans—and obviously from Stalinists of the left—and yet joins him to all human beings; it is a politics of love—and Rexroth is the poet of devoted eroticism. "When We With Sappho" begins by translating from a Greek fragment, then continues into a personal present:

". . . about the cool water
the wind sounds through sprays
of apple, and from the quivering leaves
slumber pours down . . ."

We lie here in the bee filled, ruinous
Orchard of a decayed New England farm,
Summer in our hair, and the smell
Of summer in our twined bodies,
Summer in our mouths, and summer
In the luminous, fragmentary words
Of this dead Greek woman.
Stop reading. Lean back. Give me your mouth.
Your grace is as beautiful as sleep.
You move against me like a wave
That moves in sleep.
Your body spreads across my brain
Like a bird filled summer;
Not like a body, not like a separate thing,
But like a nimbus that hovers
Over every other thing in all the world.
Lean back. You are beautiful,
As beautiful as the folding
Of your hands in sleep.

This passionate tenderness has not diminished as Rexroth
has aged. His latest book includes the beautiful "Love Poems
of Marichiko," which he calls a translation from the Japanese; however, a recent bibliography lists the translation of
Rexroth's Marichiko *into* Japanese: in the middle of his
eighth decade, the poet has written his most erotic poem.

His work for forty years has moved among his passions for
the flesh, for human justice, and for the natural world. He
integrates these loves in the long poems, and sometimes in
briefer ones. "The Signature of All Things" may be the best
of all.

My head and shoulders, and my book
In the cool shade, and my body
Stretched bathing in the sun, I lie

Reading beside the waterfall—
Boehme's "Signature of all Things."
Through the deep July day the leaves
Of the laurel, all the colors
Of gold, spin down through the moving
Deep laurel shade all day. They float
On the mirrored sky and forest
For a while, and then, still slowly
Spinning, sink through the crystal deep
Of the pool to its leaf gold floor.
The saint saw the world as streaming
In the electrolysis of love.
I put him by and gaze through shade
Folded into shade of slender
Laurel trunks and leaves filled with sun.
The wren broods in her moss domed nest.
A newt struggles with a white moth
Drowning in the pool. The hawks scream,
Playing together on the ceiling
Of heaven. The long hours go by.
I think of those who have loved me,
Of all the mountains I have climbed,
Of all the seas I have swum in.
The evil of the world sinks.
My own sin and trouble fall away
Like Christian's bundle, and I watch
My forty summers fall like falling
Leaves and falling water held
Eternally in summer air.

———————

Deer are stamping in the glades,
Under the full July moon.
There is a smell of dry grass
In the air, and more faintly,
The scent of a far off skunk.
As I stand at the wood's edge,
Watching the darkness, listening
To the stillness, a small owl
Comes to the branch above me,
On wings more still than my breath.
When I turn my light on him,

His eyes glow like drops of iron,
And he perks his head at me,
Like a curious kitten.
The meadow is bright as snow.
My dog prowls the grass, a dark
Blur in the blur of brightness.
I walk to the oak grove where
The Indian village was once.
There, in blotched and cobwebbed light
And dark, dim in the blue haze,
Are twenty Holstein heifers,
Black and white, all lying down,
Quietly together, under

The huge trees rooted in the graves.
When I dragged the rotten log
From the bottom of the pool,
It seemed heavy as stone.
I let it lie in the sun
For a month; and then chopped it
Into sections, and split them
For kindling, and spread them out
To dry some more. Late that night,
After reading for hours,
While moths rattled at the lamp—
The saints and the philosophers
On the destiny of man—
I went out on my cabin porch,
And looked up through the black forest
At the swaying islands of stars.
Suddenly I saw at my feet,
Spread on the floor of night, ingots
Of quivering phosphorescence,
And all about were scattered chips
Of pale cold light that was alive.

It is the strength of Rexroth's language that it proscribes
nothing. Starting from his reading in a Christian mystic
(Jacob Boehme, 1575–1624) he writes vividly of the natural
world, he refers to *Pilgrim's Progress*, he ranges out into the

universe of stars and focuses back upon the world of heifers and minute phosphorescent organisms. It is a poetry of experience and observation, of knowledge—and finally a poetry of wisdom. Nothing is alien to him.

Rexroth's characteristic rhythm moves from the swift and urgent to the slow and meditative, remaining continually powerful; his line hovers around three accents mostly deployed over seven or eight syllables. It is remarkable how little his line has changed over forty years, in a world of changing poetic fashion. This steadfastness or stubbornness recalls his patience over publication: he did not publish a book of poems until 1940, when he was thirty-five years old, although he had been writing since the early twenties. Later, in *The Art of Worldly Wisdom* (1949), he collected and published work from his cubist youth. Some had appeared in Louis Zukofsky's *An Objectivists' Anthology* (1932).

When we try to describe a poet's style, it can be useful to name starting points, but it is not easy with Kenneth Rexroth. He has said that Tu Fu was the greatest influence on him; fair enough, but there is no analogy between the Chinese line, end-stopped, with its count of characters, and Rexroth's run-on syllabics. In temperament and idea Rexroth is close to D. H. Lawrence, about whom he wrote his first major essay in 1947; but Lawrence's best poems take off from Whitman's line—and Rexroth's prosody is as far from Whitman's as it can get. Perhaps there is a bit of William Carlos Williams in his enjambed lines; maybe Louis Zukofsky. We could say, throwing up our hands, that he is a synthesis of Tu Fu, Lawrence, and Mallarmé. To an unusual extent, Rexroth has made Rexroth up.

He was born in Indiana in 1905 and spent most of the twenties in Chicago's Bohemia—poet, painter, and autodidact. Late in the decade he moved to San Francisco where he has lived much of his life, travelling down the coast to Santa Barbara only in 1968. He was the poet of San Francisco even before Robert Duncan, Philip Lamantia, Kenneth Patchen, and William Everson (Brother Antoninus). For decades he has advocated the poetry of the West, the elder literary figure of the city where poetry came to happen: Jack Spicer, Philip Whalen, Michael McClure, Lawrence Ferlinghetti, Lew Welch, Joanne Kyger. . . . His influence on the young is obvious, clearest in Gary Snyder who is worthy of his master. When young writers from the east arrived in the fifties—Allen Ginsberg, Jack Kerouac, Gregory Corso— they attended gatherings at Rexroth's house, and it was Rexroth who was catalyst for the 1955 Six Gallery reading that was the public birth of the Beat Generation.

Later, alliances altered. . . . Talking about Kenneth Rexroth, it is easy to wander into the history of factionalism, for he has been partisan, and few polemicists have had a sharper tongue. Inventor of *The Vaticide Review* (apparently *Partisan*, but it can stand in for all the quarterlies) he wrote in 1957 of poet-professors, "Ninety-nine per cent of them don't even exist but are androids manufactured from molds, cast from Randall Jarrell by the lost wax process." On the West Coast he has been a constant, grumpy presence. If the West has taken him for granted, the East has chosen to ignore him, perhaps because he has taken potshots at the provincial East forever and ever. The *Harvard Guide to Contemporary American Writing* (1979), which purports to cover the scene since 1945, will do for an example; the poetry critic quotes *none* of Rexroth's poetry but sputters about his "intemperate diatribes." Nor does Rexroth make the *New York Review of Books* shortlist of Approved Contemporaries.

Which is a pity, because he is better than anyone on it.

Taste is always a fool—the consensus of any moment; contemporary taste is the agreement of diffident people to quote each other's opinions. It reaffirms with complacency reputations which are perceived as immemorial, but which are actually constructed of rumor, laziness, and fear. As a writer ages and issues new volumes, he or she is reviewed as if the writing has remained the same, because it would require brains and effort to alter not only one's past opinion but the current professional assessment.

Perhaps the consensus of our moment, product largely of

the East and the academy, is especially ignorant, especially gullible. Or perhaps it is only—in the matter of Kenneth Rexroth—that the tastemakers are offended by Rexroth's morals. In fact they *ought* to be, because the ethical ideas that Rexroth puts forward with such acerbity are old-fashioned and individual—anathema to the suburban, Volvo-driving, conformist liberalism of the academy. He stands firm against technocracy and its bureaus, of which the university is as devoted an institution as General Motors. Rexroth's morals derive in part from Indiana before the First World War, in part from centuries of oriental thought, and in part from the radical non-Marxist thinking of late nineteenth century Europe.

He has not been wholly without attention. Morgan Gibson wrote a Twayne book about him which lists many reviews and articles about his poetry; a magazine called *The Ark* has recently devoted an issue to his work, with tributes from John Haines, W. S. Merwin, William Everson, the late James Wright, and many others. His reading aloud to music, which is superb and innovative, is available on several tapes and records.

James Laughlin of *New Directions* has been his loyal publisher, and keeps his poetry in print, including paperback editions of the *Collected Shorter Poems* (1967) and the *Collected Longer Poems* (1968). The long poems are five in number, including "The Phoenix and the Tortoise," a thirty-page meditative philosophic poem from the early forties, and "The Dragon and the Unicorn," from the second half of the same decade, which describes European travel and argues on a high level of abstraction. Best of the long poems is the latest, "The Heart's Garden, the Garden's Heart" (1967).

There are many volumes of prose: *An Autobiographical Novel* (1966), several collections of essays both literary and political, and a rapid, polemical literary history called *American Poetry in the Twentieth Century* (1971). There are volumes of translations; Rexroth has translated from Latin, Greek, French, German, Spanish, Swedish, but it is his work in Chinese and Japanese which is deservedly best known—

beginning with *One Hundred Poems from the Chinese* (1956). Certainly his verse translations remain among the best in an age of translation.

However, if we look for his best work, we look to his own poems. To end with, here is a lyric from his *New Poems* of 1974:

> *Your Birthday in the California Mountains*
>
> A broken moon on the cold water,
> And wild geese crying high overhead.
> The smoke of the campfire rises
> Toward the geometry of heaven—
> Points of light in the infinite blackness.
> I watch across the narrow inlet
> Your dark figure comes and goes before the fire.
> A loon cries out on the night bound lake.
> Then all the world is silent with the
> Silence of autumn waiting for
> The coming of winter. I enter
> The ring of firelight, bringing to you
> A string of trout for our dinner.
> As we eat by the whispering lake,
> I say, "Many years from now we will
> Remember this night and talk of it."
> Many years have gone by since then, and
> Many years again. I remember
> That night as though it was last night,
> But you have been dead for thirty years.

Archibald MacLeish

It is a fine day early in March. We drive west to Vermont, south along the Connecticut River on Route 91, past Bellows Falls and Brattleboro, into Massachusetts. One exit after Greenfield we turn off for Conway, a small farming town that has been home base for Archibald and Ada MacLeish since 1927. At the end of town, following directions, we find a road with the sign: NOT PASSABLE IN WINTER AND SPRING. The road climbs steeply between snowbanks, and when it reaches Uphill Farm it stops abruptly. The town plow has gone no farther. We park behind the house, stretch ourselves into the bright air, and the back door of the farmhouse opens: Archibald MacLeish bounds out—a tweed jacket over a sweater, brown beret tilted on his head, his step springy, eighty-five years old.

When MacLeish came to Harvard as Boylston Professor in 1949—at fifty-seven—I enrolled in his first writing class. A year after graduation I stopped at Uphill Farm for lunch. From time to time, over twenty-nine years, we had seen each other elsewhere, and we corresponded from time to time. I had not seen him for a dozen years. And he astonishes me. His body moves like that of a forty year old—and it does not relapse into age after creating an impression. His eyes are bright and quick. His skin shows something of years in the sun; under his chin eight decades have dropped a small sac of flesh; his hearing is faintly impaired; but his body is lithe and his eyes are strong. His voice astonishes me most: it has not aged; it seems not to have aged since its twenties. Now I remember that his voice was always youthful; it remains light, quick, flexible and with none of the crags and fissures and gutterals of age.

Archie escorts us to a small, sunny library at the front of the house, where Ada MacLeish awaits us. She too seems not to have changed in the last twelve years. When we sit, I ask about this house. Uphill Farm was built in 1771—the original saltbox—founded on stone ledge, its timber cut from its own hills. Somebody built onto it in 1826. A century afterwards, when the MacLeishes moved here, they added the large music room for Ada's singing.

Archie's connection with Conway begins even earlier. In 1892, the year he was born, his maternal grandfather, Elias Brewster Hilliard, became minister to Conway Congregationalists. Looking for a place to come back to from France, in 1927, they heard about Uphill Farm, and bought it with its 250 acres for $5,000. When they met the neighbors, Iz Boyden told Archie, "Your grandfather married me."

For fifty-one years, Uphill Farm has been the granite foundation of a busy life, and a loved place. "I've been wanting to write a poem about this house," says Archie. He shakes his head, aware of a houselife separate from his own. "I'm afraid to. Something would kick me downstairs."

We look out a window at the broad hill descending a wide white acreage toward town. At the back of the room near the fireplace, in a bookless patch of wall, there is a photograph of Earth from space—that familiar image of the late twentieth century, the green and isolated sphere that we are riders on. While Archie fetches some wine, we chat with Ada. Archie has brought up the subject of memory. Now Ada speaks lightly of the loss of short-term memory in one's eighties—this elegant warm woman—and of the strategic placement of notes reminding what's to be done.

MacLeish returns with a tray of Dubonnet and vermouth. I ask the MacLeishes about their winter. Until last year, they had wintered for almost thirty years in Antigua. Last year, when their borrowed Antigua house was unavailable, they tried Bermuda instead. It was all right, but a bit lonely; they missed Antigua acquaintances. (They made friends in Antigua despite their refusal to attend cocktail parties. "Twenty-six years in Antigua," says Archie, "and not one cocktail party.") They had made arrangements by telephone with the Club in Bermuda and were advised that one always dressed for dinner. Adaptable, they packed evening wear, only to sit night after night in the Club's dining room alone, two old and handsome people splendidly dressed in solitary luxury. "We became close friends with the headwaiter."

It is time for lunch. We walk from the library's flowers, past flowers in the hallway, to the dining room at the back of the house, with flowers on the dark table. It is after the noon hour, and the sun begins to reach the western slope that slants upward from Uphill Farm. A woman moves quietly from the kitchen and serves us with chicken and broccoli in a yellow sauce, carrots cooked with chunks of pineapple. Archie uncorks a Vougeot '72.

Sitting over a good lunch, talking about Antigua and Uphill Farm, I think how fortunate they are. After sixty-two years of marriage, each is healthy and alert—and each has a companion who is healthy and alert. Still, they are in their ninth decade; if one forgets, there are things to remind one. In order to live in this house, the MacLeishes need help. A year ago, the couple working for them decided to retire. It is extremely difficult, in this day and age, to find a couple—man to garden, care for lawns, do upkeep; woman to cook and clean house. By great luck they found two superb people, but there had been a time of anxiety. Archie said he would die if he had to live somewhere else. Ada said she would die if she had to take care of this house by herself.

The problem solved, life becomes livable again. Now they look forward to summer, to getting out of doors. The two of them garden, both flowers and vegetables, with help from their help because Ada's trick knees preclude kneeling. The carrots we eat today were frozen from their garden last summer. And when the snow pulls back, it will unloosen the swimming hole behind the house, where in their middle eighties Archibald and Ada MacLeish still take a dip before breakfast every morning, Ada tells us, "as nature made us."

After lunch Archie takes us to the music room for talk. We pass through a hallway of framed degrees and citations, signed and unsigned pictures that delineate MacLeish's several lives: Yeats, Frost, Joyce; Roosevelt, Dean Acheson. The music room is high and cavernous, full of books and flowers and pictures. Gerald Murphy's painting "The Pear and the Wasp" used to hang in this room until the MacLeishes donated it to the Museum of Modern Art, as Murphy lay dying.

I ask MacLeish, is Uphill Farm the place for work?

Yes, he tells me, this has always been the place for work. "'J.B.' Much of the 'Collected Poems.' 'Conquistador' began in France, but everything *real* was lacking in it. The real part came here, after a visit to Mexico." Did he work in Antigua? "Antigua was all right for reworking things. Antigua was perfection, but two or three months is all you can stand of perfection." Here he works in a one-room stone house, 250 yards away from the farmhouse, far from telephones. He likes to be at work by eight o'clock in the morning, to work on poems *before* he works on anything else.

I ask him what he knows now about writing poems that he didn't know at the beginning. He laughs and says that he may know "a little more at the end than at the beginning." He pauses. "I think I know one simple thing that I hadn't. This may strike you as odd because I used to talk about this as if I knew. When you're beginning, you *think* you're after scope or direction. You're *really* after a believable speaking voice, a voice that will collect feelings, the way lint collects on certain fabrics. Re-reading Alexis St. Léger's [St.-John Perse's] 'Anabase,' I see what amazing powers lie in the discovery of the voice. It is a *dominant figure.* That voice is not the voice of anyone who ever lived, but of humanity, in relation to basic experience—salt, fire, the sea."

"And there's another thing." He tells how he took Robert Fitzgerald's translation of the "Odyssey" to Bermuda, in order to read it aloud to Ada with the sound of surf in the background. Reading it, he found a line that he had never seen before, a line translated differently by other translators. In the 11th book, Odysseus tells his story to Alkínoös, who answers him saying that Odysseus has told his story, "As a poet would, a man who knows the world."

MacLeish pauses to let the line sink in. He shakes his head. "These are the words that I needed for years. Who *does* know the world? Not the businessman. Not the scientist. Yes—Shakespeare, Homer, Dante. This is what makes greatness in a poet: *to know the world.* And yet, this is not what people have been saying about the poet. The orthodox view is that the poet knows how to write, but has nothing to do with reality."

I ask him the question writers always hear: What is he working on now? He waits only a moment.

"You're aware," he says, "that people who've lived on into old age have stopped writing. You don't face up to it; you don't know what to *face.* You don't want to risk despair. Then you must face it: It is not happening."

He has been unable to write poetry for the last year. It has been a bad year, the worst year, because of the long and terrible death of their son. Kenneth MacLeish—Ada and Archie's sixty-year-old firstborn, editor and writer for the National Geographic—died last August after five years' struggle with cancer. "At the time that happened, I was putting prose pieces together. That occupied me." He did not recognize, at first, that the poems had stopped. "Then I had to face it. What do you do? Do you consciously accept silence? Wait? Begin all over again, as if in a new experience of life? How would you *use* that new experience in life? Nothing needs understanding . . . more than that dwindling."

He does not seem to have dwindled away. I suggest that sometimes extreme pain makes poetry impossible, but that it may return.

Yet he is right that few poets have written well in old age. Walter Savage Landor died just three months short of ninety and wrote exquisite, lapidary poems almost until the end. Tennyson lived to be eighty-three; there is a fine love poem to his wife ("To you who are seventy-seven") composed in his eighty-second year. Robert Frost lived to be eighty-eight and published a successful book the year before he died—but the quality of the late work shows decline. By and large, it is observable that poets in their seventies or eighties either cease to write or write badly. The great exception is Thomas Hardy, 1840-1928, who never published his poems until he was almost sixty, and who wrote many of his best poems— some of the greatest lyrics in the language—in his seventies and eighties. And Archibald MacLeish published a "Collected Poems" in 1976, with a section of "New Poems" apparently written since 1968, with this verse about "The Old Gray Couple":

> Everything they know they know together—
> everything, that is, but one:
> their lives they've learned like secrets from each other;
> their deaths they think of in the nights alone.

Archie hears me talking. He allows that I could be right— about the pain preventing poems, instead of age—but I can tell that he does not believe me. "I haven't been *able*," he says, "to get back to verse. Yet I have the compulsion." "There are poems that come from terminal experience."

Both of us think of Yeats. Though Yeats died at seventy-four, he had been ill, and he wrote magnificently "from terminal experience." Archie remembers a story and tells us now about hearing Yeats lecture at Yale in 1915—Yeats was fifty then, Archie twenty-three—and of relaxing with him later at the Elizabethan Club and how Yeats recited Tennyson's song from "The Princess" ("The splendour falls on castle walls") with a tender mockery of the Laureate's mellifluousness. We laugh, hearing in his youthful voice an American imitate an Irishman mock an Englishman: "Blow, bugle, blow. . . ." But when we stop laughing MacLeish's voice comes weaving back to thoughts of life and death and poetry.

"From the beginning of time the old have been laughed at for their forgetfulness." Short-term memory is the key; perhaps the conditions of aging *preclude* poetry, because of short-term memory's relationship to the poetic process. "When you get older, it's hard to come back to the work; when you are young you walk in the woods and you are surrounded by the poem you are trying to write; it flies around your head. When you are older you forget you are working on it."

After a pause, he thinks of Rilke and Rilke's obsession with astronomical predictions of the sun's death—the end of everything. "Rilke felt that the human role was to create a world that would survive time and disaster. *Survive.* A series of vast shadows. Perhaps there *is* an excuse for human labor." He pauses; I wonder if he can hear the wordplay he makes, on the death of the sun. Then he continues, vigorous: "There *is* sense in being alive, justification in being alive. There has been created in the human mind—in however short a time, only ten thousands of years—a world that could live without the world. Mozart has vanished; his music endures. There is a world that has been made by poets, musicians; that world *exists.* Are we to suppose this world will not survive us?"

Afternoon darkens, and it is nearly time to leave. We stand, shake hands, make plans to see each other again. MacLeish has one more thing to say: "There is also the consolation of *having been.* It is a consolation limited to old age. The haunting sense of extinguishment is there. Something in you *does* marshall, against it, an unarguable sense of *having been.*"

An Interview with Robert Louthan

(1978)

Robert Louthan: In Remembering Poets, *one of your new books of prose, you write perceptively of Dylan Thomas's suicidal urge. Have you considered committing suicide?*

Hall: In my early forties, I thought of it continually. That was a time in my life when I was very low, when suicide was the only thing that kept me living. That is, I had the *daydream* of suicide. I could go to that daydream at the most extreme pain, and it would relieve the pain. And I was terribly . . . I know it is a bad thing for your children if you commit suicide. And I am fond of my children. So I was determined, in my daydream, to think up ways in which I could kill myself without appearing to kill myself, making it look like an accident. One way was driving. But I was too *moral* to drive into another car, you see. So I was looking for bridge abutments that were not guarded by a guardrail—concrete which, if you hit at ninety miles an hour, would presumably take care of you. One day I was checking out bridge abutments on highways, finding ones that looked as if they would work; I must have been coming to the end of my despair, because I allowed myself to see that I was driving ten miles under the speed limit, as I was daydreaming suicide by fast driving. I realized, at that moment, that I did not want to. I laughed aloud in the car, and I felt at the same time a sadness, or a pain, that I had to give up this dream.

How had this affected your writing?

The despair affected the writing I was able to do, and affected me by probably preventing me, also, from writing. At the time I was drinking a great deal, which is not conducive to writing or anything else.

You've said that a poem is never about anything, and that "the poem is a monument to its moment." Several of your own poems are monuments to your visits, as a youngster, to your grandparents' farm in New Hampshire. Also, you've agreed with Vernon Watkins's statement that all poems derive from one experience. . . .

If poems are not about anything, how come they can all derive from a single experience? I accept the contradiction!

Constantly we read anthologies in which poems about war are lumped together, poems about love are lumped together, poems about death are lumped together. Thematic anthologies. Also, people are always asking me, "What do you write *about?*" My statement that poems are not about anything is an irritable response to all that. Poems are not about *anything* because they are each about *everything.* In a poem of any length and complexity, there is liable to be some murder and some love, some war and some peace—some of everything, come together. If it's not true to say poems are not about anything (*some* poems are not about anything), I do think an enormous amount of the satisfaction I take from poems has nothing to do with what they are about. It has to do with them being "about" serious things—profound and moving things, and often painful things—but then, by movement, by sound, by imagistic progression, *resolving* everything. That is, an enormous amount of the pleasure of poems comes from that resolution which is formal.

Yet I must immediately say that the formal resolution of cotton candy is trivial; it is not pleasurable. A cone of cotton candy may be beautifully resolved, and whole, but it's made of nothing but sponge sugar, and to hell with it! Apparently, I want and I need—we want and we need—the *materials* of that formal resolution to be profound human materials.

I certainly have written a lot out of that farm in New Hampshire. There were experiences of solitude and inwardness associated with that place. That place is also associated with my mother because that is where she was born and grew up. And with my maternal grandparents, who loved me and left me alone, and allowed me my own solitude there. There is, then, mother love, and the shadow of mother love through the maternal grandparents, and the solitude and the love— all at the same time. I had my own secret place, my own little womb, perhaps, in which I was served and waited on and taken care of. But I could also take part in the working of that system, I could take part in working on the farm, and I felt connected to the land, as I never did in the suburbs, as it's very difficult to do in the suburbs, where I lived with my parents most of the year. This farm became the place of poetry. When I wrote overtly *about* the farm, I was indeed writing *about* the farm. Many other times, when I was writing from other subjects, I was also writing out of that experience, and in a way, writing *about* the farm. The feeling-farm.

Your grandparents have died, and you've returned to live at the farm forever. What is it like for you there now?

Now I feel terribly much at ease where I am, in my body, in my house, in my landscape, in my community—in these Chinese boxes of four things. An extraordinary feeling, an extraordinary contentment. I worry about having no irritation, that it's unfair, that it's not belonging to the twentieth century. People tell me, "Ah, shut up, don't worry about it, just be happy with it."

The sense of connection that's come into the writing, some of the new poems . . . I think a lot of the new poems, in *Kicking The Leaves*, have to do with what endures and what does not endure. But there's a great deal, also, that makes connections with the past, and increasingly with the idea of endurance into the future. *Temporal* connections across time, from way back to the present. This began to happen, in my poetry, before I went back to the farm, but it did not happen until I knew I was going back. I can first see it in a poem like "Eating The Pig," which was written in Ann Arbor before I came to the farm, a year before. I knew I was coming. As I got to the farm and the experience deepened, connections seemed enormously there. I suspect they will continue to be. It's not exactly a subject; it's a relationship among subjects.

There are several prose poems in The Town Of Hill, *and some are quite fantastic. In your new book,* Kicking The Leaves, *there is only one prose poem, and you're down to earth again. Why?*

I don't admire *The Town Of Hill* very much. I like some of the poems in it. Godine wanted a chapbook. I sent it to them, and they took it. Getting those poems out of the house was an incredible release. Very soon, immediately, I felt this wonderful access of language. Words began coming to me. At the same time I began "O Cheese" and "Kicking The Leaves." They came in a long line, which I'd never written in before.

You said that the new poems are down to earth, and—in some ways they're a throwback to the old poems, but I like them better than the old poems, than the poems they're a throwback to. They *do* have more of the world in them. Now, one thing that I've said about prose poems is that a lot of us have gone to them because we painted ourselves into a corner. I'm speaking of myself, but I think it's true of others too. Painted ourselves into a corner with a short, surreal, ecstatic free verse where everything is transformed; nothing is itself; everything is a contortion and a metaphor and a figure. This can be a terribly exciting kind of poetry, and it was a sustaining kind for me, for some time. But as, for me, iambic stanzas rhymed abab became a structural formula for feeling, so, for me, the short, ecstatic, transformational, surreal free verse poem became a limitation on the possibilities of experience—certainly a limitation on the possibilities of the world that you could bring into a poem directly. The door to new material always seems to me to be a particular kind of sound, which in *Kicking The Leaves* is the long line that encompasses and encloses.

Why are there so many poems about eating, in Kicking The Leaves?

The book, as it's constructed, begins with a whole bunch of poems which are full of eating—including the one where people are going to get eaten by wolves and then they wind up eating the wolves instead, and they kill a dog to do it. That's the *really* cannibalistic one. But they're all cannibalistic. I find lyric poetry incredibly full of cannibalism. It is the forbidden eating of the mother. The taboo against cannibalism comes from the baby's desire to ingest his entire mother. Start at the breast and go on and take all the rest of her inside himself, acquire her, take her in.

Russell Edson and I have decided to start a summer poetry conference in rivalry to Bly's mother conference—the cannibalism conference. Russell Edson's poetry is absolutely *full* of cannibalism. So we're going to have a cannibalism conference. We've decided to hold it at the Donner Pass, every summer. We're going to invite all sorts of people. Some people write little tiny bitsy poems, short little haiku— they're going to come as hors d'oeuvres. The contributors are going to be roasted and broiled for dinner, whereas the auditors will be probably fried for lunch. We've been working this out in letters. I got a sticker of a drop of blood when I gave blood in a blood drive, and sent it to Russell, and he decided that took care of punch.

When I began this new series of poems it seems as if I was down at that cannibalistic level in my dream life. This is part of the connectedness and universality. I notice that, in the more recent poems, the later poems in the book, there isn't so much of it.

In the poem "To A Waterfowl," in The Town Of Hill, *you make fun of your audience, as well as of yourself as a reading poet. What's your actual attitude toward your live audience?*

When I introduce that poem, I frequently say that many poets are writing poems about poetry readings, like Louis Simpson, and we make fun of readings, and I've wondered why. I've suggested that it's because we love poetry readings so much that we're ashamed of it.

I love to read my poems aloud. Audiences vary enormously. When I'm with them, I want them to respond. I like to *perform*. That is something which not every poet feels quite so much. I didn't know whether to be a poet or an actor when I was young. The part of me that wanted to be an actor climbs up there on the platform. One of the things that happens with an actor is a sense of control over the audience. My feeling for the audience is one of power and control, and a resilience—not a resilience—a *reciprocation*, back and forth. This is separate from having any real feelings about them as people. Sometimes there are people out there that I know, but when I'm performing to them they're not the people I know; they're audience and I'm actor, performer.

Where is the audience for poetry?

Literally the audience is largely around colleges and big cities. Of course there are people stuck in places where they can't hear poetry readings and can't get to bookstores, all over the country, who want to read it. I'm sure the audience could be larger if, for instance, there were money available for distribution of books, distribution of magazines, for widespread poetry readings. Many things irritate me about the smallness of the audience. Some institutions are not doing their work. I'm irritated by general magazines—like *The Atlantic*, really, *The New Yorker* in the last 10 years—that have virtually stopped reviewing poetry. *The Atlantic, The Saturday Review* get out all over the country to small towns in the countryside and so on—to people who are there, who used to read poetry when they were in college, who are still potential readers of it. Well, they don't read much about it in the magazines. *The New Yorker* prints many poems, of course, *The Atlantic* prints some, but they don't *review* what's happening. People can't keep up with what's happening—unless they really try hard, or unless they're in some urban center.

Who has the audience?

There's a variety of audiences, and poets speaking to separate ones, and then general ones. Who's selling the most, I don't really know. Gary Snyder, Laurence Ferlinghetti . . . I think Snyder is a wonderful poet, and I don't think Ferlinghetti is a very good poet. Both of them have very large audiences. Robert Bly has a large audience. Robert Lowell has quite a large audience—not so large as you might think.

Some poets I would expect to be more popular than they are. There's a wonderful poet, William Stafford, who seems to me to write a kind of poem which ought to be popular, acceptable to many people, an easy pleasure to read and still good poetry—and yet I don't think that his audience is very great. I have no idea why. Robert Frost was an enormously popular poet, but his popularity had to do with things that are irrelevant to the value of his poetry. Maybe that will always be true if somebody good is popular.

You've said that poetry books are selling more now than ever. But what about, for example, the Pitt prize, when 900 manuscripts were submitted, but only 200 copies of the winning manuscript were sold?

I meet people all the time who are poets, who have a record collection that costs $2,000 and own fifteen books of poetry. There is a convention that you don't buy books. Buying books seems somehow bourgeois. Certainly you don't buy hardbacks. If you buy hardbacks, it means you're a Republican or something.

Yes, there are many contests for which more manuscripts are submitted than copies are sold. I don't mean to suggest that everybody who submits a manuscript has a duty to buy a copy; but I think that the two figures are appalling. It could be a happier experience for publishers to publish poetry, there would be more poetry read, if, somehow, conventions were changed, if we could call people's attention to the conventions whereby they will spend their money for other things—equivalent things like records, or unequivalent things like booze and grass—but they won't spend their money on a book.

Can an audience be created?

Audiences are continually created. I don't know if they can be manipulated from a publisher's office in New York. There are strange social movements. During the time that I've been grown up, and awake, and a poet, I've seen the audience for poetry enlarge a great deal. The most fantastic thing I've seen has been the audience for poetry *readings*. When I was in college—I happened to be in a college where they had two poetry readings a year, and that was extraordinary—most of the poets who came to read would probably do two readings a year at the most, though they were well known. Only, say, Carl Sandburg and Robert Frost were reading very often. Therefore the poets all read badly, didn't have any practice. But as I got into my thirties, and the world got into the fifties, we were reading constantly, and we now read to five or ten thousand faces a year. It's an extraordinary change in audience.

There are almost no non-involved audiences for poetry; the audiences seem to be made up almost exclusively of people who either write or teach poetry. Do poets actually try to find audiences, or do poets go out of their way to alienate audiences?

I've seen some poets alienate audiences that were the involved ones that you *speak* of. Some people want to be loved and feel ashamed of wanting to be loved, and therefore make a practice of turning people off. They shouldn't read their poems. They shouldn't accept money to do that kind of thing.

Some people have been going out to find audiences with the help of institutions like the Poetry in the Schools programs. Part of it has been to get kids to write poetry, and that's the part that we're most aware of right now. But the program also brings live poets into the schools so that, when the kids are studying poetry—this is not kindergarteners we're talking about, older kids—they meet somebody who's actually working, who is not dead words in a book or a picture of an old man with a white beard, but somebody alive who comes in and says, "Yes, I'm a poet. Poets are real; they're not just things your teacher made up." *That* is an attempt to find and create new audiences.

When I talk about creating audiences, I don't want the poets to write differently, so as to suck up to audiences that have not previously liked poetry; I want to find an audience that will like real poetry, good poetry. To discover this audience, or to create it. But I don't want to cheapen poetry in the process of finding an audience. That is the danger of the whole movement.

What about the inbreeding involved in being a poet who writes for other poets?

Wordsworth wrote with his neighbor Coleridge partly in mind, and Coleridge with his neighbor Wordsworth partly in mind. I don't feel too bad about it. Poets have often come in groups, and have been friends, and have thought of each other as their particular readers. But is anybody stupid enough to think of himself as *just* writing for other people who write poetry? One has an idea of what a good poem is, and one writes toward that idea. I'd like to be read and loved by everybody in the world, for goodness sake. But I don't want to give up my idea of a good poem for that, and my idea of a good poem is in a sense my audience. My idea of an audience may limit my audience; it's unlikely, you know, that anybody's going to read any one poem well unless he or she has already read many other poems. The more poems you read, the better you are able to read the next poem you read.

Magazines and small presses are dying every day. More are taking their place—for now. But, will we get to the point of entropy, where the outlets for work can no longer sustain the amount of work being poured out? Will the producers lose interest, will the audience be lost?

Many magazines and presses have a small audience now, and they *deserve* a small audience. I imagine—I don't know this for a fact—that there are more magazines and small presses now than there ever were. When the markets dry up, when a group of poets in a city cannot find places to publish, there's always something that they can do about it. They start a magazine and publish themselves. Of course most of this material is no good, it's terrible. New magazines and presses come along all the time; I don't particularly celebrate it or lament it. I think it improbable that they will dry up.

By economic necessity, most magazines are local and limited. But I like to see one or two magazines that are national, which can be read by almost everybody, so that one can keep in touch, see what's happening. *APR* performs that function. Everybody wants *APR* to be better, including me. But it performs some of that function.

How would you have the APR *be better?*

I would have *APR* publish better poetry. I like some of the poetry in it, there's a lot of it I don't like so much. *APR* is edited by committee, and I'm friends with one of the editors there, and I continually argue with him, feeling that if one person edited it—if that person were *any* good—he or she would do better than any number of good people working in committee. And he says—I'm sure he's right—there's too much work to go around to one person. You would have to—this is me talking now, not him—you would have to have enough money to *hire* people to read for you; then you could reject their recommendations, and impose particular taste.

If people work together without being paid, they've got to have a voice and a power. I understand that. But I think *APR* suffers from committee editorship.

You've written that "poets read their contemporaries for confirmation or for contradiction." Who do you read for each?

I just read James Wright's new book with the greatest pleasure and delight. Confirmation. I don't think I really write *like* James Wright, or he like me, but obviously we write more like each other than either of us writes like Bob Creeley. I read Bob Creeley for contradiction. I love his poems, but he does things that I don't do—that maybe I ought to do. He can do things *without* metaphor. I rely on metaphor so much, and on description. I *love* Charles Reznikoff's poems, which are extraordinarily flat. There's a poet in Vermont, called David Budbill, author of *The Chain Saw Dance*, who has been writing an absolutely strange line—nothing interesting in line breaks, just flat, prosaic stuff—and I think it's beautiful. The content—the order of event and so on—contributes a kind of resolution. Then there's Frank Bidart, whose work I like very much. Frank Bidart uses language of no interest whatsoever, but he uses semicolons bravely. These are people who are doing things I can recognize as beautiful, and I don't know how to do them. I don't know how *they* do them. And I'm puzzled, and I go back over them, and over them, and try to figure out what's going on.

You've written that Bidart's language is "boring," and that it is "careful to be plain." Do you think it's careful to be boring?

Not really. Inch by inch, or quarter inch by quarter inch, it's boring. But the story, the anecdote, the character—this is what he's doing—develops with an absolute honesty through his plainness of language, and through his brilliant spacing and pausing and punctuation. The music, the rhythm, especially the pacing of the rhythm, contributes what the language lacks: a kind of specificity and precision and exactness.

Almost all language is dead metaphor, and the rest is live metaphor. How is Bidart, who uses no new metaphor, extending the language? If he isn't, what is his contribution?

Well, he's not extending the language on the level of new metaphor. Neither is Creeley. He is protecting and preserving language by speaking only with great precision and accuracy, by measuring everything that he does by the highest standards. Bidart's punctuation is terribly important. Punctuation is language as much as metaphor is; pause and commas are language as much as metaphor is. And it is precision of language which the poet is after. Purifying the language of the tribe. By his commas you shall know him, as well as by his metaphors.

In defending Bidart's poetry, you've written that "everything truly new has always begun as 'not poetry'." It seems too easy to say that; the converse, that everything that's not poetry is new, isn't true.

Sure. It *doesn't* prove, as you say, that everything that is not-poetry is any good.

Many readers are delighted to find some reason to reject anything new. I was like that when I was in my twenties. I have tried to learn a lesson, not to be like that any more. One doesn't *want* to let anything new in; it disturbs one's universe. But, you're right: not-poetry is not necessarily good; "new" is not necessarily good either.

In your column in APR, *you pointed out that "many poets write short lined, rhapsodic, fantastic, surrealistic free verse when they would do better writing sonnet sequences to Celia." You said that "the question is how many poets of* APR, *Seneca, Kayak, etc. would be better poets if they let themselves write in forms temporarily on the index." Do you have an answer to that question?*

I see a lot of sameness in young poets. A lot of poems belong to the air, to the age, to the *period*. Looking at styles of painting, you can say, "This isn't a genuine Ruebens"—or somebody—"it's just *period*." It apes Ruebens manner. I don't really think that there are poets around who are consciously aching to write sonnet sequences to Celia, but who suppress the desire and write surrealism instead. But I wish that people would feel more able to flout fashion, that more poets would take as their starting point anything in literature that appealed to them, do their own versions in their own voices of whatever has been done and could be done. It seems unlikely that there is now only one way to write a poem, and that five years from now there will be one *other* way to write a poem. I wish people had more courage. I was addressing myself when I wrote that piece, trying to give myself courage to be free, to do the unfashionable thing. When I talk to myself, about poetry, I talk to myself in public. If it means anything to anyone who overhears it, that's fine.

Looking for Noises

(1981)

Beginning. When I was twelve I was a loose aggregate of ambitions with no direction to them. I wanted to be an actor, a politician, a writer. At fourteen I decided to be a poet. Although I have since taught at a university, advised publishers, edited magazines, and written prose—fiction, biography, journalism, children's books, plays—poetry has remained at the center of my life.

When I was sixteen I published free-verse poems in small magazines like *Trails, Experiment*, and *Matrix*. I thought of the poet as alienated from middle-class culture and therefore innovative. At seventeen I discovered metrics. It was the midforties then, when the dominant American poets wrote rhymed stanzas, and I studied at a boarding school where the English teachers formed a coven of Robert Frost worshippers. Although Frost was a good poet, my teachers admired him for silly reasons—because he was not T. S. Eliot—and, alas, they looked upon Stephen Vincent Benét as the heir apparent.

If Eliot would not do, Ezra Pound and E. E. Cummings were unmentionable, and no one had heard of William Carlos Williams. At Harvard my poetry teachers dedicated themselves to discovering irony, complex textures, and the iambic foot. By the time I was graduated, I knew the way to write poems.

And so did most of my generation, and like most of my generation I have changed.

At Harvard during my four years I knew other undergraduate poets: Peter Davison, L. E. Sissman, Adrienne Rich, Frank O'Hara, Kenneth Koch, John Ashbery, and Robert Bly. Robert Creeley had dropped out the year before and lived in New Hampshire; I met him at the Grolier Book Shop in Cambridge in 1949 and we talked poetry for an hour. John Hawkes was beginning to write fiction; John Updike arrived as a freshman when I was a senior. Richard Wilbur was a graduate student, later a junior fellow. John Ciardi was my first writing teacher; two others in that class were O'Hara and Edward Gorey. Archibald MacLeish arrived as Boylston professor in my junior year; Bly and I took his course. Frost lived nearby in fall and winter; Eliot visited every spring.

But it was the other undergraduates who mattered most. We were serious about our writing, and hard on each other. Many of us worked together on a student magazine, the *Harvard Advocate*, and we would argue til four in the morning about publishing a particular poem. I suppose we were self-important—as if our decisions *mattered*; yet I learned more in these arguments than I learned in classrooms.

When I left Harvard and spent two years at Oxford I was appalled by the amateurishness of the young English poets. (There were exceptions: Geoffrey Hill was at Oxford, Thom Gunn at Cambridge.) Oxford was poetry-crazy: it was the only place I know where writing poems was a form of social-climbing—and in a variety of publications Oxford published more than four hundred student poems a year. At Harvard our one magazine grudgingly published twenty or so.

Most young English poets in 1951 were sloppy indeed, sub-Georgian, without skill or brains or talent for verse—and I hurled the word *amateurish* at them. In my American way it never occurred to me to doubt professionalism. But my view of poetry was distorted by notions borrowed from businessmen, from professionals like doctors and lawyers and engineers—and from the universities which manufacture them. It took years before I could see that by the standard *professionalism*, which emphasized craft or technique, I wedded myself to safe old ways which precluded change or growth.

Entrepreneurship. Once a good poem is made—with its sweet sounds, its miseries and joys, its spirit and shapeliness, its *new word*, its luck—it enters the marketplace. People do not like to hear this. Many poets avoid public appearances in the marketplace, although their poems appear there. There is always a marketplace—publishing houses, magazines, anthologies—and someone will always run the store. From my years at college on, as editor of magazines and anthologies, as advisor to publishers and sometimes to foundations, I have judged other people's poems, published them, reviewed them, rewarded them. I have tried to persuade others of my taste.

In small part I have concerned myself with older poets. I interviewed Eliot, Pound, and Moore for the *Paris Review*, and later wrote reminiscences of Dylan Thomas, Frost, Eliot, and Pound. For the most part I have tried to judge and discriminate among the poets of my own generation and the generations that follow. In 1957 I edited (with Robert Pack and Louis Simpson) *The New Poets of England and America*. This was the anthology which became known as academic, as opposed to Donald Allen's *New American Poetry*, three years later, which became known as beat. Our book included good poets, but it became known for the poets it left out, an astonishing list: Frank O'Hara, Kenneth Koch, John Ashbery, Robert Creeley, Denise Levertov, Robert Duncan, Gary Snyder, Allen Ginsberg, etc., etc. For the most part we left these poets out—not having read their work—sometimes from provinciality and sometimes from preconceptions. But that is another story. Although it was not our intention, our exclusiveness proved useful: it drew Donald Allen's counter-anthology out of the air, which presented an array of alternative poetries. No longer would it be easy to think that one knew the way to write poems.

A few years later, in 1962, I made an eclectic anthology for Penquin called *Contemporary American Poets*. By this time I loved Creeley's work, Snyder's, Levertov's, Duncan's . . . I am glad that I could now see past my own atelier, because many people took from this anthology their sense of American poetry after the war. But as a literary event, the more biased an anthology is the more powerful it is; and my Penguin suffered from the blandness of eclecticism.

In the meantime I was a member of the editorial board of the Wesleyan Poetry Series, to which I brought books by Bly, Wright, Simpson, Dickey, and others. Then I became an advisor to Harper & Row. I edited poetry for the *Paris Review*, I wrote book reviews, gave lectures and interviews . . . And I continue—although I have learned with age that even my most passionate prejudices are subject to change.

Changing. As my taste in poetry changed, so of course did my poems. Here is a poem, "My Son, My Executioner," that I wrote in 1954 at twenty-five, when I had been working with Yvor Winters.

My son, my executioner,
 I take you in my arms,
Quiet and small and just astir,
 And whom my body warms.

Sweet death, small son, our instrument
 Of immortality,
Your cries and hungers document
 Our bodily decay.

We twenty-five and twenty-two,
 Who seemed to live forever,
Observe enduring life in you
 And start to die together.

Meter, rhyme, paradox, irony, abstraction. I no longer quite know the person who wrote this poem, though I remember him dimly, as if recalling not a person but a photograph. In 1957 I began to write poetry which I associated with Surrealism; the first was "The Long River," finished in 1958:

> The musk-ox smells
> in his long head
> my boat coming. When
> I feel him there,
> intent, heavy,
>
> the oars make wings
> in the white night,
> and deep woods are close
> on either side
> where trees darken.
>
> I rowed past towns
> in their black sleep
> to come here. I rowed
> by northern grass
> and cold mountains.
>
> The musk-ox moves
> when the boat stops,
> in hard thickets. Now
> the wood is dark
> with old pleasures.

Although this poem is twenty-two years old now, it does not feel alien to me. I no longer use this sound—short-lined, enjambed, percussive, with emphatic monosyllabic assonance—but I can still hear myself in it.

I had a number of reasons for changing. And as I changed, so did the poets with whom I talked poetry. We had written iambic stanzas; now we seemed to feel that we had come to the end of something. Independently and simultaneously we moved into free verse, following various masters, and most of us began to incorporate fantasy in our poems. In my metrical verse I had come to feel limited by my associations of subject and structure with metrical form. Now I felt free, loose, improvisational, excited, and a little frightened.

We changed, I think, independently—but of course we spoke to each other. About 1957 I talked about the poetry of fantasy with Robert Bly and later with James Wright. Bly and Wright translated Georg Trakl, and Bly among others translated Pablo Neruda. I learned from these poets and from others of Spain and Latin America. A little later I found another source of change. In 1960 I met the English sculptor Henry Moore, when I interviewed him for a magazine. In the early sixties I spent much time with him and wrote a book about him. Several poems, like "Reclining Figure," came directly out of his work.

> Then the knee of the wave
> turned to stone.
>
> By the cliff of her flank
> I anchored,
>
> in the darkness of harbors
> laid-by.

Moore told me, paraphrasing Rodin, "Never think of a surface except as the extension of volume." I wanted to write a poetry with an articulated surface under which one could sense a volume of emotion pressing upwards.

In the thirties both Constructivism and Surrealism thrived briefly in London. Of course they were at war—the poles of modernism—but Moore showed sculpture in both camps. While I wanted for my poetry the emotion provided by expressionist distortion, I wanted as well the resolutions of a constructed object. Thus the small poem above improvises formal resolution by drumbeat and assonance. As Moore never abandons reference to the human form, I never intend—in the pursuit of resolution—to leave behind intensity of feeling. For me the extremes seem to touch in a poem's sound—as vowel and consonant both "rhyme" and provide the catalyst to feeling.

Noises. As my writing has changed, I have noted that changes announce themselves first as changes in sound. It seems as if, when my mouth begins to make a new noise, something inside me begins to speak, something that was previously dumb. When a new noise begins, I feel full of energy and ideas; everything I look at blooms with poetry: I write and write. Over years the energy drains from the new noise—not all at once, and by no means with a steady decline. Eventually I feel as if I had painted myself into a corner, as if the new noise—at first mysterious and undefined—became more restrictive the more I knew about it. Knowledge or self-consciousness erects rules. About 1970 or 1972 my poems could *only* be short-lined, monosyllabic, assonantal, and fantastic; of course such a rulebook restricts subject matter.

For a number of years I flailed about, writing in several manners without settling into any. I wrote prose poems; I revisited meter and felt the old grievances rise again. Then in the autumn of 1974 a new sound started—and I wrote the poems of *Kicking the Leaves* (1978): long-lined poems, asymmetrical, various in intensity, with many flat passages, less "constructed" in the intimate collision of syllables, perhaps more inclusive and architectural in the large scale. These poems are longer and more various—in detail and in tone—than anything I have written earlier. They differ from one another, but I have room only for one. I pick "The Black Faced Sheep"; here are the first and last sections of that poem:

Ruminant pillows! Gregarious soft boulders!

If one of you found a gap in a stone wall,
the rest of you—rams, ewes, bucks, wethers, lambs;
mothers and daughters, old grandfather-father,
cousins and aunts, small bleating sons—

followed onward, stupid
as sheep, wherever
your leader's sheep-brain wandered to.

My grandfather spent all day searching the valley
and edges of Ragged Mountain,
calling "Ke-*day!*" as if he brought you salt,
"Ke-*day!* Ke-*day!*"
. . . .
At South Danbury Church twelve of us sit—
cousins and aunts, sons—
where the great-grandfathers of the forty-acre farms
filled every pew.
I looked out the window at summer places,
at Boston lawyers' houses
with swimming pools cunningly added to cowsheds,
and we read an old poem aloud, about Israel's sheep
—and I remember faces and wandering hearts,
dear lumps of wool—and we read

that the rich farmer, though he names his farm for himself,
takes nothing into his grave;
that even if people praise us, because we are successful,
we will go under the ground
to meet our ancestors collected there in the darkness;
that we are all of us sheep, and death is our shepherd,
and we die as the animals die.

Making a Living. From 1957 to 1975 I taught at a university.
At first it was good, as I learned by speaking what I did not
know I knew; but repetition was inevitable, and when I spoke
what I knew I would speak, I learned nothing. In 1975 I
moved to the New Hampshire farm where my family has
lived since 1865, and I support myself by writing prose, by
editing, and by reading my poems aloud.

Most days, now, I write all day.

Adding Eden On

(1976)

Some time ago in this column* I made a claim for poetry as progressive in the evolution of consciousness. Over the months, I have accumulated a few arguments to go with the assertion.

Let me start with notions of Eden. Our minds are crowded with paradises. Many of them are banal: for an alumnus, maybe college was paradise; for a lover, a weekend ten years ago in Worcester, Mass. Other paradises are more nearly universal, as when Wordsworth remembers childhood. If Edens are human nature—greater and lesser ones—we must ask what Eden *means*, in our consciousness, and what it *was*, in the history of racial consciousness.

When we have cleared away the paradisal debris of mere youth—as with the alumnus—I think the identity of the ur-Eden becomes clear. It represents in our psyches the old world of instinct and imagination, the world before reason, the world without planning ahead, without regret, without rational thought, the world in which desire and act are the same. This is the country of Yeats's imagination, which he describes so often:

---

* This was the last in the series of "Knock Knock" columns written for the *American Poetry Review*.

> Labor is blossoming or dancing where
> The body is not bruised to pleasure soul,
> Nor beauty born out of its own despair,
> Nor blear eyed wisdom out of midnight oil. . . .

This "where" in our waking lives is nowhere at all. We catch a glimpse of it when the dancer is the same as her dance; we lose it when the dance ends, and the dancer sits in her dressing room, smoking a cigarette and thinking about tomorrow. We see this paradise only in the visions of poets, who repeatedly imagine such a place of continual, instantaneous insight, spontaneous connection with the universe of things—Wordsworth in his reminiscences of childhood, Blake in his anarchic utopian vision, Lawrence.

If this is the mental Eden, we can still speculate on the historical one. Let us assume that myth is coded history, and that persistent psychic habits represent the development of the race. Many people have speculated about the historical Eden, taking off from similar assumptions. I remember that Erich Fromm placed the Fall at about 3000 B.C., when Babylon changed from a hunting culture to an agriculture. I guess many people have associated the Fall with the institution of agriculture.

The assumption is attractive. Hunting requires first of all quick reactions, instincts and sharp senses. Animals are model hunters. Animals are not model farmers. You must be expert at deferring pleasure, if you can save seed instead of eating it. To choose the best shape of land for planting, or to set the pyramids to predict the seasons, you must squint into the sun for many centuries.

But in my own subjective history, I will set the Fall backwards in time by hundreds of thousands of years. Pre-men had gathered in the savannahs and conspired to hunt animals hundreds of thousands of years earlier. They drove elephants into swamps, and hacked living meat from the bodies of elephants stuck in the mud; they hacked the meat with tools carved from stone and bone. Eden trembled when

Australopithecus sharpened the stone; Eden fell when the small creatures gathered to drive the elephant.

Doubtless some of my facts are wrong or at least conjectural; I am not trying to carbon-date the apple and the snake. I am concerned only to push backward in time the original Fall, because this altered perspective seems to make necessary an alteration in the accepted notion of art's psychic function and place.

Art is more recent, in man's development, than reason is.

The first art I know about is the decoration carved on ancient tools. (After a while, decoration on certain knives rendered them useless as knives; once a tool becomes useless, we can call it art for sure!) Later of course there are cave paintings and early sculpted figures. If we had painting and sculpture thirty thousand years ago, I suspect that we had poetry also, at least in conjunction with dance and music. Men must have shuffled to the sound of bones clacking, and themselves voiced noises, for hundreds of centuries, before these noises told stories about Achilles and Hector.

But we had tools—planned and crafted for their functions—*millenia* before we had decorated tools. We conspired to hunt elephants *millenia* before we had poems.

Art is more recent than reason, by hundreds of thousands of years. Poetry as we know it is three or four thousand years old. As for the powers of reason, every time a Leakey makes a discovery, the beginnings of reason move back ten thousand years.

But art, we have been told forever and ever, is *primitive*. For all his love of the products of artists, Freud condescends to their brains. The Freudian theorist of artistic creativity, Ernst Kris, reduces artistic creation to the formula: "regression in the service of the ego."

But Kris's formula explains nothing. To regress is to become infantile; to serve the ego is to be adult. Regression which is involuntary, painful, and destructive characterizes the schizophrenic. The artist resembles children or schizophrenics because his waking consciousness sometimes finds dream available to it, and the mechanics of primary process thinking. Metaphor, for instance, resembles the thought processes of dreams, of small children, and of schizophrenics. Kris merely observes that the artist does something which resembles what the schizophrenic does; only when the artist does it, it helps him out.

Or consider the analogy of artist and child. It is not until a child reaches an age roughly ten to twelve that he begins to organize thoughts in a disciplined fashion. When the nine-year-old still thinks by leaps and associations, the twelve-year-old courts chronology. Similarly, man's intellectual development through ages of paleolithic time, to recent neolithic times, must have been painful and slow. As the child learns to put away childish things, so our race—over hundreds of thousands of years—learned to put away irrational things. It put them away by hiding them. Reason is a survival-oriented characteristic, just as brain-size is. It helps you avoid death—whether by lions or by floods—by acting according to remembered precedent, and by planning ahead.

The artist does not give up reason in order to become a six-year-old again. Children do not write great poems or paint great pictures. Adults do. Adults do when they add Eden on.

Instead of regressing to an infantile state, *artists have the ego strength to add the irrational to the rational*. Strength of ego, among other matters, distinguishes the artist from the schizophrenic. Where id was, let there ego be. The artist opens up and explores dark continents which we hid, ages ago, in order to survive.

As instinct was the thesis, and reason the antithesis, art is the synthesis. We march to the drum of the dialectic.

I suggest, then, that art is a survival-oriented characteristic, and an indication of evolutionary direction. Far from primitive, it is futuristic. It is progressive, not regressive. If reason began to grow a million years ago, and depended for its growth on drowning the shadow that ruled before it—the new god must always kill the old—then art is a comparatively recent development, beginning perhaps only thirty thousand years ago. It is *evidence* of the new synthesis.

It is not art itself which leads to survival. Poetry is not itself the messiah; certainly religious thinking is synthetic also. Art is an *embodiment* of the two parts become one—the insight combined with the organization—which is necessary to human development.

For instinct is spontaneous and imagination deals simultaneously with wholes. Reason has the characteristic of dealing with parts in order. For man to survive, he must be able to release and use imaginative vision, and yet retain the tools and efficacies of reason. Surrealism maps or puts into shape the contours of dream, and can be read only with intuition. But reason—whether the surrealist denies it or not—is necessary to language itself. The combination *adds* to human consciousness. Therefore it advances human consciousness. Nothing else is worth doing.

The Nation of Poets

(1977)

A foggy liberalism denies the profundity of nations. Whether we like it or not, poems often get written in history's blood, out of bodies fed on regional and religious particulars, out of souls that speak God's Word in warring dialects. We deny the old countries, in order to deny our parents. Few Americans, committed to poetry bother even to *read* contemporary English—or Scots, Welsh, or Irish—poetry. More profess Andalusian, more profess T'ang. Fewer still understand that Irish is a poetry profoundly separate from English. But separate it is—even more separate than English and American, and for similar reasons. The separateness of Scots from English seems to me more arbitrary, even voluntary. A Scot can move to London, work for the BBC, and almost adopt another nation. But the Scot or the Welshman is the exception; for most writers, there is nothing voluntary about the literature they belong to. A New Zealander in London for forty years remains a New Zealander whatever he wishes he were. An Irishman must write *Irish*, whether his Irish be Celtic, English, or French.

And the Irish were a subject people until fifty years ago, and part of the island is subject still. What a complex fate, to be Irish and to be a writer, to write under the two empires of London and Rome, to write in the language of one empire squished by the moral thumb of another, and all the time

45

suffused with a repressed nationality—nationality like Seamus Heaney's bog people, preserved in the flesh, the tongue for most of them virtually dumb. I think of the nation of black Americans inside white America, speaking the language of the slaveowners; at least in America color delineates races.

So politics runs through John Montague's *Book of Irish Verse* (New York: Macmillan, 1977). Half of the book is translated from native Irish into the enemy tongue—with a sweetness that seems pure paradox. Certain themes, like hunger, seem to be present even before the English; later they *become* political. In the editor's translation, here's a piece of the twelfth-century "Vision of the MacConglinne."

> The fort we reached was beautiful—
> Thick breastworks of custard
>   Above the lake
> Fresh butter for a drawbridge
> A moat of wheaten bread
>   A bacon palisade.
>
> Stately and firmly placed
> On strong foundations, it seemed
>   As I entered
> Through a door of dried beef
> A threshold of well-baked bread
>   Walls of cheese-curd.

The Big Rock Candy Mountain turns up in numerous visions—before it becomes for Yeats an island, a culture, a mountain top, or John Kinsella's vision.

Another theme is the difficulties of language. Here's part of a song (18th century, I think) translated by Donagh Mac-Donagh—a minor poet of considerable beauty, whom no one reads:

> When I was at College they taught me English
> And praised my accent, but with that first sight
> The only language that I knew was love-talk
> And all my thoughts were turned to birds in flight.

Or here's a poem by the editor, who suffers from a stammer.

(Dumb,
Bloodied, the severed
head now chokes to
speak another tongue:—

As in
a long suppressed dream,
some stuttering, garb—
led ordeal of my own)

An Irish
child weeps at school
repeating its English.
After each mistake

The master
gouges another mark
on the tally stick
hung about its neck

Like a bell
on a cow, a hobble
on a straying goat.
To slur and stumble

In shame
the altered syllables
of your own name;
to stray sadly home

And find
the turf cured width
of your parent's hearth
growing slowly alien:

In cabin
and field, they still
speak the old tongue.
You may greet no one.

To grow
a second tongue, as
harsh a humiliation
as twice to be born.

Decades later,
that child's grandchild's
speech stumbles over lost
syllables of an old order.
"A Grafted Tongue"

Politics is psychosomatic in Ireland.

Vital speech continues in Ireland among contemporary poets like Derek Mahon, wonderfully represented here, and Paul Muldoon—and the marvelous Kinsella, and the editor himself, and Seamus Heaney, and several others. The island blooms with poets; only the brightness of Yeats has kept Americans from seeing two dozen others. These others are various enough, heaven knows—but they share one thing: an intense regard for the beauty of language, for richness of vocabulary and metaphor. American poets lack precisely this Irish richness, as Americans struggle *against* the dominant language of commerce, *toward* a purity which is largely negative. The Irish poet paradoxically uses and brightens the oppressor's language, as he struggles to maintain Irish identity.

I say "he" with good reason. Where are the women? Curious. Montague's preface tells us that in medieval Ireland women were prominent among the poets. But in Montague's selection, among the last fifty-six poets—from Yeats (born 1865) to Gregory O'Donoghue (born 1951)—only *one* is a woman. (Gaelic names and spellings may have deceived me; I don't think so.) Is this pathology national or editorial? I suspect that the problem is national, and that Irish culture has erected a monstrous male supremacy, in that Maryolatrous green land.

In *The Book of Irish Verse*, Yeats has nine pages. The selection is a fascinating disaster: selections from "Meditations in

Time of Civil War," all of "Nineteen Hundred and Nine-
teen," the doggerel "The Curse of Cromwell"; absent, to
name one or two: "Among School Children," "Lapis Lazuli,"
"Sailing to Byzantium." The selection, you might say, is
political. Yeats is beaten out by Austin Clarke, who has eleven
pages. If you don't know Austin Clarke, try this poem:

> When the black herds of the rain were grazing
> In the gap of the pure cold wind
> And the watery haze of the hazel
> Brought her into my mind,
> I thought of the last honey by the water
> That no hive can find.
>
> Brightness was drenching through the branches
> When she wandered again,
> Turning the silver out of dark grasses
> Where the skylark had lain,
> And her voice coming softly over the meadow
> Was the mist becoming rain.
>
> "The Lost Heifer"

Or take another, as different as we are likely to find, called
"Aisling," which translates a "vision" or "dream":

> Morning had gone into the wood before me,
> The drip-drop answering its ray. I saw
> Greenness that lettered greener greenness open
> With sudden beam as if trees had been sawn down.
> Glints echoed from the thickness as I followed
> Under the green-brown twistiness by twisted
> Fern-rusty paths and, dazzling out of foresight,
> A woman rounded whitely from the mist.
>
> Unbraided tresses, gold chasings of her curls,
> Encircled her with light that feared no error,
> Half hid untouchable breasts as white as curds
> Or April snow we see on Errigal
> And Nephin, restraining all that glory of swirl.
> Her nipples were pinker than the bramble flower.

One slender hand below her navel curved
Lightly to drape her virtue with a cloudlet.

Leaf-stirring in that wood, I asked: 'Are you
A goddess come from Greece, Perimela,
Tella, or dearest of the Nine, Euterpe?
Sky-woman from our land? One of the pair
Who fled to love, the mountain-lost, yew-hidden
Grainne or Deirdre who threw away a sail
North of Loch Etive with a noble youth'—
I frowned— 'their widowed bodies given for sale?'

She smiled and took away her happy hand:
The red-gold curlets changed to modesty.
'Are you the morn personified in handsome
Robes?' 'Veilless, you see again my naked body.
Do you not recognise me now?' she answered,
Unrobed. I heard the ripples of a beck
Repeat the syllables of her high glance
That was all books and every beckoning.

I read her name that held my hushed voice, saying:
'When shall I feel at last upon this brow
Visible comfort of your touch, presage
Of a single leaf plucked from the sacred bough,
Though years of pen and disappointment press age
On it?' She vanished. Suddenly for the taking
I glimpsed Hesperidean fruit beyond our age,
Then, morning emptied my grasp and wakened me.

Another *belle-dame* poem, it compares well with Yeats's
"Aengus," or with Keats for that matter. (The Clarke poem
may be a translation. The note does not tell me; translations
and adaptations and originals wander among each other,
difficult to tell apart. This annoying lacuna indicates collec-
tive and traditional assumptions common to Irish poets.)
But why must I ask—by mentioning "Aengus"—that we
compare him to Yeats? For years and years, I have been
unable to read Austin Clarke, to catch his tune. It has helped
me to read him, *not* in the light of his Anglo-Irish elder, but

in the light of *The Book of Irish Verse*. With the aid of Montague's anthology, I can begin to be able to read his *Selected Poems* (Winston-Salem, N.C.: Wake Forest University Press, 1972), helpfully introduced by Thomas Kinsella. Outside Ireland, few people seem to have read him. Here's a poem on that subject, not one of Clarke's best, but a poem typical in its topical density, in its allusiveness and privacy:

> Criticus smiled as he wrote, and remarked
> In the Literary Supplement
> Of the London Times that Mr. Clarke was
> A garrulous rambling old Irishman.
> No doubt I have become too supple
> For the links of those boastful manacles
> That hold back meaning, but I prefer it
> To being a silent Englishman
> Who cannot untie his tongue. So I pen
> On, pen on, talkative as AE was,
> When old. Because there is no return fare,
> Few friends come out to the Isle of AEaea
> Where lately my desires have been penned by
> A Temple ogre who is one-eyed, filthy.
> Whenever Circe has a night-party
> And entertains with her famous snake-dance
> Clubbable guests that show the kind
> Of wallowers they are, when she's half-naked,
> She forgets to give us our fill. But I
> Have liked her and sometimes she is kind.
>
> "A Jocular Retort"

He writes as if everyone knew him, and knew what he had in mind—which, given the size of Ireland, may have been true of his primary readership; or he writes as if he did not give a damn whether anybody knew what he was talking about or not, which is probably truer. Little details of the life lived abound in these poems; for me—reading without a brogue and in New Hampshire—many poems remain mysterious in their allusions. But there are also autobiographical poems which are not mysterious, like the poems about encounters with Yeats, with Maud Gonne, and—believe it or not—with Winston Churchill.

Some of the best of these poems are late, satirical, funny, and sexual. "The Dilemma of Iphis" (owing its origin to Ovid) talks about a sex change that would account without prejudice for the change from matriarchy to patriarchy. "The Healing of Mis" is bawdy and tender in its sexuality; a wild girl, daughter of a king, wanders in a forest out of her mind for three centuries. Then she is saved and civilized by a harper named Duv Ruis. It's another story of the triumph of patriarchy, written with more tenderness than such tales usually muster, even with some harperly mothering:

> 'Wait here. I'll bring you venison.' She leaped over
>   The quicken-tree with lifted head. He hurried
> To pick up kindling in the forest, gather arm-loads
>   Of withered branches, fanned them into up-rushers,
> Cracklers, with a flick of his flint, set large stones
>   For a nearby cooking-pit the Fianna
> Had used, then waited, uneasy as his shoes. At last
>   She rose above the rowan branches,
>
> Lightly bearing a buck on her shoulder. 'Here's a meal
> For both our bellies . . . Look, day is aflame on the edge
> Of night. Run, run!' 'It's only faggots turned into heat.'
>   He poked the stones from the ash and the slope sent
>   them,
> Red-hot, into the paven pit. He coiled up
>   Each sweeping tress from her filthy body, saw
> Her nipples harden into blackberries. 'Bogholes have
>   spoiled them.
>   But soon that pair will be redder than haws . . .
>
> I stumbled on a helmet in sand near to washed-in
>   wreckage,
>   Brimmed it from a high cascade, going
> And coming patiently to fill your bath.' He shoshed
>   Himself as he lathered her down, soaped the skin of her
>   back
> With a lump of deer-fat, washed the crack between the
>   slurried

Cheeks, like a mother, turned her round, picked crabs
        from
Her sporran, nit-nurseries hidden in tiny flurries
    Through tangled tresses, then began

All over again. He soaped her body, washed it down,
    Drawing the wad of deer-skin to-and-fro
Softly between her glossing thighs, turned her around
    And frizzled her neglected faddle, noticed
It needed a thorough-going cleansing inside and out,
        scrubbed
    And douched it, cursing her ignorance, lack of care.
Then coiled her tresses neatly after he currycombed them
    As if she was a gainly mare.

'Now canter into dryness, my filly.' She galloped, instead,
        up
    The smooth slope, became a momentary
Speck on the summit, then flew down again into his arms—
    The favourite no ostler had led across the Curragh
Or mounted yet. 'Lie down with me under the blossoms.'
    He entered so quietly she never felt it
Until a pang shook her. Fearing involuntary loss,
    He waited, obedient as she helped

Him through the hymen. Then at the thrusting of the wand,
    Her eyelids closed in bliss. The flowers of the quicken-
        tree
Were poppies. Both drowsed but how could they stop
        fingers that wandered
    Until their passion was no longer tender?

'Buck, buck me,' she cried, 'as the stag in rut.' Wildly
        crouping
    Herself while he husbanded roughly, she spent with him
        in the spasm
That blurs the sight. They lay without words. Soon limbs
        drooped
    Towards sleep in the deepening grass.

They woke for late supper. He cut and crusted two fillets
        in dampish

Clay, left them to bake until the savour
Called to their mouths. He gave her thick slices of bannock.
    When
The hot meal was over, she said.. 'Why do you delay
The feat of the wand again?' 'We must prepare the bridal
    Bed.' Waist-deep in ferns, he gathered sunny swathes.
She ran to pull the fennel bloom, wildering woodbine
    And made a border of braided daisies.

Clarke's not an easy poet to read, but if we're going to know what's good in modern literature, we must read him.

The same season that brought America *The Book of Irish Verse* brought a new collection of poems by its editor, *A Slow Dance* (Winston-Salem, N.C.: Wake Forest University Press, 1975). Montague's an Irishman born in Brooklyn, educated partly in Iowa, and in recent years largely domiciled in Paris; insofar as geography can contribute to identity, his peregrinations only increase his Irishness. *A Slow Dance* is beautiful, poems unafraid of poetry, unafraid even of a refrain that recalls Yeats, in a poem called "Courtyard in Winter":

> I plunged through snowdrifts once,
> Above our home, to carry
> A telegram to a mountain farm.
> Fearful but inviting, they waved me
> To warm myself at the flaring
> Hearth before I faced again where
>
> *Snow curls in on the cold wind.*
>
> The news I brought was sadness.
> In a far city, someone of their name
> Lay dying. The tracks of foxes,
> Wild birds as I climbed down
> Seemed to form a secret writing
> Minute and frail as life when
>
> *Snow curls in on the cold wind.*

Ireland fills Montague's veins, and the veins his lines, as he motions his words in short lines down an eloquent page:

for Patrick Collins

> The sounds of Ireland,
> that restless whispering
> you never get away
> from, seeping out of
> low bushes and grass,
> heatherbells and fern,
> wrinkling bog pools,
> scraping tree branches,
> light hunting cloud,
> sound hounding sight,
> a hand ceaselessly
> combing and stroking
> the landscape, till
> the valley gleams
> like the pile upon
> a mountain pony's coat.
>
> "Windharp"

Montague is virtually unknown and unread in this country. And he offers what we need, a richness of vocabulary and line which combines a love of poetry itself—the made space of lyric on the air, footbeat and mouth croon—with a passion of place and vision, love of land and people; love and hate together.

Of young (male) poets Ireland has plenty. The last fifty pages of *The Book of Irish Verse* includes Ciarán Carson, who has published a first book called *The New Estate*. Here's a new poem from Ireland:

> I wonder if they see me.
> Fluttering like swallows
> Behind a window, their wings
> Take the invisible
>
> Curtain of water
> Heavily as silk, as air
> Before a storm, for their
> Own weathers move them only

Slowly, their mouths opening
And shutting like an eyelid.
The branches where they nest
Half-asleep are those of

An ornamental garden;
Where they drift,
Miniature trees
Flower as paint through water;

The thin bubbles
Rising in scales to the surface
Mime various bird-musics.
Suddenly I felt helpless

As if, seeing an accident
Outside, my mouth was pressed
To the glass, my hands uttered
Dialects of silence.
                    "Fishes in a Chinese Restaurant"

But politics, the violent results of politics, puts its heel on this
book. As with Seamus Heaney, the current troubles make
their way into poems:

Is it just like picking a lock
with the slow deliberation of a funeral,
hesitating through a darkened nave
until you find the answer?

Listening to the malevolent tick
of its heart, can you read
the message of the threaded veins
like print, its body's chart?

The city is a map of the city,
its forbidden areas changing daily.
I find myself in a crowded taxi
making deviations from the known route,

> ending in a cul-de-sac
> where everyone breaks out suddenly
> in whispers, noting the boarded windows,
> the drawn blinds.
>
> "The Bomb Disposal"

It should be noted that Carson is a northerner, born in Belfast, who attended Queen's University there. Troubles kill innocent people; troubles also seem to make poems and poetry. The greatest flowering of Irish poetry today happens in the murderous North. Out of the north comes Seamus Heaney.

North (New York: Oxford University Press, 1976) is Seamus Heaney's fourth book of poems. *Death of a Naturalist* was his first, a fully achieved book, followed by a second volume—so often observed in young poets—which was hasty and inferior, *Door into Dark;* followed in Heaney's case by an excellent third volume, *Wintering Out*, and now by *North* which is the best of all. One has the sense in Heaney that politics is forced upon him by the combination of nationality and circumstance. (One has the sense with other poets that when the times are apolitical, apolitics will become the political subject: "Romantic Ireland's dead and gone" called for a terrible beauty to be born.) Circumstance invades this volume.

> Archimedes thought he could move the world if he
> could
> find the right place to position his lever. Billy Hunter
> said Tarzan shook the world when he jumped down out
> of a tree.
>
> I sink my crowbar in a chink I know under the
> masonry
> of state and statute, I swing on a creeper of secrets
> into the Bastille.
> My wronged people cheer from their cages. The guard-

dogs are unmuzzled, a soldier pivots a muzzle at
the butt of my ear, I am stood blindfolded with my hands
above my head until I seem to be swinging from a
                                        strappado.

The commandant motions me to be seated.
'I am honoured to add a poet to our list.' He is
amused and genuine. 'You'll be safer here, anyhow.'

In the cell, I wedge myself with outstretched arms
in the corner and heave, I jump on the concrete flags to
test them. Were those your eyes just now at the hatch?
                "The Unacknowledged Legislator's Dream"

The second and final section of this book recounts such
moments. It is good poetry—and there is not a single poem
among them that ranks with Heaney's best. It's a poetry
written out of social necessity. No man or woman in North-
ern Ireland at this time could avoid social statement without
loss of humanity.
But when mad Ireland teases Heaney into the truest poetry,
in *North* it is confrontation with the long dead which pro-
vides us the favor. Heaney writes of the bog people, corpses
preserved in the humus of Ireland.

As if he had been poured
in tar, he lies
on a pillow of turf
and seems to weep

the black river of himself.
The grain of his wrists
is like bog oak,
the ball of his heel

like a basalt egg.
His instep has shrunk
cold as a swan's foot
or a wet swamp root.

His hips are the ridge
and purse of a mussel,
his spine an eel arrested
under a glisten of mud.

The head lifts,
the chin is a visor
raised above the vent
of his slashed throat

that has tanned and toughened.
The cured wound
opens inwards to a dark
elderberry place.

Who will say "corpse"
to his vivid cast?
Who will say "body"
to his opaque repose?

And his rusted hair,
a mat unlikely
as a foetus's.
I first saw his twisted face

in a photograph,
a head and shoulder
out of the peat,
bruised like a forceps baby,

but now he lies
perfected in my memory,
down to the red horn
of his nails,

hung in the scales
with beauty and atrocity:
with the Dying Gaul
too strictly compassed

on his shield,
with the actual weight
of each hooded victim,
slashed and dumped.

> "The Grauballe Man"

Here in the short lines, sentences elegantly broken across them, contemporary man touches down at an ancient source. In the title poem he makes the same motion downward through to the "longship's swimming tongue," which weds him present and past to poet's journey and task.

I returned to a long strand,
the hammered shod of a bay,
and found only the secular
powers of the Atlantic thundering.

I faced the unmagical
invitations of Iceland,
the pathetic colonies
of Greenland, and suddenly

those fabulous raiders,
those lying in Orkney and Dublin
measured against
their long swords rusting,

those in the solid
belly of stone ships,
those hacked and glinting
in the gravel of thawed streams

were ocean-deafened voices
warning me, lifted again
in violence and epiphany.
The longship's swimming tongue

was buoyant with hindsight—
it said Thor's hammer swung

to geography and trade,
thick-witted couplings and revenges,

the hatreds and behindbacks
of the althing, lies and women,
exhaustions nominated peace,
memory incubating the spilled blood.

It said, "Lie down
in the word-hoard, burrow
the coil and gleam
of your furrowed brain.

Compose in darkness.
Expect aurora borealis
in the long foray
but no cascade of light.

Keep your eye clear
as the bleb of the icicle,
trust the feel of what nubbed treasure
your hands have known."

"North"

In a dedicatory poem, he looks at the Irish present with eyes
gifted with linkage, and makes for us all the human cove-
nant, found in a particular natural place:

They seem hundreds of years away. Breughel,
You'll know them if I can get them true.
They kneel under the hedge in a half-circle
Behind a windbreak wind is breaking through.
They are the seed cutters. The tuck and frill
Of leaf-sprout is on the seed potatoes
Buried under that straw. With time to kill
They are taking their time. Each sharp knife goes
Lazily halving each root that falls apart
In the palm of the hand: a milky gleam,

And, at the centre, a dark watermark.
O calendar customs! Under the broom
Yellowing over them, compose the frieze
With all of us there, our anonymities.

"The Seed Cutters"

Reading the English*
The Continental Drift of the Poetries

(1979)

I

The poetries of England and America have become discontinuous. If Americans read English poetry without a preconception of discontinuity, they read very, very bad American poems; perhaps they leave grudging space for Charles Tomlinson or Tom Raworth. If Englishmen read American poetry without expecting differences, they praise John Crowe Ransom and find Whitman "untidy"—as C. H. Sisson does, in *Parnassus* Spring/Summer 1978.

I address Americans, as an admirer of many contemporary English poets, wanting to convince doubters that English poetry is worth reading. Of course there are Americans who read and admire English poets—John Matthias knows more English poetry than anybody else—but most who read it are merely Anglophile; they also admire British Railways tea. The prevailing wisdom among us says that the energy left English poetry some years back—when Blake turned in his chips, some would say; others would allow Hopkins; some go as far as Auden—and traveled cross-channel to

---

* And Scots, and Orkneymen, etc. . . . . I cherish a dislike for the word "British."

Ireland and cross-ocean to these parts. It is a received idea that English poets for fifty years (or a hundred and fifty) have been interior decorators unskilled in interior decoration. Back in the Sixties this view was advanced with special fury; I was living in England when a chap showed up from the Pacific Northwest, looked around him for a week, and announced with some disdain that there were more good poets in *Seattle* than there were in the United Kingdom.

At the same time, it used to be progressive and fashionable for English critics to agree with American self-esteem. Now, when Americans are less excited to prove their point, it would surprise most American readers to learn that England has recovered some of its old arrogance, or confidence, and—with an ignorance almost as gross as our own—looks upon contempory American poetry as pretentious and barbaric. Witness, for instance, a mind-boggling survey of "Recent American Poetry," printed in the *PN Review* by a fellow named Andrew Waterman. Recent American poetry consists of six poets: Margaret Newlin, Ernest Sandeen, Frederick Morgan, Michael Mott, Anthony Hecht, and Robert Bly. On his way to attack Bly and Merwin, Waterman—who apparently considers them influenced by William Carlos Williams—tells us: "American poets and readers have harkened too readily to the Williams keynote of the false-naive (I mean, *flowers* and things, gee I feel sort of rapt and *grateful*, I don't need to *make* anything of it *artistically*, that'd be sort of *artificial* for Chrissake, destroy its validity as, like, *experience*. What you want, *poetry* or something?)." This is music-hall xenophobia, attributing to Williams or to Bly or to Merwin (or all of them) the prepschool idiom of Holden Caulfield, slightly afflicted with rumors of the Sixties. This sort of language has nothing to do with Williams or with Bly or with Merwin—three rather different cases, one might think—and reveals an ignorance as profound as its malice; and Waterman reviews Bly's *This Body is Made of Camphor and Gopher Wood*, without reference to Kabir.

Nothing is accomplished by know-nothing condescension, beyond devious and shaky support for national self-esteem. It will be unfortunate if such bigotry persists, because an informed engagement with the other literature may be useful, for poets and critics alike. An injection of T'ang once helped the poet from Wyncote; the Singer of St. Louis found himself when he discovered a Frenchman on the shelves of the Harvard Union library. I mean to say that English and American literatures have moved far apart; and influences are often useful in proportion to the distance they travel. Because prevailing English modes are as distinct from prevailing American modes as haiku from Icelandic saga, American readers must learn to approach English poets *as if* they were reading translations from the Polish—with a generous and larcenous eye. Generous, Americans will learn to recognize excellence; larcenous, they will learn (as they have learned from Chileans and Czechs) to steal what they lack and to improve their poems.

I recommend an attitude. I realize that to read a poem in something which *resembles* your own tongue is not the same thing as reading a translation. And I welcome the difference. The qualities we can learn from the English differ from the qualities we can learn from Czechs and Chileans. It is a characteristic flaw among young Americans, however accomplished and innovative, to lack resourceful *sound*. Tin ears make bad alloy with golden metaphors. Allied is the lack of resourceful syntax, reliance instead on simple and compound sentences. I suppose that a number of reasons account for these weaknesses, and I suppose the chiefest reason is that the *literary* sources, for many of these poets, are translations or readings in languages half-learned.

I underline *literary* sources because literature forms only one of the tributaries contributing to the new poem. One's own common speech, one's culture, one's society, one's common life, one's uncommon psyche add their own waters. But a paucity of English-language *literary* sources may well account for the diminished sound of contemporary American verse. Cadence translates only rarely and partially; good translations attend to image and overall structure, in cadences managed in the language translated *into*. Generally if the translator is a good poet he improvises versions of his own characteristic cadences. To learn sound from Chilean and Czech, one need listen with knowledgeable ears to the original language. If the literary sources of a poet's particular ear are the half-energies of translated sound, that poet loses a portion of his possible education.

Now the sounds of English poetry are not the same as American sounds because the noises of the two nations differ. But the relationship among a poem's sounds persists. If an English poet makes assonance on a particular English vowel sound, the sound is different when an American reads it—but for the most part assonance is preserved because vowels for the most part change consistently. Consonants vary less than vowels. Therefore an American reading Donne or Wordsworth or Keats or Hardy (none of whom spoke like BBC actors) hears a music of resolution which resembles the original, perceivable as formal and phonic resolution. So with line and line-break. English syntax has not yet wholly parted company from American syntax (though English melody expresses syntax through pitch in patterns unlike American melodies), and American poets, reading the English, can find coherences on a level of syntax as well as sound. These are coherences which they can steal, which they can learn from, which they can transfer to their own practice without losing national identity.

II

National identity is crucial, and nationhood is a mystery. Until America rebelled and became an independent nation there was no American literature. Anne Bradstreet is colonial, Philip Freneau is colonial. We may quibble about the exact date American literature began, but our candidates for the first American book were published within a few decades of each other. I would make Hawthorne the beginning, thinking of Poe as limited not by nationality but by obsession. Longfellow lived and died a colonist, making Americanist epics in English idiom and rhythm. In Hawthorne, Poe, Melville, Whitman, Dickinson, there were elements that derived from English sources, portions of the tradition, but in each writer was a national identity which was firmly and finally un-English.

American literature differs from English not only because of the difference between the traditions, but in the extent to which tradition informs the work at all. An English writer's soil is layered with Roman bones, Celtic and Danish. You cannot dig down two feet in England without digging into the centuries. When England goes socialist, it not only progresses toward something in the future but it follows something in the past—a reaching back to notions of common ownership which were medieval, the people only expropriated during the reign of Whig landowners and manufacturers. Now the dispossessed begin to repossess, the idea of common ownership and commonwealth a confluence of progressive Marxism and medievalist reaction. But when Americans are socialist, their socialism arrives horizontally, across the waves, from ideas and books.

The tradition that matters most, to a nation's literature, is not the style or the content of its great writers. It is the soil of its history, the bones of its dead ground up in that soil, and the ideas and passions, the battles and revolutions, the glories and defeats of nation and spirit. Our tradition (like it or not) is enlightenment, protestant, industrial, and capitalist. In England tradition is inevitably layered. Last year I returned to a town called Bradwell-super-Mare in Essex, to a place I remembered. Here it was that Roman invaders built a fort called Othona against Danes invading across the North Sea. It was the last fort the Christianized Romans abandoned when they left England about 400 A.D. Then the area went pagan again, for a time, until a Celtic bishop named Cedd sailed down the east coast in the Seventh Century to bring the gospel. At Othona he built a church, using Roman bricks still there, perhaps restoring a cornerhouse of the old fort.

Then, then, then . . . sometime in the Nineteenth Century, an antiquarian reading old chronicles tried to figure out where Cedd might have built his church; the scholar determined a place on the map, visited it, and found there a barn full of a farmer's hay—and the barn made of Roman brick, three arches at one end of it bricked in . . . . In ditches on the approach to the church there are concrete pylons which the Home Guards set in the fields against Hitler's gliders in 1942; there are WW II pillboxes all around; and when they dug seatrench in 1942 against the tanks invading, they dug up hills of Roman sea wall erected against invaders coming from the same sea. . . . The place is a cross-section of two thousand years, of soldiers in varying costumes, of worship and watchfulness.

And when I write of it here, I sound like the tourist I am. For the literate English, this layering of the past is the air breathed and the ground walked on.

America begins with the encroachments of industry and in a secular time. We are not only English in background, we are not only white, we are not only Christian. Our DNA derives largely from Europeans who turned their backs on the past, who said goodbye, who left it all. We are their descendants who keep moving always, who think of settlement as death, who praise living in the present. To praise the present—which is after all the only place any of us lives—is only to dispraise thought of the future and memory of the past. It is our nature, and from our natures we make our poetry.

On the other hand, English poets work with (and against) thousands of years of history and five hundred years of literature. The burden is considerable. American poets have a century and a quarter of literature; otherwise, what do we have? Probably a sense of nakedness, a sense of the necessity for originality and innovation, a sense of tradition as jail or subservience. We must keep moving, to prove to ourselves that we are free. This sense of adventure and originality, of literature as the voyage across seas to the unknown place, makes our literature energetic, attractive, brave, and romantic.

III

For evidence of the discontinuity of English and American poetry, I recommend C. H. Sisson's remarks in the Spring/Summer 1978 issue of this magazine. Sisson is a fine poet, little read in this country, and a literary and social critic whose prose is a continual, quirky pleasure. (Carcanet has just published a monumental volume of collected essays called *The Avoidance of Literature*; for an example of classic English prose, read Sisson's essay on William Barnes.) But his *Parnassus* essay on American poetry proves again that even Homer nods. When Sisson comes to Whitman he exclaims—"this loud, untidy writer . . . a sinister portent of worse to come . . . A lout of the Western Protestant decadence . . . What an unpleasant man!" This last dismissal apparently responds to a line in which Whitman mentions privies.

Possibly most of us are loud, untidy, unpleasant louts. (Europeans have been known to say as much.) Our tradition *is* protestant, Western, and doubtless from Sisson's Anglican viewpoint, decadent. We are all offspring of that monstrous marriage between Mr. Whitman of New York and Miss Dickinson of Amherst, Massachusetts. Of Emily Dickinson Sisson hints darkly: "I say only that she has to be read with, and judged against, Christina Rossetti. . . ." As it happens I have been reading Ms. Rossetti, with mild pleasure, discovering that the critical patriarchy has overlooked a poet of talent. But the achievement of Emily Dickinson—originality, energy, range, and intelligence—is vaster by far, a fact apparently not discernible to the English mind. Wallace Stevens we find ". . . one of the Great Names whose work I have never been able to stomach. . . ." And Robert Frost gets the Emily Dickinson treatment, comparison with a minor homeboy: "for proper evaluation Frost . . . needs to be set beside Edward Thomas"—the small, pleasing poet whom Frost created.

Sisson of course claims that the poetries are continuous, and bases his claim on a reason that seems to me preposterous: "the language spoken on the two sides of the Atlantic . . . is such as to permit of a more or less unimpeded conversation." The statement pretends that the identity of a literature is its approximate lexical continuity. But how much besides the O.E.D. enters our poems! Besides the merely personal elements of poems—perhaps distasteful but usually undeniable—there is the national and the historical. Precisely the reader who finds Whitman a loud lout is unable to hear what he says and how he says it for reasons of nationhood. In his political writing, Sisson is eloquent on national identity, on the matter of England, as it were, the matter of France. Are we seriously to suppose that the difference between French and English poets depends only on Larousse and the O.E.D.? Is there no national character? History? American and English are not so far apart in the lexicon as English and French; at this moment, they may be further apart in history.

Then Sisson says that we do not consider St. Augustine an African writer, nor Seneca nor Martial Spanish writers. I find this suggestion curious. Was Dante a Latin writer when he wrote Latin, Italian when he wrote Italian? Was Milton Latin when he wrote his Latin poems, and only became English when he wrote in English? St. Augustine, Seneca, and Martial were Latin writers, wherever they were born, because they were citizens of an Empire—Roman or Holy Roman: *ubicumque lingua romana, ubicumque roma*. But the British Empire is dead; it is not true, as Sisson in his enthusiasm would have it, that where the English language is, there is England.

For contrast let me quote another Englishman, another good poet, this one a student of American literature who has lived in this country and perceives the separateness of the literatures. In a review of Edward Dorn, in the *Sewanee*, Donald Davie cites a sloppy text, and quotes a flippant poem, and mentions that many of his friends do not share his admiration for Dorn. "Dorn knows England well, and . . . defines his own tradition, and indeed his own language, as firmly distinct from theirs—as American. . . ."

IV

One other matter, for which I will again make use of Sisson's essay; he writes of Whitman: "One knows he is lying when he goes on: 'And in my soul I swear I will never deny him.'" (Whitman has been going on about the "cleaner of privies.") Well, I am not so sure he is lying. In Sisson's own remarkable poems, I am struck with his self-accusation and self-distrust. He displays an emotion or an idea, then sees through himself to report on his own dishonesty or vanity or greed or egotism; distrust has the last word. In the best English poet of all, Geoffrey Hill, this self-distrust is almost the basis of the style, of the grammar, clauses balanced so that the final antithesis contains in a precise doubleness both the statement and an acidulous criticism of the statement. I suppose this is called irony—but I want a more serious word: an ironic American tends merely to display a consistent tonal sarcasm, saying something and denying its seriousness, wearing protective covering. In Sisson and in Hill this irony is deadly serious, not mask nor armor plate but vision.

Romantic Americans like Whitman typically want to become better than they are. They are not occupied with seeing through themselves, but with self-improvement. Obviously this endeavor presupposes that the self needs improving, but the emphasis is not on error but on possible rectification. As irony can become a self-cancelling tic, so can this emphasis on betterment become wearisome. Many contemporary American poets write a narcissistic flat line full of images which tell us what a fine fellow the poet is, or will shortly become. He may be a drunk, he may be cruel to women, but somehow or other through it all his golden heart shines triumphant. . . . I do not praise this garbage, but I suggest that this garbage comes from a portion of the national character that creates Whitman's true desire to become generous and accepting. Whitman made an imagined self which was *good*, made a model of tolerance, acceptance, and celebration—a moral idea. (This is not all Whitman did.) It may well be an Emersonian by-product of a history which is decadent, enlightenment, and protestant—but it is not, I think, a lie. It is national character. I think of Ezra Pound who started with an esthetic program for betterment, turned ironic about it in *Mauberley* (his most popular poem in England), and then sought to cure the world's diseases by social credit.

I have used words like "typically" to cover myself. No generalization about national character will hold. But America, where psychoanalysis has thrived as it never has in England—and Scientology and Coué and EST and Jim Jones— is populated by people who believe that they can *change*, that they are not doomed by circumstance, that they can by understanding or imagination or transcendence remove or replace or at least alter the old Adam. Obviously such a belief—in the pursuit of happiness, I suppose—is vulnerable to charges of naiveté and self-delusion. I assert its pervasiveness. After all, Americans carry in their genes the DNA of people who believed that by emigrating they could change and improve their lives.

The two poetries are discontinuous because they emerge from different gene pools.

V

I had intended to hold up for display a number of young English poets, and instead I have spent my time on matters of nationality. I will at any rate mention one or two—but first I need to speak of some older poets, almost equally unread in this country. There is, for example, W. S. Graham, who is a superb poet. He is a Scot who has lived for many years in Cornwall, in his sixties now, and has just published his fourth book with Faber, *Implements in Their Places*. When he published his first book in 1949, *The White Threshold*, Dylan Thomas had risen from the burnt Apocalypse, the war deaths of Sidney Keyes and Keith Douglas left English poetry impoverished; the movement hovered in the wings with its inept imitations of Empson. Graham seemed a late Apocalyptic then, out of place; he has continued for thirty years to write, out of place and time, no Apocalyptic but an original, varied, Romantic voice. In his new book he ruminates language, stubbornly and playfully arguing with silence:

> What is the language using us for?
> Said Malcolm Mooney moving away
> Slowly over the white language.
> Where am I going said Malcolm Mooney.
>
> Certain experiences seem to not
> Want to go in to language maybe
> Because of shame or the reader's shame.
> Let us observe Malcolm Mooney.
>
> Let us get through the suburbs and drive
> Out further just for fun to see
> What he will do. Reader, it does
> Not matter. He is only going to be
>
> Myself and for you slightly you
> Wanting to be another. He fell
> He falls (Tenses are everywhere.)
> Deep down into a glass jail.
>
> I am in a telephoneless, blue
> Green crevasse and I can't get out.
> I pay well for my messages
> Being hoisted up when you are about.
>
> I suppose you open them under the light
> Of midnight of The Dancing Men.
> The point is would you ever want
> To be down here on the freezing line
>
> Reading the words that steam out
> Against the ice? Anyhow draw
> This folded message up between
> The leaning prisms from me below.
>
> Slowly over the white language

Comes Malcolm Mooney the saviour.
My left leg has no feeling.
What is the language using us for?

His loneliness is gregarious, his silence gabby, and his particular music is created by syntax struggling over line breaks. Anyone will need to read thirty pages before learning to hear this music. Probably it is useless to quote this eccentric master, but I cannot forebear:

I have my yellow boots on to walk
Across the shires where I hide
Away from my true people and all
I can't put easily into my life.

So you will see I am stepping on
The stones between the runnels getting
Nowhere nowhere. It is almost
Embarrassing to be alive alone.

Take my hand and pull me over from
The last stone on to the moss and
The three celandines. Now my dear
Let us go home across the shires.

"The Stepping Stones"

The title poem is long. Here is the seventy-first numbered section out of seventy-four.

I can discern at a pinch you
Through the lens of the ouzo glass,
Your face globing this whole Piraeus
Taverna of buzzing plucked wires.
Here we are sitting, we two
In a very deep different country
At this table in the dark.
Inevitable tourists us,
Not in Scotland sitting here
In foreign shadows, bouzouki
Turning us into two others

Across the waiting eating table.
At home in Blantyre if your mother
Looked at the map with a microscope
Her Scotch palate would be appalled
To see us happy in the dark
Fishing the legs of creature eight
Out of the hot quink ink to eat.

Parse the last sentence!—where "eight" comes out as a hasty parenthesis—and its use of "appalled" with "dark."

No one in America publishes this fine eccentric Scot.*

I attempt no survey, heaven knows. Even a list would only frustrate. I have written elsewhere about Geoffrey Hill, C. H. Sisson, and Basil Bunting. Charles Tomlinson and Charles Causley are published here, and even R. S. Thomas appears in some anthologies. Thom Gunn lives in this country, which has allowed us to know him a little. Although Donald Davie lives here much of the year, it is my impression that his excellent poems are little read, that he is better known as a critic than as a poet. Of course Ted Hughes and Philip Larkin are our token Englishmen. (It will be noted that I list no women. I have recently read twenty-seven new books of poems sent by English publishers; not one was written by a woman. Nor do I think this sample a misrepresentation. I am otherwise aware of several English women poets. Fleur Adcock has recently published a book of which I have seen agreeable reviews. As I finished proofreading this essay, I received in the mail a good book by Jenny Joseph, published by Secker and Warburg. Of course there are others—but there are not very many others. Published English women poets, published *at all*, are rare. The United States has been sufficiently chauvinist in its history, literary and otherwise— but it seems another mystery of national character that

---

* In the autumn of 1979, Faber has published W. S. Graham's *Collected Poems 1942–1977*, which includes selections from two early books I was ignorant of.

American women are quicker to make poems than English women. In America now, the best younger poets are largely female. In England nothing comparable appears to be happening. Or is it that English women are writing the poems, and that they are not being published?)

But nobody in the United States reads George MacKaye Brown. This prognathous Orkneyman, in his early forties I should guess, has written remarkable books of poems, most recently *Winterfold*. As R. S. Thomas takes his poems from the hills of Wales, Brown is a Viking poet from the spare islands: this is the third poem from a sequence called "Vikings":

> Remarking, 'It is not to my taste
> To wheeze on a white pillow
> Nor to toil gravewards on a stick, murdered slowly
> By avarice, envy, lust,'
> Elinar ran where the swords fell thickest.
>
> An Irish axe
> Struck the right shoulder of Sweyn the skald.
> 'In future,' said Sweyn,
> 'I will write my poems with the left hand.
> I will sup a sinister broth.'
>
> Near the end of the battle.
> Rolf returned to the ship, downcast.
> 'Gudrun,' he said, 'is a proud woman.
> She will not bed with boys.
> Hard wounds I sought
> For thigh and chest and forehead today.
> All I have got
> Is a broken tooth, an eye blue as an oyster,
> And my pinkie scratched.
> From now on, Gudrun,
> I will court less particular girls.'
>
> "A Battle in Ulster"

This poem is further from London than Kansas City is. From

"The Sea: Four Elegies":

> Think of death, how it has many doors.
> A child enters the Dove Door
> And leaves a small wonderment behind him.
> For soldiers and airmen there is the Door of Fire.
> Most of us, with inadequate heart or lung or artery
> Disappear through the simple Door of the Skull.
> There is the Door of the Sheaf: the granary is beyond.
> The very old enter, stooping,
> Harvesters under a load of tranquil sorrows.
> For islanders, the Door of Water.
> Beyond a lintel carved with beautiful names
> The sea yields to the bone, at last, a meaning.

"The Door of Water"

Religious feeling and religious thought dominate Brown even more than Orkney does. Although in contemporary England culture is even more secular than in the United States, where most American poets seem as irreligious as the universities they work for, the best English poets like Hill and Sisson run counter to their culture; perhaps this phenomenon derives from or agrees with the English poet's closeness to centuries, soil, and history. Here is one more poem by George MacKaye Brown:

> Cool water over my fingers flowing
>
> The upstart
> Had ruined a night and a morning for me.
> I thrust that stone face from my door.
>
> I was told later he bent a knee
> Between the cupid and the rose bush.
> The gardener told me that later, laughing.
>
> And that a woman hung upon him like a fountain.
>
> What is it to me, who helps this king

Or strikes him down?
I reduced majesty to a driven shadow.

Another woman stood between him and the sun,
A tree, sifting light and shadow across his face.

Outside the tavern
It was down with him once more,
Four holes in the dust.

More women then, a gale of them,
His face like a scald
And they moving about him, a tumult of shadows and
    breezes.

He clung close to the curve of the world.

The king had gone out in a purple coat.
Now the king
Wore only rags of flesh about the bone.

(I examined cornstalks in the store at Tarsus
And discovered a black kernel.

Of the seven vats shipped from Rhodes
Two had leaked in the hold,
One fell from the sling and was broken.)

And tell this Arimathean
He can do what he likes with the less-than-shadow.

No more today. That business is over. Pass the seal.

"Pilate"

David Wright is in his fifties, lives in the Lake Country, and has been deaf most of his life; he came to England from South Africa as a boy. (Many other "English" poets come from Australia, New Zealand, South Africa.) Carcanet published David Wright's selected poems a year or two ago. Here is a poem from a sequence about revisiting Africa:

Three stunted jacarandas, planted this year,
And, red as its corrugated iron roof,
Raw ground surrounds the Anderson bungalow,
And aloes, evergreen scrub; not green enough.

A few profitable shares will cultivate
(The monocled colonel is a stockbroker)
This acre of quartz outcrop. Shovel and pick
Level and break soil, rocks. These white splinters, stone,

In earth like drying blood, or scratched flesh, or both:
A wound extended daily by hired convicts
For lawns, parterres, and pools for fish to swim in.
Cheap, says the colonel.
                            I saw his D. S. O.

Bland on plump satin, forty years ago.
'The district's not what it was. Jews, Italians.
The houses faded, derelict stucco fronts,
Nobody you'd know now.' The colonel's garden

A waterfall of leaves; over the cracked tiles
Virginia creeper; vines bind the pergola;
Those heavy and deciduous trees, full grown,
Might hide a Ligurian or Etruscan villa.

                    "Terrace Road, 1928, 1970"

And another, on two American expatriots:

Old whitebearded figure outside the abbey,
Erect, creating his own solitude,
Regards, tremulously, an undistinguished crowd,
Literati of the twentieth century.
They have come to pay homage to his contemporary;
He, to a confederate poet who is dead.
The service is over. Fierce and gentle in his pride,
A lume spento, senex from America,

He can only remember, stand, and wonder.
His justice is not for us. The solitary
Old man has made his gesture. Question now

Whom did the demoded Muse most honour
When she assigned with eternal irony
An order of merit and a cage at Pisa?

"E. P. at Westminster"

This measured eloquence of tone and this dignified wit seem
qualities generally lacking in contemporary American verse.

Carcanet—which now publishes more good English poets
than anybody else—has also brought out a new volume by
John Heath-Stubbs, from which I must print two small ex-
amples. Like David Wright's, it is a kind of verse Americans
do not write:

Old men, as they grow older, grow the more garrulous,
Drivelling *temporis acta* into their beards,
Argumentative, theoretical, diffuse.

With the poet, not so. One learns
To be spare of words; to make cold thrusts
Into the frosty air that comes.

The final message—a few strokes on the sand;
A bird's footprints running to take off
Into the adverse wind.

"A Few Strokes on the Sand"

Hearing a nightingale one evening sing,
A frog from its puddle opined:
'Among those senseless twittering roulades
Occasionally you note
A deep hoarse croaking, which evinces
Definite marks of talent.

Eh me, what a frog is lost in him!'

"The Frog and the Nightingale"

Donald Davie's latest volume, also from Carcanet, contains a poem addressed to us, from "Depravity: Two Sermons":

> The best, who could, went back—because they nursed
> A need to find depravity less dispersed,
> Less, as it seemed, diluted by crass hope.
> So back went Henry James to evil Europe,
> Unjust, unequal, cruel. Localized,
> The universal could be realized
> In words and not in words; not by the Press
> Nor the theatrical Pulpit. Prefaces
> Delineate the exquisite pains he took
> To bottle up a bad smell in a book.
> Inordinate pains! For Paris, London, Rome
> Were not much less disorderly than back home;
> There too, already, what he sought was traced
> Upon no maps, but must be found by Taste,
> A nostril lifted to the tainted gale
> Of words, of words—all shop-soiled, all for sale.
> Each year that he survived, things fell apart
> Till H. G. Wells was 'Life', and he was 'Art'.
> 'Life'! Is it something else than life, to live
> On the scent always of that faint, pervasive
> Smell that alone explains what we've become?
> What ought to be, and once was, axiom?

"Americans: for their Bicentennial"

But Carcanet mainly publishes the young. Let me end this little sampler with examples of two young English poets. First, here is Robert Wells:

> Inopportune desire! It runs to waste
> Too cold for love, too bold for secrecy
> And falls from fresh to salt, an altered taste
> Where grassy covert gives to barren sea.

"The Stream"

What a bad American poem. Learn to read English, and it is not bad at all. Or:

Dry sticks laid across
A piece of paper stained with oil
And a fire where we halt.
The sweat falls off and we drink
A mouthful of water and feel the cold.

The mule suddenly seems a lighter colour.
In the half dark
The fire paints strokes over the long muzzle
And flat hard forehead
And the forelegs

And the men move
Like more than men possessed
By their own lives,
Become what is evidenced by the rounded stones
Close in the path

And the rough stones lying like scree
At the side.
There are meetings here and things said
Though full light brings
Them back to themselves.

"Cattlemen"

He wakes in the last instant of a dream
And feels its diminishing explosions
That shake his sleep across the sudden distance
Like bridges blown, securing a retreat.

"A Dream"

My favorite of the young (living in New Hampshire, I have
doubtless missed one or two) is Jeffrey Wainright, who re-
cently published *Heart's Desire* with Carcanet. He has
learned from Geoffrey Hill, not to the point of imitation:

That is her lover lying there,
And she beside him lying close.

They do not speak, or move, or touch.
The lucid grass between them flows.

To lie, in stillness, breathing just,
Might motion time towards desire.
The air now barely moves the grass.
The sun in white draws off its fire.

"Illumination"

(It is always necessary, reading English metrical verse, to
remind oneself that "towards" is a two-syllable word.) Or this:

I.

Just above where my house sits on the slope
Is a pond, a lodge when the mine was here,
Now motionless, secretive, hung in weeds.

Sometimes on clear nights I spread my arms wide
And can fly, stiff but perfect, down
Over this pond just an inch above the surface.

When I land I have just one, two drops of water
On my beard. I am surprised how quick
I have become a flier, a walker on air.

II.

I see my brother crawling in the woods
To gather snails' shells. *This is not
A vision.* Look carefully and you can tell

How he is caught in the roots of a tree
Whose long branches spread upwards bearing as
Fruit gardeners and journeymen, merchants

And lawyers, jewellers and bishops,
Cardinals chamberlains nobles princes
Branch by branch kings pope and emperor.

Reading the English, it is useful to start with the magazines. Three of them are essential to anyone who wants a window onto English poetry. The old wonder is *Agenda*, splendidly edited for many years by William Cookson. (Subscriptions: Cranbourne Court, Albert Bridge Rd., London SW11 4PE, U.K.) *Agenda* is respectful of its elders, and has done special issues on Pound and David Jones when they were alive, on Basil Bunting recently. It has printed much of the best Geoffrey Hill, much Davie. Also essential is the new wonder *PNR*, *Poetry Nation Review*, published by Carcanet in Manchester. (Subscriptions: 5 Elton Rd., Clevedon, Avon, BS21 7RA, U.K.) Editors are Michael Schmidt—young and energetic, also editor for books with Peter Jones—and Donald Davie and C. H. Sisson. *PNR* is loaded with criticism and social argument, with a tendency toward the political right. (Jon Silkin has been annoyed with its monarchism.) Some of its young critics have discovered Yvor Winters. With its energy, its vigor, and its youth, it is spotty—I quoted earlier from a bigoted review of American poets—and it is the liveliest magazine of poetry in the language. Finally, among essential magazines, there is Jon Silkin's *Stand*, politically left, with reviews, poems, and much translation from continental literature. (Subscriptions: 19 Haldane Terrace, Newcastle upon Tyne, NE2 3AN, U.K.) Another place to read young English poets is Faber's series of anthologies called *Poetry: Introduction*—of which I have so far seen four. Each paperback includes six to ten poets, with a generous selection of poems by each. Needless to say, neither these magazines nor the Faber series is notable for printing women.

My premise has been that Americans can learn from the English (as of course English can learn from Americans) once they agree that the poetries are separate. It is a social disease to be an American Anglophile to the extent of imitation. But through their poetry we have access to their tradition, their Europe, and their Latin; we can learn to read them as well as we can learn Spanish, possibly better.

Geoffrey Hill
Naming The Devils

(1980)

Tenebrae is Geoffrey Hill's fourth book of poems, issued in the United States by Houghton Mifflin, which had the good sense to collect Hill's three earlier volumes into *Somewhere is Such a Kingdom* in 1975. *For the Unfallen* (1959) was Hill's first book, containing early poems like "Genesis," "Merlin," and "In Memory of Jane Fraser" which are lush and powerful, and remain Hill's anthology pieces. Later poems in that volume include "Of Commerce and Society" and "Two Formal Elegies"; they are less grand than ironic, less vowel than consonant—better and less anxious to please. His second collection was *King Log* (1968), from which Hill's critics often single out "The Songbook of Sebastian Arrurruz" and "Funeral Music." The volume which brought widest notice in England was *The Mercian Hymns* (1971), a sequence of prose poems or canticles which juxtapose an ancient King Offa with twelve centuries of English history. In *Tenebrae* Hill returns to the metrical line; some of the best new poems are sonnets.

Hill's poems are complex in syntax and lexicon, dense with allusion to literature of the past, to English history, to European history and religious thought. American poetry, over the twenty years of Hill's publication, has largely moved into simplicity of diction and grammar, and into discourse which has rid itself of allusion: a poetry largely without

85

history, founded often on notions of historical discontinuity, sometimes on defiant ignorance. These purities have made a powerful American poetry, though it is possible that their utility has exhausted itself; but I do not contrast Hill with American practice in order to beat the one with the other. I call attention to the contrast because it is great enough to make Hill appear all but unreadable—pretentious, affected, impenetrable, reactionary—to Americans unfamiliar with, say, English religious poets of the seventeenth century.

Actually, American readers looking for a door into Hill need not go so far away; early influences on Hill were paradoxically American: Allen Tate, for instance—who went to school to the seventeenth century—and early Richard Eberhart. Geoffrey Hill even resembles the young Robert Lowell of *Lord Weary's Castle*, not because Hill learned from Lowell, but because both poets departed from Tate. Still most contemporary Americans will be put off by Hill when they first read him. We must approach him acknowledging that he is alien; we must remain undeceived by contemporaneity, or by the apparent similarity of English and American languages. Only by admitting his distance may we come close enough to Hill to love his poems and make use of them.

Hill's major subjects, out of which his poems weave a continuous cloth, are erotic and spiritual love, history as suffering, and the lives and deaths of the martyrs. His poetry is suffused with religion, but it is not a poetry of belief; it is a poetry of struggle and pain, obsessed with Christianity in which it takes no comfort or solace. History is England first, by means of various archaeologies from a half-mythical Mercia to nineteenth-century factories and twentieth-century motorways. Through ecclesiastical history Hill's time recedes backward—as his language sometimes approaches Latin—as far as Calvary. Europe is Roman or Holy Roman, with local tribes speaking their Frankish and Anglish dialects. But Anglish indeed prevails: toward the end of the *Mercian Hymns*, he told us about a grandmother "whose childhood and prime womanhood were spent in a nailer's darg."

Hill's martyrs begin with the Saints from Sebastian

through Southwell, and continue to Dietrich Bonhoeffer. They are not only Christian; the overwhelming event of modern history is Hitler's final solution; contemporary suffering and martyrdom center on Dachau and Belsen. And many martyrs elegized are the twentieth-century poet-victims of tyranny: Mandelstam, Desnos, Hernandez. This history is real, yet it fulfills some of the functions of myth. As C. H. Sisson says in an essay about Hill, both history and myth are "repositories of the common experience which gives meaning to what we feel as individuals." Although the poems are strongly emotional, they are general rather than confessional. When Hill doubts his martyrs, we understand that his scepticism is self-directed, but we do not hear details of his life.

If he doubts the motives of martyrs—that ecstacy of submission—or his own motives for lamentation, he doubts *everything*. Self-mistrust is the slogan on his shield, and he entertains no subject without suspecting his own entertainment. His St. Robert Southwell wrote that "a poet, a lover and a liar are by many reckoned but three things with one signification. . . ." If Hill takes poetry as seriously as anyone alive, he doubts in particular that part of himself that takes poetry seriously—"the tongue's atrocities." In his early "Orpheus and Eurydice," Hill's Orpheus approaches the "still moist dead," "to be judged / For his song. . . ." He is, indeed, "Serene even to a fault."

In mentioning Hill's concerns, I have left sexual love until last; it is strongest of all. Of course it is intertwined with suffering and suspicion and everything else, but this is a poetry of sensuality as well as sensuousness. The natural world in Hill's poems is fecund and thick with the blood of sex, wounds, and sexual wounds, both attractive and repellant, "an earth of sickly richness" Jeffrey Wainwright calls it. I am aware of no recent poetry which more belongs to the body, both in its texture of mouthy rhythm and in its imagery, yet it is also a poetry repelled by body.

In general, it is a system of such oppositions which creates Geoffrey Hill's poems. In "Veni Coronaberis" two relatively simple quatrains name some of Hill's contraries:

> The crocus armies from the dead
> rise up; the realm of love renews
> the battle it was born to lose,
> though for a time the snows have fled
>
> and old stones blossom in the south
> with sculpted vine and psaltery
> and half-effaced adultery
> the bird-dung dribbling from its mouth;

The middle couplet of the first quatrain reflects the conflict which Hill continually embodies, representing it smoothly in military metaphor. When the metaphor moves to flower and stone, the language becomes more typical of Hill, as his last line contradicts in its scrupulous ugliness the beauty of the earlier lines. Statement and denial are of course properties of irony. "Hill's use of irony," says Jon Silkin, "is ubiquitous, but it is not, usually, of the non-participatory and mandarin sort. It articulates the collision of events," and it is precisely participatory, an alert self-mocking corrosive moral concern.

To read Hill you must immerse yourself in his actual language, because its quick alternations of tone, its sudden and frequent reverses, work to *prevent* paraphrase; no sooner do you think you have accomplished paraphrase than you realize that you have allowed a qualification to escape notation; it is like trying to summarize a Beethoven quartet. I find myself considering music's kind of statement, when I read Geoffrey Hill—the way music in its articulated structure of pitch continually abolishes itself, sketching the way by traveling, rubbing itself out as it travels. Flailing about for analogies, I think also of a literary image from atomic physics: a billion particles in constant motion, like the desk I write on, find stasis in contradiction. If C. H. Sisson compares Hill to Crashaw in his fastidiousness—"a mind in search of artifices to protect itself against its own passions . . ."—I find Hill's passions perceivable in the mind's desperate artifice, and not beyond it. And if in the end he has contradicted everything that he has said, including his own contradictions, he has made an articulated structure, or representation, of the modern mind unable to find rest or resolution, defeated and beautiful in stillness.

Here is a whole brief poem in which the statement is plain and the oscillations less swift than usual; it will hold still to be talked about. "Christmas Trees" is about the German theologian Dietrich Bonhoeffer, former pacifist who plotted and spied against Hitler, was imprisoned and executed.

> Bonhoeffer in his skylit cell
> bleached by the flares' candescent fall,
> pacing out his own citadel,
>
> restores the broken themes of praise,
> encourages our borrowed days,
> by logic of his sacrifice.
>
> Against wild reasons of the state
> his words are quiet but not too quiet.
> We hear too late or not too late.

Jeffrey Wainwright calls attention to Hill's strategic metrical variation in the next-to-last line. After a poem disciplined into smooth octosyllabic tetrameters, regular and soft-spoken, the extra syllable and the feminine ending of "his words are quiet but not too quiet" are mimetic of the motion from lamentation and praise to the proper notation of our hearing, our response or our non-response. The variation, in its scrupulous reservation, is almost comic—and exactly appropriate. Hill is simply too *responsible* a thinker and poet to leave his words ringing with praise. I use the word "mimetic"quoting Hill, who wrote in an essay: "If language is more than a vehicle for the transmission of axioms and concepts, rhythm is correspondingly more than physiological motor or a paradise of dainty devices. It is capable of registering, mimetically, deep shocks of recognition . . ."

"Christmas Trees" is one of six short poems in *Tenebrae*. Most of the book is four major sequences ending with the title poem. The first is "The Pentecost Castle," which is erotic, sensuous, and lethal; a love poem in which eros and innocence are slaughtered together, it makes a plaintive sound:

> I was going
> to gather flowers
> my love waited
> among the trees
>
> down in the orchard
> I met my death
> under the briar rose
> I lie slain

The dead lover speaks, living, and dies again. Perhaps because he has been praised for his intricate and expressive punctuation—both Christopher Ricks in a long lecture reprinted in *TLS*, and Jon Silkin in his essay, praise and explicate Hill's devoted use of brackets—Hill writes here without punctuation. His rhythm substitutes the frequent pausing of dimeter lines for the pauses and pitch-changes required by comma and bracket; he retains control. Here is the last of the fifteen twelve-line sections:

> I shall go down
> to the lovers' well
> and wash this wound
> that will not heal
>
> beloved soul
> what shall you see
> nothing at all
> yet eye to eye
>
> depths of non-being
> perhaps too clear
> my desire dying
> as I desire

The lines move down the page erasing themselves; if we go

down, yet it is to a *well*; we may *wash* a *wound*, but it is a *wound* which *will not heal*; if the *soul* is addressed as *beloved*, it is told that it will *see nothing* in the water; if it will *see nothing*, it will *see* it *eye* to *eye*—which on reflection suggests that the *beloved soul* is also *nothing; depths*, yes, but of *non-being*; and he ends with the magnificent, inclusive ambiguity of "as"—my desire dying as I wish it to; my desire dying in the act of desiring. It may be noted that only motive or circumstance is ambiguous: in both readings desire dies.

Lachrimae is a series of seven sonnets. It begins with a subtitle out of Dowland, who also supplies some section-titles; there is an epigraph from Southwell, one line of which is repeated in reverse later in the poem; the sequence quotes from sonnets by Quevedo, Lope de Vega, and an anonymous Spanish sonneteer; and there are allusions to a masque by Ben Jonson and Inigo Jones. A flesh of gathered allusion, yet the result is coherent and single-voiced; Hill is saturated with literature—but when literature reconstitutes itself to emerge from his mouth, it has turned through passion to a new articulation.

The question in much of the poem is the sincerity of tears, as Hill worries the notion of self-seeking martyrdom and self-seeking lachrimosity. "Crucified Lord," the poem begins, "you swim upon your cross / and never move." The image suggests that the hanged God is about to commit a backstroke—but it is only an illusion of our tears that puts him in water: therefore the lines suggest that everything else about this image may be illusion.

> Crucified Lord, you swim upon your cross
> and never move. Sometimes in dreams of hell
> the body moves but moves to no avail
> and is at one with that eternal loss.

And the water image extends to allude to Cowper's great poem of predestined damnation:

> You are the castaway of drowned remorse,
> you are the world's atonement on the hill.

This is your body twisted by our skill
into a patience proper for redress.

Christ as the damned soul! Perhaps His damnation results from our false remorse, "drowned in tears"; if it is drowned then our remorse is already dead. The last two lines of the octave show Hill at his most complex: to "redress" is to "dress again" or to "re-clothe" as a pun; but it is also to "set straight" what we have "twisted." And "twisted" is "distorted" as in the image of swimming, and of course as in a distortion of meaning, and perhaps most of all as in "tortured"—all of it, in Hill's self-doubting morality, "by our skill."

Of the seven sonnets, perhaps the third is best of all:

> The Jesus-faced man walking crowned with flies
> who swats the roadside grass or glances up
> at the streaked gibbet with its birds that swoop,
> who scans his breviary while the sweat dries,
>
> fades, now, among the fading tapestries,
> brooches of crimson tears where no eyes weep,
> a mouth unstitched into a rimless cup,
> torn clouds the cauldrons of the martyrs' cries.
>
> Clamorous love, its faint and baffled shout,
> its grief that would betray him to our fear,
> he suffers for our sake, or does not hear
>
> above the hiss of shadows on the wheat.
> Viaticum transfigures earth's desire
> in rising vernicles of summer air.
>
> Martyrium

This martyr, this imitation of Christ, turns into an artwork, which turns into ruin, and that very ruin—"a mouth unstitched . . . / torn clouds the cauldrons of the martyrs' cries"—turns back into emblems of suffering.

The next sequence is thirteen sonnets gathered under Pugin's title, "An Apology for the Revival of Christian Architecture in England." The title is ironic, because contemporary England admits of no such revival. The poem uses the dream of a mythic England, Coleridge's "spiritual, Platonic old England," as a criticism, not just of the modern world but of the real England (or real world) of any time. Because the myth is golden, Hill's language must become on occasion lavish:

> Platonic England grasps its tenantry
>
> where wild-eyed poppies raddle tawny farms
> and wild swans root in lily-clouded lakes.

If I think this "Apology" least of the major sequences in this book, it is least obsessed, distanced by its fastidious dream. The sequence ends:

> In grange and cottage girls rise from their beds
>
> by candlelight and mend their ruined braids.
> Touched by the cry of the iconoclast,
> how the rose-window blossoms with the sun!

Hill's opportunities here make me remember Seamus Heaney's account of Hill's language: "Hill addresses the language like a mason addressing a block. . . . Words in his poetry fall slowly and singly, like molten solder, and accumulate to a dull glowing nub. I imagine Hill as indulging in a morose linguistic delectation, dwelling on the potential of each word with much the same slow relish as Leopold Bloom dwells on the thought of his kidney."

The final sequence gives the book its title. *Tenebrae* means shadows or darkness in Latin, and in the Christian lexicon it refers to darkness at the crucifixion, repeated each year in Holy Week by ritual in darkness. Because *Tenebrae* means shadows, and possibly because of its association with the resurrection, the word can also refer to ghosts. *Tenebrae* shows Hill alive with allusion, passionate, learned, and unredeemed; and his language enacts the continuity of the ancient world into the mind of Europe:

> Veni Redemptor, but not in our time.
> Christus Resurgens, quite out of this world.
> 'Ave' we cry; the echoes are returned.
> Amor Carnalis is our dwelling-place.

Here is the fifth section of the poem, which demonstrates all that restless, musical motion of statement and contradiction which ends in a tormented stasis.

> Stupefying images of grief-in-dream,
> succubae to my natural grief of heart,
> cling to me, then; you who will not desert
> your love nor lose him in some blank of time.
> You come with all the licence of her name
> to tell me you are mine. But you are not
> and she is not. Can my own breath be hurt
> by breathless shadows groaning in their game?
> It can. The best societies of hell
> acknowledge this, aroused by what they know:
> consummate rage recaptured there in full
> as faithfulness demands it, blow for blow,
> and rectitude that mimics its own fall
> reeling with sensual abstinence and woe.

He names and addresses his own devils, whose ironic love torments him by substituting itself for the love and the presence of a woman desired and not possessed. (In an epigraph for "The Pentecost Castle," Hill quotes Yeats: "It is terrible to desire and not possess, and terrible to possess and not desire.") There is ironical play upon nature and "natural," which in its geography is "desert" and in eternity the equivalent "blank." The poet's own breath or spirit is damaged by bodiless and spiritless chimeras. Look at "acknowledge," where the snake of knowledge is hell's creature, a hell in which the societies are precisely "aroused by what they *know*." Psychological hell comes to resemble the hell of a punitive God, where fallen rectitude, as in the mind's compelled rehearsals, repeats in its misery and in its breathless absence of love the act of its falling. Consider the structure of the last sentence: the word "this" refers us back to the two-word sentence that proceeds it, and is followed by a clause ending in a colon which leads us four lines down the page to the end of the poem. "What they know" is the last quatrain. The "societies" are "aroused," in a hint of sexuality, but if there is rage it is also "consummate" with all the ambiguity of that revived cliché; but it is, in military term, "recaptured," and it is also subjugated, ironically, because of "faithfulness," a militant faithfulness which exchanges "blows." Parallel to rage is "rectitude" that repeats its falling, "reeling" like a leaf falling from a tree.

Hill follows this section with a simpler song, commenting on the section just quoted:

> This is the ash-pit of the lily-fire,
> this is the questioning at the long tables,
> this is true marriage of the self-in-self,
> this is a raging solitude of desire,
> this is the chorus of obscene consent,
> this is a single voice of purest praise.

It is not Hill's meaning—but I will be happy to leave *Tenebrae* at this last line.

Earlier, I wrote that to read Geoffrey Hill you have to immerse yourself in his language. As it happens, there is a new way to accomplish this soaking, which I suspect may be helpful. Caedmon has just issued an LP and a cassette (Caedmon CDL5 1597) of Geoffrey Hill reading his own poems— half of the first two volumes, all of *The Mercian Hymns*, but regrettably none of *Tenebrae*. As it happens, he reads very well. He has a sonorous voice, capable of pitch variation and mostly pitched low. He has, I suppose, read his poems on the BBC, with the help of a director. As with any particular reading, there are imperfect moments—haste at the beginning of *The Mercian Hymns*, for instance—and there are moments when I would prefer a different reading: in some of the early poems, where rhetoric mounts to glory, Hill's voice studiously underplays his old grandiloquence. All in all it is first-rate reading.

Rhythm and tone are a central matter in Hill, and probably a central problem for American readers. Hill's reading, sensitive to rhythm and fully capable of supplying tone, will help anyone enter the music of these poems. The reading like the poems makes a complicated texture, as the voice in its rapid oscillations of tone equals the rapid qualifications of the poetry. Listening to the poems, preferably listening to them over and over again, we may enter Hill's poetry by way of Hill's voice, experiencing through that voice the poetry's genuine emotional wholeness. Let us worry about the import later on.

Poets Aloud

Coming to Harvard in 1947 I discovered the Poetry Room, originally located high in Widener Library, then expanded in the new undergraduate Lamont Library. For four years I dropped by once or twice a week, clamped earphones to my head, and listened to Ezra Pound boom out his poems while beating on a drum: "The Seafarer," "Sestina: Altaforte," parts of "Mauberley" and the Cantos. . . . I heard Eliot's voice mimic its way through the "Fragment of an Agon." I heard young Auden, Spender, MacLeish, Stevens, Williams, Moore. . . . With rare exceptions these recordings were unique and not for sale. An enterprising man named William Packard began recording poets on wax at Harvard in 1926—an expensive and difficult process. In 1933 Packard began to issue 78 rpm discs for sale on the Harvard Vocarium label. Most of his recordings, however, were available only to those who had access to the Poetry Room, administered by its curator Jack Sweeney.

At Lamont we read poetry with our ears as we sat on blue chairs in a room with furnishings designed by Alvar Aalto. Even if some poets spoke their poems badly, even if some voices were monotonous, with pauses inappropriate to line structure, the voices were the poets' own—and we incorporated their poems without benefit of print. Of course we had all grown up ingesting poetry through print only. Ingestion by ear had its uses. For the very reason that the listener rarely stops and reverses the tape—while the reader may easily interrupt his reading or vary its pace—listening to poetry enforces the voice's tempo on the mind's receptor. And we hear real voices, real accents—especially useful for the American hearing Auden or for the Englishman hearing Williams. Of course reading silently, we must hear in the mind's ear—but the mind's ear and the ear's ear differ sufficiently. If the mind's ear is at once too ideal and too idiosyncratic, then the ear's ear can alter and revise the mind's.

Those recollections occur because I have been listening to these recordings again. Three years ago the Harvard University Press released a collection of six cassettes—stored in a case shaped like a book, under the title *The Poet's Voice*—which includes Ezra Pound's 1939 readings, earlier and later recordings by Eliot, and readings by many others—a wonderful collection, which I will return to later, when I list and discuss other tapes and LPs as well. For the time of the tape is upon us.

As well it might be. In the past twenty years reading-aloud has become the main form of publication for American poets. More contemporary poems go public in readings-aloud than in readings-silent.If recent college generations have grown up on poetry readings, there ought to be an audience for records and tapes.

But of course we must realize the dissimilarities of tape and live reading. We might consider the recording as an abstraction of a reading—a black and white reproduction perhaps, or a copy diminished in size like a television version of a stage play. The recording cuts away face and gesture, leaving only voice. But it is useful, I think, to approach recorded poetry as a thing in itself. It is no more a diminishment or abstraction of a public reading than a printed book is, but simply another form of publication.

I will seem to change the subject if I say that, by and large, English poets do better on recordings than Americans do. I am not changing the subject: when a poet reads his poems into a microphone in a studio—to record them on tape that

an engineer wearing earphones attends to, not to amplify
them for college students sprawling in their bluejeans—the
poet is doing not "a poetry reading" in the absence of a body,
but something like "a radio program." There is all the dif-
ference in the world; because of the BBC, English poets have
had the practice.

In England, poets for some decades have made a portion
of their incomes from radio. An English poet does not
merely read his poems on the radio; he may interview others,
review books, criticize films and stage plays; he may work for
the BBC as a producer—like W. R. Rogers, Louis MacNeice,
Dylan Thomas, Anthony Thwaite, Patric Dickinson, George
MacBeth. . . . The Poet Laureate made his name giving BBC
talks about church architecture; other poets do twelve min-
ute talks between movements of a symphony on Sunday
afternoon, on a childhood in Bhutan, perhaps, or the advan-
tages of tinned peaches over fresh ones. Whatever you do for
the BBC, you rehearse for a producer who makes notes on
his copy of your manuscript and gives you notes on your
performance before you tape. If you are an old hand, you are
likely to rehearse once and then go directly to taping, or you
may rehearse it again and again. You are always well directed.
If you are an English poet, you are an old hand at radio.

Speaking or reading to a microphone in a studio is an ex-
perience wholly separate from addressing a roomful of peo-
ple. American poets are used to roomfuls, both as poetry-
readers and as teachers. If you approach the recording
microphone as if it were a crowd you will sound pompous,
remote, inflated, and false. Of course you can learn to do
both things—as intelligent stage-actors can learn screen or
radio technique—if you take the first step of acknowledging
the difference.

I believe that the differences are the kind of losses which
can be turned into gains. If we receive no message from the
collaboration of eyes/mouth/hand/shoulders, perhaps the
resultant concentration on voice alone makes the voice capa-
ble of a thousand subtleties. Voice is quieter and capable of
more modulation; tiny changes in pitch and volume, under

the ear's sole attention, take on the expressive power of body's leaps and arms' wing wheeling. When gesture bodies itself into voice alone, the voice grows shoulders, hands, mouth, and eyes.

When you speak to a BBC microphone, even if you talk on the elitist network, at least twenty thousand people hear you; if your words are recorded, posterity may increase your audience to millions. But by the paradox of this genre, *the audience for the studio performance is one person.* The audience is the woman sitting by her radio in Northumberland, or the man driving alone playing a cassette in New Hampshire. When you learn microphone technique you learn to address this solitary audience. Sitting in the soundproof antisepsis of the studio, with an earphoned technician behind glass as the visible audience—he not listening to words but to sounds—you learn to speak as if to a person dear and even intimate; you learn to address the microphone personally—to persuade it, love it, and curse it.

If you are a platform professional, wishing to acquire studio technique, you need practice and intelligent direction. Alas, most American recording is undirected or directed incompetently, and the result is that much of our studio recording is poor. Many American poets fifty and younger, expert at reading to audiences, go dry in the studio or fake their feelings. The late James Wright, who read brilliantly on the platform, recorded a session with Caedmon in which he seems to push his voice toward feeling, with a strain that never troubled him on the platform.

And on the other hand the English poets are superb because they have learned to use a microphone. Although I do not admire John Betjeman's verses, I enjoy hearing him say them. When I reviewed Geoffrey Hill's *Tenebrae* in these pages, I recommended his Caedmon LP/cassette as a way to introduce yourself to Hill. A wonderful recording. If anything Ted Hughes is even better (Caedmon lists two records or cassettes—one from *Crow* and *Wodwo,* the other from earlier poems.) The Yorkshire accent is essential, and Hughes reads with a strict and powerful thrust—he records with his jaw I think—yet without muscular strain. His reading is intimate, forceful, passionate, restrained, appropriate, and expressive of the poetry's intelligent strength. Marvelous inflection, pitch-range. . . . Never corny, he reads to the imagined listener, addressing neither a convocation of the dead nor a cold microphone.

American poets, on the other hand, show at their best in the recorded live reading. The poetry reading is what American poets do best. Audience response bodies forth a remembered relationship, as we listen to the record, which recurs in the psyche of the listener; the listener becomes part of the audience, participates in laughter, hush, in-drawn breath, and applause. If the studio reading has the advantage of intimacy, one person speaking to one person, the taped public reading has the advantage of community.

Because taped live reading can be pleasing, perhaps we should just hope that Caedmon, when adding American poets, will give up the studio for the concert hall. Perhaps. But if the market for recorded poetry expands, American poets can learn to use the microphone. The sound of a studio recording is better and more accurate, but I do not praise this method only for its sound: I think that studio-intimacy is best for bringing out a poem's inwardness: the solitary listener resembles the solitary reader. When American poets address *all* their poems to an audience packed with twenty-year-olds, this notion of audience begins to corrupt their poems. Perhaps the studio's single focus of attention is more appropriate to poetry's best nature. Perhaps recorded poems are more likely to be taken internally. I suggest that for the poet the studio's absences may be a useful antidote to the dangers of platform experience.

Everyone knows that a current temptation in American poetry—some of these tapes provide shocking examples—is corruption by celebrity culture, whereby the poet becomes a platform Johnny Carson responding to Professor Mac-Mahon's rousing introduction. Because audiences are largely kids, naive and impressionable, we can easily win applause by being the Goofy Grown-up. We can win applause by alluding to our fondness for drink or drugs, or by performing that fondness; we can win applause by acting out the fantasies of middle-class children and their professors. We can ingratiate ourselves by flattery, or we can win applause by being fools.

But the studio microphone is cold-hearted to such appeals; the microphone does not think that one is cute. Two late recordings by Robert Lowell are hard to bear because of the dreadful playing-up to an audience that overcomes so many poets late in their lives, the narcissism that begs for the rote love of a celebrity-dazzled audience. (Some old poets like Williams and Pound and Eliot never seemed to struggle with this problem; sometimes Frost played Mortimer Snerd to please his audiences; at other times his pride saved him.) It is easy enough to understand why poets pursue cheap applause. Poetry is difficult enough, and reward comes late. When recognition arrives—daily letters solicit your manuscripts, academics beg to write about you, everyone drops your name—it is understandable that you may wish to enjoy the rewards of a life's labor. Because Lowell suffered so greatly with mental illness, his pandering is all the more understandable. . . .

But there is also X, there is also Y, poets of decent work, who perform contemptibly at the Folger Library. They cuddle up to the audience while they condescend to it. They are cute for laughter and applause; they belittle their own poems, and poetry in general, by playing to idiots who laugh whenever an authority-figure asks for laughter. When we sit in the audience we may accept this behavior, for we are pulled along by the community we sit with. Each of us becomes an idiot dressed in an audience suit. But when we listen in solitude to the poet at his most ingratiating, we detest the push-overs who coo at every cuteness; and the very isolation of the voice reveals its coy manipulations.

Harvard's *The Poet's Voice* makes a good beginning to any collection of the out-loud word. The first of the cassettes has Eliot on one side and Pound on the other. Eliot recorded on three occasions: in 1933, in 1947, and in 1948—the years in which he turned 45, 59, and 60. He always read well, and I enjoy hearing the difference of the younger voice. (The two Caedmon records of Eliot are undated, an annoying habit of Caedmon's.) For our Eliot collection, we need these minor poems—"Gerontion" and "The Hollow Men" among others from the 1933 reading; the great performance of "Fragment of an Agon" from 1947—to go with *The Waste Land* and the *Four Quartets* available from Caedmon. Because the body of Eliot's work is small, we are able to hear his voice speaking most of his poetry.

Ezra Pound's Harvard recording took place on May 17, 1939. Pound was making his megalomaniac return from Italy to this country in order to prevent the second World War. More successful than the diplomacy, the reading is vigorous, dark, studied, intense. The Pound readings include the "Sestina: Altaforte"which he later tried to suppress: "War is no longer amusing. . . ." They suffer a little from bad acoustics, which make the drum which he pounds sound metallic and thin. But Pound's eccentric voice and manner hammer through and succeed. As he ends his final poem— "When I think of what America would be like / If the classics had a wide circulation . . . ," he and his audience— Mr. Packard?—suffer a wonderful tiny collapse into laughter. He reads his translation of "The Seafarer" powerfully, and some of the "Moeures Contemporaines" with great humor and intelligence. He reads from the Cantos. On the other hand, Caedmon has a whole Pound LP recorded in the fifties, also marvelous and equally essential. In the Caedmon, Pound makes a fine studio reading—doubtless profiting from the studio experience he acquired between 1941 and 1944.

Most of the poets on the Harvard tape read for about half an hour. Roethke and Jeffers read less and share a side. The 1941 Jeffers studio recording provides some of most boring noises ever heard from a poet. The studio Roethke is good if a little staid—"The Long Alley" and "The Shape of Fire" done as early as 1948. Intelligent notes tell us the date and the circumstance of each recording. The 1941 Auden, recorded in a studio, includes poems later revised or suppressed; the 1970 Auden is live. Jarrell's 32:50 minutes combine a 1946 studio reading with a live reading from 1964. John Berryman's long side—35:20—comes entirely from *77 Dream Songs*—a live reading in 1962. There are sides by Williams, Moore, Stevens, Frost, and Plath. The Lowell reading is late and live; I will speak of it later in connection with other Lowell readings.

The most monumental of all spoken-poetry publications is the *Spoken Arts Treasury of One Hundred Modern American Poets Reading Their Poems*, published several years back. This wonderful dinosaur not only presents the inevitable—Pound, Eliot, Frost, Williams, Moore, Stevens—but more importantly, preserves the evitable. If we become curious about the sounds of Witter Bynner or Max Eastman or James Weldon Johnson or Dorothy Parker or Donald Davidson, we will find them all here. The eighteen long-playing records of this collection are still available—and cheap.

For a briefer general anthology there is the two-record Caedmon *Treasury of Modern Poets Reading Their Own Poetry*, like the Spoken Arts compendium not a recent release. It is also essential, including the few Yeats performances available to us, and Auden's "Elegy for W. B. Yeats," and Sitwell, Thomas, MacNeice, Graves, Eliot reading "The Waste Land," Stein, MacLeish, Cummings, Moore, Empson, Spender, Aiken, Frost, Williams, Stevens, Eberhart, Pound, and Wilbur. Except for the Eliot, each poet struts a brief minute or two; it is a monster literary party, entertaining in its guest list, frustrating because you don't get to *know* anybody.

Many imprints have issued many titles. After Harvard Vocarium's beginning, in the forties, the Library of Congress issued a number of albums on unbreakable 78 rpm discs, and have reissued some on 33 ⅓. In the mid-fifties, Caedmon and Spoken Arts started issuing records of poets reading. Then in the sixties there were good records from Folkways, Yale published a series, Stanford University made a series including a good Adrienne Rich, and Caedmon went into a funk from which it has lately recovered.

There are many newer publishers now. *Black Box* is a cassette magazine, featuring poets reading their own work—both conventional and experimental—with remarkable pizzaz. Its associate, *Watershed*, publishes cassettes mainly recorded live at the Folger Library in Washington. Because publications become too numerous to list in an article, we are fortunate that *Watershed* and *Black Box* have spawned a third entity, a mail order house for all sorts of different recording companies. If the poetry reading is on tape, they claim, they will get it for us. (Write for their catalog, *Poetry on Tape*: Box 4174, Washington, D.C. 20015)

New Wilderness publishes innovative sound-poems. Innovative or experimental work is difficult to describe. Maybe the electronic event, executed by electronic means in a studio, makes a separate art form. John Giorno's *Dial-a-Poem* also seems purposeful, directed, and diverse—but I need to hear more and to live longer with these notions before I can say anything sensible about them. Let me say only that these tapes show technology catching up with imagination. Dada's simultaneous readings required the tape recorder.

On Caedmon's poetry list Dylan Thomas is still the star, but the catalog is solid with other English and Americans. Two records of Cummings provide an overview of the poet's whole work, a way to touch down on what he did and did not do. The voice snarls like Thersites—contemptuous and affected and vigorous. The William Carlos Williams record—like the sessions available from Harvard and Spoken Arts—reaches no great height of performance, but he reads with a shy gusto in his strange, high, boyish, old-man's voice. He begins stiff and relaxes as he goes on, the strangeness of the studio seeming to wash away.

On the other hand, the Caedmon record of Robert Penn Warren sounds impossibly self-conscious. Warren speaks between the poems as if he were reading from a teleprompter, then recites with violent and inappropriate emphases of pitch and volume; then it gets worse. There are other recent tapes by Margaret Atwood, who is stiff and distant in the studio, and by Galway Kinnell, who reads *The Book of Nightmares* at three-quarters of his usual excellence; it is a studio recording, as is Philip Levine's Caedmon record, which is no disaster—but low-energy.

On the other hand, there is Philip Levine recorded by *Watershed* as he reads his poems to an appreciative crowd at the Folger Library. Here Levine performs his poems with the attention and the intensity they deserve. Between poems— commenting at that lower intensity which is a rhythmic and emotional necessity—he is charming and madcap, spontaneous and pleasant yet not too damned pleasant; chit-chat which is light without being ingratiating makes essential contrast to the stark and pointed attack of the poems.

Watershed's tapes cover the waterfront, and most of them are good. Ann Darr, Kenward Elmslie, Theodore Enslin, Reed Whittemore, Carolyn Kizer. Not everything works. John Logan's reading misses the man; Marvin Bell lacks power. But Maxine Kumin brings a platform professionalism thoroughly across on tape and makes a model of the poetry reading. Marge Piercy's considerable success is wholly different, a rough pleasure rather than a smooth one, a voice that comes through in this abstracted performance with all the poignant and vulnerable specificity of her photographs. William Bronk's cassette is low-keyed, not especially interesting for voice or expression, but the quietness suits the poems of this good and neglected poet. Charles Simic and Russell Edson make two of the best live readings yet recorded.

Many poets like Philip Levine exist in different versions— Roethke on *Folkways* and *Caedmon*, Wilbur on *Caedmon* and *Spoken Arts*; Robert Graves on numerous different labels. Sylvia Plath is on *Harvard, Caedmon, Spoken Arts,* and the obscure label of *Credo*. And *Credo* is the one to listen to. The others are early recordings of *Colossus* poems, and they suffer from the same tight, controlled competence that makes *The Colossus* inferior work. The *Credo* recording was made shortly before her death, and includes readings, commentary, and an interview. Done for the BBC, the record's sound and the performance are equally fine. Plath had lived in England for some years, she and Hughes living by their wits, and Plath had learned to talk to a microphone. She speaks and reads with a fierce clarity, a chilling and exhilarating performance. Some of the poems differ from printed versions: "Lady Lazarus," for instance, and "Daddy."

Another poet multiply available is Robert Lowell: *Spoken Arts, Harvard, Caedmon,* and the *Library of Congress* labels. The *Harvard* and *Caedmon* were recorded late in the poet's life, *Harvard*'s twenty-four minutes taken from a reading in 1977, and *Caedmon*'s his last New York reading at the Poetry Center in 1978. It is difficult to listen to the latter because it sounds like death—shortness of breath, continual panting—and because he is ingratiating. Fortunately there is a good two-record set of Lowell available from the Library of Congress. This hides behind the ugliest jacket in the history of record jackets, but it is essential to a collection. The recordings took place over many years. In 1955 Lowell taped "The Quaker Graveyard" at his house in Boston. Already he found his early poems melodramatic, and as he reads the surging, Marlovian lines of his elegy, he tends to downplay the strength, to read over-modestly; still the reading is intimate and attentive, close to the work's grammar and thrust. Then there is a cluster of poems read to a live audience in Washington in 1959, rich versions of *Life Studies* poems and "For the Union Dead." A 1961 Johns Hopkins reading follows, maybe best of all, at which Lowell wonderfully reads "When the Rainbow Ends," "Ford Madox Ford," and "Skunk Hour."

So there is a central recording of Lowell; eventually there should be more—and there should be more of everybody we want to listen to, because of all the archives of colleges and private collectors. The potential for audiotapes of American poets is endless, because for two decades many poets have recorded at least thirty readings a year. Whichever poets survive, they should exist on hundreds of live recordings. The great poems will be heard with a thousand subtle differences of expression; the poet's varying comments or patter will be analyzed for clues to his development; certain audio scholars, wizards of the ear, will claim to tell how many martinis the poet consumed beforehand. I wonder if anyone has begun to catalogue the tapings held by colleges in this country. Surely a catalogue is the place to begin, to be followed—after interminable troubles with permissions and technology—by a series of anthology albums. Let us hear *Best Readings from Tucson*, and *Live from the Poetry Center*. Let us hear *Collected Outloud Works of James Wright*, and the *Five Foot Shelf of Best Talking Poets*.

Russell Edson

(1977)

Poetry reviewing in the United States is a disgrace. Poetry's doing all right, but who knows it? Poetry reviewing is almost exclusively small circulation literary magazines—*Parnassus, Ohio Review, Iowa Review, Georgia Review, Hudson Review,* and so forth. Sometimes small political weeklies lend a hand, but bigger national publications have defected totally. *Atlantic* and *Harper's* review virtually no poetry. The *New Yorker,* which once printed Louise Bogan's reviews quarterly, has not reviewed poetry for many years (these facts and opinions are as of 1977). The *New York Review of Books,* after Robert Mazzocco stopped reviewing for them, has fallen to printing reviews by academics out of touch with new American poetry. The *New York Times Book Review* is spotty and usually poor. (Recently, two reviews by Robert Pinsky made exceptions.) You can count on the *New York Times Book Review* only for the predictable thing—like Hilton Kramer's assemblage of clichés about Robert Penn Warren.

Thus too few Americans—interested enough in poetry to go to readings, to read reviews if they were public; not committed enough to keep up with small magazines and small presses—even know that Russell Edson is *there.* I don't know whom to call the best contemporary American poet—and as Dylan Thomas used to say, "Is it a contest?"—but among the best I daresay Russell Edson is the most original, astonishing, extraordinary, and inimitable.

I suppose one could question—if one were taken with such questions—whether he writes poems at all. When New Directions published *The Very Thing that Happens* in 1964 (score another for New Directions) the jacket spoke of "Fables." Now that the prose poem is a dominant American literary form, we call Edson a prose poet, but he is doing precisely the same "Fables"—short stories of extraordinary fantasy and caprice—that he was doing in 1964, or in 1969 when Jargon published *What Can a Man See*, or in the several pamphlets which Edson published on his own, and in the more recent large collection of "prose poems" published by Wesleyan and Harper. If you count everything, Russell Edson has published eight volumes of prose poems—I'll settle for that label—and one New Directions collection of plays. The eighth book of poems, *The Intuitive Journey*, was the first ever reviewed in the *Times Book Review*—May 1, 1977, on page sixty-nine in a seventy-two page issue, a one-paragraph review, perfunctory and condescending, which did not quote a word.

There's been much talk in recent years of surrealism in American poetry—and little surrealism. American poetry has *used* fantasy in the course of poems otherwise directed by reason or recollection or straightforward narration. I don't mean to put down this use of fantasy, only to say that it does not undertake the pressure and limitation of surrealism. After all, Pablo Neruda was usually an adjectival surrealist, his poetry surrealis*tic* rather than pure surrealism. Fantasy can be used the way an expressionist uses his palette and his broad brush, to distort in order to embody feeling. But Russell Edson, whatever his method of writing, makes surreal poems. Few poets have *ever* written as Edson does, out of a whole irrational universe—infantile, paranoiac—with its own small curved space complete to itself, impenetrable by other conditions of thought.

Take "Mr. and Mrs. Duck Dinner":

An old woman with a duck under her arm is let into a

house and asked, whom shall I say is calling?

Mr. and Mrs. Duck Dinner.

If you don't mind my asking, which is which?

Pointing to the duck the old woman says, this here's my husband.

A little time passes and the butler reappears, yes, come right in, you're expected, the kitchen's just this way.

In the kitchen there's a huge stove. The butler says, I'm sorry, we don't have a pot big enough for you; so we're using an old cast-iron bathtub. I hope you don't mind? We have a regular duck pot for your husband.

No no, this is fine, I'll make pretend I'm having a bath.— Oh, by the way, do you have enough duck sauce? says the old woman.

Yes, plenty, and the cook's made up a nice stuffing, too.

My husband'll need plucking; I can undress myself, says the old woman.

Fine, that'll be a great help; we'll have the kitchen girl defeather your husband.—By the way, what would you suggest with duck? asks the butler.

Wild rice, but not too wild, we wouldn't want any trouble in the dining room; and perhaps asparagus spears . . . But make sure they're not too sharp, they can be quite dangerous; best to dull them on a grinding wheel before serving . . .

Very good, Madam.—By the way, do you think that having the kitchen girl defeather your husband might be a little awkward, if you know what I mean? She is rather pretty; wouldn't want to start any difficulties between you and your husband, says the butler.

No worry, says the old woman, we're professional duck dinners; if we started fooling around with the kitchen help we'd soon be out of business.—If you don't mind I'd like to get into the oven as soon as possible. I'm not as young as I used to be, not that I'm old, but it does take me a little longer these days. . . .

This narrative spectacle refers to nothing outside itself. It is reflective, creating out of a personal cosmos a dangerous world where everything and everyone is perfectly exchangeable, renewable, and eatable. There's a good deal of cannibalism in Edson, among other taboos broken. Look at "The Dogs' Dinner":

> An old woman was just cooking her dog's dinner when she decided to review the general decline of things in her west window.
> Yes, there the old sun bleeds and dies of childbirth.
> In the east the anemic child rises, stillborn . . .
>
> When she turns back to the pot where she cooks her dog's dinner she discovers that it is her dog that she is cooking for her dog's dinner.
> How strange that when cooking a dog's dinner one cooks the very dog for whom the dinner was being cooked . . .
>
> She takes the steaming pot off the stove and puts it on the floor, thinking that the dog will not be having its dinner tonight, thinking that the dog cannot eat itself . . .
>
> She draws a chair to the pot, and sits there soaking her feet, seeing her dog floating at her ankles in the mist that rises from his dinner.
>
> She thinks, if I cooked the dog, how is it I didn't cook myself? . . . Perhaps next time. . . ?

Other poems *include* cannibalism, background music of an ingestive dream, while other magic transformations take center stage. In his large recent volume *The Intuitive Journey*, one of my favorite poems, at once terrifying and funny, is called "Hands":

> An old woman buys an ape's hand for supper. It will not be still, it keeps clenching and unclenching its fist. It might want to pinch her too, she thinks.
> Be still, you silly thing, while I clean your fingernails. She wants to clean it up and pluck the fur off it to make it ready for the pot.

She doesn't know whether she'll fry or boil it, or just simply hurt it, stick it with a fork or a hat pin. She'll hurt it if it doesn't be still!

Be still, you silly thing!

Now the ape's hand is pointing with its forefinger to the cupboard.

The cupboard, huh?

And she is trying to see the angle of the forefinger to see where it points. It points high, something at the top of the cupboard.

What's there? She starts to climb the cupboard, using the shelves as a ladder.

What's up here so grand to be pointed at?

The ape's hand has become a fist and is pounding the table.

I'm looking for it! Stop pounding the table, you silly thing!

The ape's fist continues to pound; the room shakes with it.

Please, please, I'll fall, cries the old woman.

At the top of the cupboard she finds an old dried-out hand covered with dust.

Is this what you want?

The ape's hand on the table opens and closes, as if it would grasp what she has found; and then pounds the table as if to say, hurry, hurry, bring it down to me!

All right, all right, I'm coming.

Finally she puts the dried-out hand into the ape's hand. The ape's hand lays the dried-out hand on its back, and strokes the insides of the fingers and palm, until the hand begins to be alive. Then the two hands close into a clasped set, the short blunt thumbs twirling at each other . . .

The old woman sits watching the hands, with their short blunt thumbs twirling, late into the night, until she falls asleep in her chair. . .

Everything is potential in Russell Edson, everything possible in his infantile magic. Everything is possible in imagination—but the world remains sometimes intractable, even in the universe of these poems. When the magician fails, the result can be poignant, as failure brings ordinary human feeling into Edson's poems. For example, "Bringing a Dead Man Back into Life":

> The dead man is introduced back into life. They take him to a country fair, to a French restaurant, a round of late night parties . . . He's beginning to smell.
> They give him a few days off in bed.
>
> He's taken to a country fair again; a second engagement at the French restaurant, another round of late night parties . . . No response . . . They brush the maggots away . . . That terrible smell! . . . No use . . .
> What's wrong with you?
> . . . No use . . .
> They slap his face. His cheek comes off; bone underneath, jaws and teeth . . .
>
> Another round of late night parties . . . Dropping his fingers . . . An ear falls off . . . Loses a foot in a taxi . . . No use . . . The smell . . . Maggots everywhere!
>
> Another round of late night parties. His head comes off, rolls on the floor. A woman stumbles on it, an eye rolls out. She screams.
> No use . . . Under his jacket nothing but maggots and ribs . . . No use . . .

Most of us would have known it couldn't be done—but in Edson's universe nothing seems impossible until we have tried it out. How hard we try. How discouraged we become, when death and decay persist in spite of our wish that they should go away. How cruel we are to the dead: "They slap his face, His cheek comes off . . ."

Poetry exists to extend human consciousness, and it extends human consciousness in one particular way. The words of poetry—words in general, language—belong to the upper air of light, to the developed human brain. Infants don't talk. But infants think, and infants grow upward into speech. When they have grown upward into speech, they suppress after a while infantile forms of thought. Infants think the way Russell Edson thinks—or they would if they could talk. (Robert Bly said somewhere that Edson writes the kind of poetry a chicken would write, if a chicken could write poems; he was of course being complimentary.) Poetry adds to the light of consciousness the darkness of metaphoric and fantastic thought which belong to pre-verbal states; these states exist full-blown in the infant, and possibly in the chicken, and we admit them as adults only in the disguises of dream. And they come to the surface in poetry, in forms and in metaphors. With Russell Edson's poems, they are the meat and muscle, story and sentence of the whole poem. The superaddition of dark powers to light language—*not* the abandonment of reason to drown under total darkness; that is drunkenness, drugs, and suicide—is poetry's task. It is precisely poetry's task to enlarge consciousness in pursuit of evolutionary development. Thesis of primary process thinking added to antithesis of secondary rationalism makes synthesis of new, fully born man, Homo Poeticus. When Freud said, "Where id was, let there ego be," his injunction led toward the same goal.

Poets all over the world are engaged in this secret progressive task, psychic revolutionaries. It is a task forbidden by much of society, which fears the "madness" of the old thinking, rejects it, censors it. Plato was the Rational Censor when he banned poets from his republic. Poets, who come from the same society that fears poetry, are themselves often frightened of what they do. Often they punish themselves for doing forbidden things, and the punishment indeed can be drugs, drunkenness, and suicide. Often they escape punishment by refusing fully to understand what they are up to. Whether Edson knows it or not—down there in Stamford, Connecticut, in a house on Weed Avenue—he's doing the work, as much as anyone is.

Edson's books—the ones so far as I know which are available: from New Directions, *The Very Thing that Happens* ("Fables and Drawings"), and *The Falling Sickness* (four plays); from

Wesleyan University Press, *The Clam Theater*, and *The Reason Why the Closet Man is Never Sad*; from Harper & Row, *The Intuitive Journey* (incorporating an early Harper book, *The Childhood of an Equestrian*; two books in one.)

Robert Giroux

(1980)

When Peter Taylor, novelist, playwright and short-story writer, was recently asked about Robert Giroux, he replied simply: "the best publisher there is. . . ." Giroux is editor, publisher, partner and a major stockholder in Farrar, Straus and Giroux Inc. His authors have included T. S. Eliot, Isaac Bashevis Singer, Robert Lowell, Elizabeth Bishop, George Orwell, Walker Percy, Louise Bogan; he published the first books of Bernard Malamud, Randall Jarrell, Flannery O'Connor, Jack Kerouac and Susan Sontag. He is the only living editor whose name is bracketed with that of Maxwell Perkins.

Giroux is sixty-five years old now, an age for retrospect though not for retirement. Lunching with him a first time, in the environs of Gramercy Park and the Players Club, withdrawing to a cardroom for more talk, I am curious to discover the qualities that make a great editor. I meet a man who tells a good story, who laughs well, who shows white hair around a pink face that is open, affable, expressive, genial. The intelligence, the literary taste, the sophistication are obvious. Also, I am quickly aware of *charm*. Although his stories describe people such as Ezra Pound and Marianne Moore, although his tastes run to opera and sonnet sequences, I almost feel that I meet, not "the best publisher there is" but the best politician to come out of Boston or

Chicago in some decades. Telling about a visit to Ezra Pound at St. Elizabeth's, in the company of Robert Lowell, Giroux remembers that Pound was initially hostile when he learned that Giroux was a publisher, glaring at him, asking, "What in hell are *you* doing here?" Giroux answered, "I have come to pay homage to a poet." Pound rose, bowed elegantly, and the encounter proceeded amicably.

We meet again, a week later, at his office, a small green cubicle four stories above Union Square. From that height, Union Square is a pleasant patch on lower Manhattan, green and pastoral; one cannot make out the brown bags in the hands of the winos, or the dazed expressions of the junkies. FSG's location reveals the firm's tactic of low overhead. The ground floor is shared with a Lafayette Electronics; nearby is a McDonald's and several less elegant establishments. The facade is ugly, the foyer junky, and in the hallways exposed pipes hang dirt from flaking green-painted walls. The offices do not resemble those of Doubleday or Simon & Schuster or Holt, Rinehart and Winston—no plush, no Plexiglas, no shag carpet and virtually no space. When the Nobel Prize-winning poet Pablo Neruda came to New York toward the end of his life, he visited FSG after he had been to establishments uptown. He said, "This is the first publishing house I have seen in New York."

As a schoolboy Giroux worked for a newspaper in his native New Jersey and came to Columbia to study journalism. A classmate was John Berryman, who spent his first Columbia years in a fraternity, running on the track team and for campus office. Both young men, like so many others over four decades, owed the direction of their lives to Mark Van Doren. They took every course he offered, and this encounter with literature changed them utterly. Giroux speaks of Van Doren now as if he had just left the classroom. "The great thing about him," Giroux says, "was that he talked to young students as if they were as intelligent as he was. He made you meet *his* level. He was a marvelous talker, and he was my first encounter with a living poet."

Another influence was Raymond Weaver, who presided

over an honors course. "Weaver was the first biographer of Herman Melville, and the first person to read the manuscript of 'Billy Budd,' in 1919. This left a mark on me. I thought, 'Imagine discovering a literary masterpiece!'"

Converted to literature, Berryman and Giroux worked together on the Columbia Review, where they published Thomas Merton's first prose and Berryman's first poetry. They revived Philolexian, an ancient literary society founded by undergraduate Alexander Hamilton, and invited poets and critics to speak on campus. Berryman began to devote his life to poetry. With Giroux, it was the editing that took; he never looked for another sort of life. Eventually Van Doren's converts worked together again, when editor Giroux published poet Berryman's "Homage to Mistress Bradstreet" and all his subsequent books.

When Giroux graduated in 1936, he looked for jobs in publishing but found nothing in that Depression year. He took a job with CBS in public relations, where he helped edit two books that documented the political crises of 1938, each a footnote for historians from the Columbia Broadcasting System. Radio broadcasts, printed verbatim, made documentaries from the words of H. V. Kaltenborn, William L. Shirer and Edward R. Murrow.

One year before America entered the war, Giroux took a job in publishing. After three years on an aircraft carrier in the Pacific as an intelligence officer, he returned to Harcourt, Brace and settled down to a life of other people's books. He has written a little himself—a piece about Eliot, introductions to posthumous collections by Flannery O'Connor and John Berryman; now he is writing a short work of Shakespearean scholarship, "The Book Known as Q," the seed planted years ago in Van Doren's Shakespeare class—but he is no writer manqué. When he was a young editor at Harcourt, lunching with T. S. Eliot, Giroux asked if he agreed with the commonly expressed opinion that most editors are failed writers. Eliot's reply turns up in the Oxford Book of Literary Anecdotes: "Perhaps, but so are most writers."

At Harcourt he worked with Frank Morley, who had come to New York from Faber & Faber of London to head the trade department, and with the founders Alfred Harcourt and Donald Brace. All became models. Harcourt, Brace's small first list, when the firm began after the Great War, included Keynes's "The Economic Consequences of the Peace," Sinclair Lewis's "Main Street" and Lytton Strachey's "Queen Victoria." All Bloomsbury followed Keynes to Harcourt's door, and for a reason: The exchange rate between dollars and pounds altered so that the publisher, sticking to the letter of its contract, could have profited at Keynes's expense. Alfred Harcourt paid more than he needed to and lived up to the spirit of the contract. Keynes, dazzled by this gesture of generosity and trustworthiness, persuaded Lytton Strachey to join Harcourt; Strachey was followed by Virginia and Leonard Woolf, by Roger Fry and E. M. Forster.

Giroux took other lessons. Prone to read manuscripts late into the night, Giroux felt troubled over his difficulty keeping nine-to-five hours. Alfred Harcourt reassured him: "Bob, if you are an editor, your desk is wherever you are." Wherever he found himself, Giroux brought books to Harcourt, Brace. Authors and consultants referred young writers who became Giroux's authors. He signed up Jean Stafford, and Jean Stafford brought her husband Robert Lowell, who recommended Flannery O'Connor; Alfred Kazin recommended Bernard Malamud; the Stafford-Lowell connection was responsible for Peter Taylor and Randall Jarrell.

Giroux believes that if "War and Peace" were to be submitted today, some publishers would reject it: "Too long. Wordy. Drags." Frequently, Giroux's authors were the discards of other publishers. With the publication of Flannery O'Connor's letters, it is possible to observe how another publisher, having signed her first novel, tried to persuade O'Connor to revise "Wise Blood" into a more conventional work. His cajolery met Milledgeville asperity, which won the day, and Giroux edited another first novel. This process happened twice with Bernard Malamud. "The Natural" was signed with another publisher, who turned it down; Giroux took it for Harcourt, Brace. When the old guard passed at Harcourt, Brace, and Giroux found it difficult to work with the new regime, he joined the nine-year-old firm of Farrar, Straus and Company in 1955. (In 1964 Giroux became a partner and his name was joined to the firm.) When Malamud submitted "The Assistant" to Harcourt, Brace, the new guard rejected it. Giroux obtained it for his new firm: it became their first Natonal Book Award winner.

An early discovery at Harcourt, Brace was Jack Kerouac, whom Mark Van Doren recommended to his old pupil. Giroux published Kerouac's first novel, "The Town and the City." Editor and author worked together on cutting the novel, which had the quality and some of the quantity of Thomas Wolfe. When it was published, Kerouac composed a lyric dedication: *"Since Kindness be the / Venus-star of Friendship, / and that Bright Star / Doth light the Lowest Hill, / may Praise be Worthy / of the Highest Good. /* To my Editor, Mentor, and Friend / Robert Giroux. . . ." But Alfred Harcourt vetoed the dedication on grounds of Harcourt, Brace policy. Kerouac was upset, and Giroux had the dedication set and tipped into two copies for author and editor. In ink Kerouac added to Giroux's copy: "To Bob, dedicatee, a man immoderately after my own heart, in appreciation of everything including this special volume. . . ."

Of course, Giroux has made mistakes himself. When young Jason Epstein, fresh out of Columbia, approached him for a job, with the publishing idea of a quality-paperback series, he assured Epstein that it would never work. He recalls that Modern Age Books had flopped a few years earlier. However, he recommended Epstein to his friend Ken McCormick at Doubleday, where Anchor Books emerged. Giroux has lost authors, too. About a year after "The Town and the City" was published, Kerouac arrived in Giroux's office with the famous continuous roll of teletype paper on which he had written a draft of "On the Road." Kerouac announced that the book was divinely inspired, touched by the Holy Ghost. Giroux looked at the manuscript, as thick as a roll of paper towels, which had come uncorrected from the typewriter. Giroux suggested that "even after you have been inspired by the Holy Ghost, you have to sit down and read your manuscript." Then he suggested that the novel might need revision.

In outrage Kerouac swore that nobody was going to change a single word, and, denouncing Giroux as a crass idiot, he left the office. Giroux says now: "I realized later that he was floating on a cloud. It was stupid of me. I should have said, 'My God, you've just finished a book! This is a great occasion! Put the MS. on my desk and let's go and have a drink to celebrate.' Instead, reacting to his ultimatum, I came out flat-footedly with the most deflating statement I could have made." When the Viking Press took "On the Road," Kerouac indeed worked over the manuscript with Malcolm Cowley. Giroux and Kerouac remained friends and years later worked together again when FSG published "Visions of Gerard" and "Big Sur." Together they made a few changes in these novels. Still, Kerouac would caution, "Now, Bob, don't try to pull this apart. . . ."

By all accounts, Giroux is not one to pull things apart. Peter Taylor explains Giroux's editorial excellence as the art of non-interference: "The best government is least government." Giroux's own notion of the worst editor is the one who tries to substitute his own work for the author's. When Giroux suggests a change in someone's manuscript, he wants his suggestion to derive from the book. His favorite editorial example is Max Perkins reading the manuscript of "The Great Gatsby" with delight, making suggestions in the spirit of the novel, particularly one about a central image—the staring eyes on the billboard—to help Fitzgerald strengthen the design. Bernard Malamud remembers a Giroux contribution to "The Natural." A character early in the book disappeared never to return; Giroux felt an absence, a second shoe not dropped; Malamud revised so that the character reappeared in the novel in a dream.

A good editor's work defies job description. It goes from sheer encouragement and running interference to medical, financial and other forms of friendly assistance. "I've picked a drunken John Berryman off the floor of the Chelsea Hotel and got him to a hospital. In the aftermath of Jean Stafford's divorce from Robert Lowell, I got to know the various floors of the Payne Whitney Clinic, where Jean was under psychiatric treatment. Incidentally, on that occasion one of the tabloids ran a witty, and very literary, headline which Jean and I relished: 'WEARY OF LORD'S CASTLE, JEAN ENDS BOSTON ADVENTURE.' And the only time I've been in a padded cell was when Lowell's mother asked me to visit him at Baldpate, after he refused to see her." Giroux adds: "But I've also had some of the brightest and most pleasant days of my life with each of these writers. In a long editorial relationship you become friends—you share the ups as well as the downs."

The late Elizabeth Bishop reported that once a year Giroux asked her how soon he could expect a new volume. She also praised him for fending off the importunities of would-be biographers; she understood that considerable temper could be called into play. Giroux acted as T. S. Eliot's unpaid lecture agent during the last years of Eliot's life. (When Giroux left Harcourt, Brace for FSG, Eliot, like many authors, followed him over. Giroux is proud that they came, proud that he never asked them to.) He was shocked to hear that Eliot, who did not enjoy reading his poems, was accepting as little as a hundred dollars for a performance. Giroux promptly raised it to the then unheard-of fee of a thousand, "and a lot of people, once they heard that, wanted him to read." Often he accompanied Eliot on his American reading tours—to Chicago, to New Haven, to Dallas, where Eliot was made honorary sheriff. When the poet's doctor ordered Eliot to warmer climates, Giroux spent many winter vacations with Valerie and Tom Eliot in the Caribbean.

There are a thousand anecdotes from the life of editing. Reading Marianne Moore's correspondence with publisher Eliot, which Moore had entrusted to him, Giroux discovered that Moore wrote Eliot refusing a royalty check from Faber & Faber because she feared that Faber would lose money on the handsome volume they had produced. Eliot's reply was grave: *Never*, he told Moore, *never* return a check that you have received from a publisher. . . . The uncashed check remains among the letters.

Or there was the time Giroux published Louise Bogan's collected poems, "The Blue Estuaries," and was going over critical quotes for the jacket. Most of them seemed ordinary, but he found beautiful and apt a statement by Theodore Roethke, who had recently died. Giroux telephoned Bogan to make sure that she was agreeable, and read the passage aloud to her. As he was reading he became aware that Bogan was weeping at the other end of the line. He himself, he remembers, had found the quote quite moving—but not *that* moving. After Bogan died he discovered what he had not known before: The two poets had been lovers years before.

Publisher as well as editor, Giroux has more scope to help writers than most editors do. Many years ago Peter Taylor found himself in an author's nightmare. His short stories belonged to a publishing house that was, in effect, defunct, that existed perhaps as a sheaf of contracts in a safe. Although his volumes were listed in Books in Print, bookstores ordering received no reply; anthologists could not reprint his stories in their anthologies. Yet because the books were officially in print, Taylor could not reclaim copyright; he might as well have writ his stories on water. On Giroux's initiative FSG issued "The Collected Stories of Peter Taylor," daring the defunct firm to sue. It did not. Peter Taylor's stories were back in print, where they have remained.

Such daring is rare among publishers, and FSG is a rare publishing house. They publish no textbooks, and nowadays the text division of a house often supports the trade books. Giroux thinks that the textbook tail wags the trade dog. Of course, FSG, like any other publisher, must publish books that sell or they will not survive to publish books that don't. Faber & Faber, the great English house with which FSG shares many authors, cushioned itself with a line of nurses' manuals. FSG sells cookbooks and juveniles, which help considerably; in years past, Gaylord Hauser sold interminably; not long ago they published a nonbook called "The Best" and reprinted "Mrs. Beeton."

But the solution, says Giroux with an earned complacency, is to publish good books. FSG is especially proud of its foreign authors, who solidify the backlist: Hermann Hesse, Colette, Moravia, Marguerite Yourcenar, Pavese, Peter Handke, Solzhenitsyn. Often it takes years before they catch on. And it takes a long time to make money publishing Robert Lowell and Elizabeth Bishop. But a backlist that continues to sell, anthology rights to poems, subsidiary rights to paperbacks—these are the long-term rewards for publishing contemporary classics. "A classic," Giroux remembers Van Doren saying, "is a book that is never out of print."

"Patience is a large part of it, and judgment," says Giroux, "and *loyalty*. You have to have a commitment to the author. If you believe in the author, you are willing to wait. Flannery O'Connor is a good case. Her first book did very little, originally. Now it's a film."

If Giroux is proud of his firm, he is not so sure about the times and the country he lives in; yet he is a man of resilient optimism. Many phenomena of the moment—such as the American Book Awards, which replace the NBA with imitation Academy Awards—do not please him. He notes that they have put poetry in a second-class category together with, but after, Westerns. "They have no sense of the past," he says, "and as a great Frenchman said, if you have no sense of the past, you are a child. The world is too full of infantilism." The state of publishing, he says, reflects the state of the country: We are an illiterate people. "The biggest best seller in modern times was probably 'Gone With the Wind.' People who never read a book in their lives had to read that—and what was the sale? Maybe twenty million copies, the absolute saturation point. Put that against the total population! Compare it with the television audience!

"One worries about the deterioration of intellectual activity, the attention-span of readers and the general illiteracy—college *graduates* who cannot write or read properly.

We are victims of the history of our era." Momentarily depressed, he mentions the increase in malicious reviewing, enemies ambushing enemies. He shakes his head; then he picks himself up again, and he praises small publishers, new presses, guessing that "there will always be enough people, even if it is just a handful. There will be young publishers whose names you don't know right now." And he reminds himself that, in the old days that we praise, best sellers were novels not by Henry James but by Hall Caine and Gene Stratton Porter.

Asked about memorable occasions, he mentions E. M. Forster's special brand of humor: "Visiting him at King's College, I found him limping around in a leg cast with the aid of a cane, and his laconic reply when I asked what had happened was, 'Slipped in a belfry.' In America I took Forster to a college on Long Island, where he answered the students' questions amiably until one young Marxist delivered a lecture beginning 'Don't you agree that in our corrupt society, etc. etc.' At the end of this harangue, Forster simply cleared his throat and said, 'Next question?'"

Giroux's weirdest experience was an encounter with the Secret Service shortly after President Nixon's re-election: "Two men entered my office with their hands on their holsters. After showing me their credentials, they handed me an unsigned cable from Australia which read, 'Robert Giroux has vowed to assassinate Richard Nixon if he is re-elected.' I said, 'Is this a joke?' They said, 'What do you have to say about it? We have to follow up every single alleged threat.' I told them the charge was absolutely absurd. I said I was unable to account for it but that, as a Democrat and a former naval officer, I deeply resented it. At the mention of the Navy, the atmosphere visibly relaxed. I called in my assistant, Patricia Strachan, and showed her the cable. She went to the file and brought back a letter I'd forgotten from an author in Australia whose book I had rejected. It said, 'I will make you rue the day you rejected a great manuscript.' I gave them the letter to follow up and got their calling-card in return. I keep it to remind me of the perils of being an editor."

Now Giroux comes into the office four days a week, staying at home in his country place—an old farmhouse in New Jersey—on Fridays to read manuscripts. Soon he will read at home Mondays as well, coming to the office for the weekly FSG editorial meeting on Tuesdays. When he comes to Union Square he still looks into the slush pile from time to time, seeking the moment of discovery. Asked what characteristics an editor must exemplify, he begins with "curiosity," thinks some more, and adds "optimism." He remembers a moment from his early career at Harcourt, Brace, taking a train to Riverside, Conn., for a weekend at Frank Morley's house, opening a manuscript by an unknown author, and with growing excitement discovering Jean Stafford's "Boston Adventure." He forgot where he was and rode past his destination.

Looking back from the age of sixty-five, Giroux can recall a career in touch with the greatest literary figures of our time. But associations with these writers are not his greatest satisfaction: "Although I published T. S. Eliot, he was a monument long before I met him. And many fine writers with whom I love to work, like Walker Percy, Madeleine L'Engel, Paul Horgan, Isaac Bashevis Singer, Donald Barthelme, Grace Paley, William Alfred, Derek Walcott, and William Golding, were well-established writers before they joined our list." Yet his special satisfaction is to have discovered and published the first books of authors who went on to write better books. Sitting at his desk in his cramped, low-overhead office, he writes out in pencil, on a plain pad of paper, ten titles and authors; Jean Stafford, "Boston Adventure"; Robert Lowell, "Lord Weary's Castle"; Bernard Malamud, "The Natural"; Randall Jarrell, "Losses"; Peter Taylor, "A Long Fourth"; William Gaddis, "The Recognitions"; Hannah Arendt, "The Origins of Totalitarianism" (her first book in English); Jack Kerouac, "The Town and the City"; Susan Sontag, "The Benefactor"; L. Woiwode, "What I'm Going to Do, I Think." I note that he has forgotten to list an author of whom he is especially proud: Flannery O'Connor, "Wise Blood."

Finishing, he looks up: "When you look at work by someone never published, you always hope to pick up a manuscript you cannot put down. Cyril Connolly, the late British critic and editor of Horizon, said that the writer's job is to write a masterpiece. Editors are born to discover them."

How often in a publisher's life, I ask him—thinking of all the appointments, lunches, telephone calls, all the manuscripts read on trains or in bed at midnight—how often will you pick up such a manuscript?

"Oftener than I expected," says Robert Giroux.

James Laughlin

(1981)

When I was fourteen I discovered New Direction's *Poet of the Month* series. I do not remember if I registered the irony of the name; the bookshelves of my parents' house were filled with Books of the Month—J. P. Marquand and Kenneth Roberts rather than Berryman, Winters, and Rakosi. I delighted in my difference and James Laughlin fed my difference.

All through the 1940s, as I grew into poetry, New Directions showed the way. Probably the annuals were most important. During an illness when I was seventeen I bought *1940, 1941,* and *1942* by mail from the Gotham Book Mart and occupied myself for a month or so. I bought the three volumes of *Five Young American Poets* when they were new, finding Jarrell, Berryman, Shapiro, Goodman, Nims, Garrigue. In *New Directions* books I read Henry Miller, Kenneth Patchen, William Carlos Williams. . . . As I look around the room I write in, forty years later, I see these volumes everywhere, many of them from the decade of the forties when the sight of them made my heart pound. I remember the excitement of reading Delmore Schwartz's *Genesis,* and dreaming of the long poem . . . I remember opening the annuals, packed densely with print, to find out what X and Y had been doing since last year. . . .

Because he did not put his own name forward, for many

years I knew nothing of the figure whose taste, energy, and fortune made New Directions. Forty years after I started reading his choices, I know a little of James Laughlin's loyalty and devotion to good writers and good writing. In an era when the profession of publishing becomes the province of marketers and distributors, it is useful to praise this man who does not need our praise. For forty-five years he has stood for quality and independence and generosity and faith in publishing. No one in his time has served literature more.

This fall, "New Directions 43" will appear. In 1936, the first of these annuals included poets named Williams, Pound, Moore, Stein, Stevens, and Cummings—none of them yet the cynosures of English departments. It also published the very new: three early poems by Elizabeth Bishop and a short story by Henry Miller, whose "Tropic of Cancer" had appeared only two years earlier in Paris. At the time, the twenty-two-year-old editor-publisher, James Laughlin, loaded his Buick with 600 unpaginated copies, became a traveling salesman and persuaded bookstores to stock a few volumes—out of pity, he believes.

Laughlin, now in his sixty-seventh year, continues to reside in Norfolk, Conn., near the horse stable from which he started publication. In 1981 ND's New York editors and staff handle much of the work of publication, and W. W. Norton distributes more efficiently than the publisher had from his automobile. The annual's pressrun has escalated to 2,500 copies: 1,000 hard and 1,500 soft. The one-man rule of past years has devolved to consensus, but in a sense Laughlin has always collaborated: He has listened well.

Publishing Ezra Pound, he listened to Ezra Pound— which brought him not only William Carlos Williams but Henry Miller. Listening to Henry Miller, he reprinted Hermann Hesse's "Siddhartha," which sold as many as a quarter of a million copies a year late in the sixties. Pound's friend Mr. Eliot recommended Djuna Barnes, whose "Nightwood" has been continuously available. Edith Sitwell recommended

Dylan Thomas, and Dylan Thomas Vernon Watkins. William Carlos Williams recommended Nathanael West—as well as many terrible poets, especially from New Jersey, whom he would praise extravagantly, ending his letter, "but as you think best." Laughlin's Harvard connections—he was a sophomore when he first published a New Directions book—supplied him well. Harry Levin, who wrote his "James Joyce" for ND when he was in his twenties, supplied Vladimir Nabokov, and Albert Guerard John Hawkes—one of the younger writers Laughlin is proudest of. Laughlin met Tennessee Williams at a cocktail party—his only literary discovery with a social origin. He found Delmore Schwartz in the Partisan Review and wrote him a letter; Schwartz brought him Randall Jarrell and John Berryman. Laughlin cannot remember how he came across Kenneth Rexroth, who led him to Denise Levertov, Robert Duncan, Gary Snyder, Gregory Corso, Lawrence Ferlinghetti, David Antin, and Jerome Rothenberg.

Although New Directions started in the service of verbal revolution, it reprinted Henry James, E. M. Forster, Ronald Firbank, and Evelyn Waugh when other publishers would not; when no one would print F. Scott Fitzgerald's "The Crack Up," ND did; when "The Great Gatsby" was out of print, New Directions brought it back. For the most part the list represented the new, with Objectivists George Oppen, Carl Rakosi, Charles Reznikoff; with Robert Creeley, Michael McClure, Robert Duncan, William Everson; with Laughlin's particular friend Thomas Merton; with novelists Chandler Brossard, James Purdy, Coleman Dowell, Frederick Busch, and Walter Abish (who recently received PEN's 1981 William Faulkner Award).

Two glues held the list together: the assumption of quality and the assumption that these books would not sell in the marketplace. In bringing foreign authors to American readers in translation, ND may have made its most important contribution: not only the obvious Rimbaud, Baudelaire, Rilke, Valéry, Kafka, and Cocteau, but the less known and the unknown: Montale, Neruda, Queneau, Cardenal,

Lorca, Pasternak, Paz, Borges, Mishima, Lihn, Vittorini, Parra, Guillevic.

Because such publishing required subsidy at the start, ND's story begins with a nineteenth-century immigrant. Laughlin's great-grandfather James Laughlin—the first syllable sounds like the Scots "Loch"—understood that there was a shortage of crockery in the New World. He sold his farm in northern Ireland, bought crockery, shipped it to Philadelphia, filled a wagon with it and started west. By the time he arrived at Pittsburgh his wagon was empty and his pockets full. A devout Presbyterian, he founded a bank and a store and before he died joined forces with a Welsh iron-puddler to smelt iron. The patriarch's five sons entered the firm (Laughlin's grandfather James II became the treasurer) and made their fortunes—providing eventual support for books by Henry Miller and William Carlos Williams.

When James Laughlin IV was a boy in Pittsburgh, his father (named Henry; an uncle was James III) took the children down to the mill once a year at Thanksgiving. "It was scary—tremendous slabs of hot molten steel coming out of those giant furnaces, terrible noise, huge cranes carrying metal over your head all molten. [Although] there was never in my time any grim things such as the time when my great-uncle Frick turned the machineguns on the workers [during the Homestead Massacre], at an early age I made up my mind that I would not go into the mill."

Boyhood on the Hill, where the rich people lived, was pleasant enough, but Laughlin's life seems to have begun when he left Pittsburgh for Choate; he never came back to stay. Teaching at Choate was the poet Dudley Fitts, who had corresponded for years with Ezra Pound and later introduced Laughlin to the master craftsman. With the tutelage of Fitts and Carey Briggs, Laughlin found the purpose of his life. He edited the Choate literary magazine, wrote fiction and published a prize-winning story in the Atlantic Monthly before he arrived at Harvard.

At least as important as Choate in the long run was the alternative home provided in Norfolk, Conn., by his father's older sister, Aunt Leila Laughlin Carlisle, who had bought 360 acres in Norfolk and built herself Robin Hill in 1929. He started visiting Aunt Leila in Norfolk from Choate; he has not left Norfolk since. A town of enormous white wooden houses, it is a north-western Connecticut enclave of the rich. Here sits the large white Meadow House of James and Ann Laughlin: set back from the road, with black-green shutters, surrounded by rocky pasture with white birch growing in it, sheep and a sheep barn. The land is hilly, hemlock over the granite fields, vistas north and west into hills of western Massachusetts and northeastern New York.

When Laughlin translated himself from Choate to Harvard, he continued to take his vacations in Norfolk at Aunt Leila's, who was powerful, childless, loving, dominant ("she should have been a man running a steel mill") and eccentric. Through a medium she communicated with a spirit named Lester who wrote long letters. Years later, when she worried over the books her nephew published, Lester would reassure her, saying not to worry about James, James is going to straighten out, be patient, he is a good boy. "Oh," says Laughlin now, "she was a wonderful old woman."

Aunt Leila was literary, with the taste of her generation—Scott, Thackeray—and could not countenance ND's list. By contemporary standards, of course, ND published no dirty books—and it was Aunt Leila who was chiefly responsible. As Nabokov's first American publisher, Laughlin could have taken a chance on "Lolita"—but counseled Nabokov to publish it first in Paris. As Henry Miller's publisher, ND issued books energetic but inoffensive—"The Cosmological Eye" (the cover illustration is a photograph of Laughlin's eye), "The Wisdom of the Heart" "The Colossus of Maroussi"; fifteen titles still in print—and Barney Rossett's Grove Press published the "Tropics" when censorship diminished in America. Laughlin admires Rossett's enterprise; but "I knew that my aunt would come down on me like a sledgehammer."

At Harvard Laughlin heeled the Advocate in his freshman year, made the editorial board and "hung around a lot." James Agee was a senior that year, precocious, writing the poems of his first volume. "I was in awe of him," Laughlin says. Later Robert Fitzgerald, "began putting me onto the classics." Laughlin majored in the unusual combination of Latin and Italian, the Italian coming from his adventures on leave as a sophomore.

Despite the Advocate, Harvard in general was stuffy; it was a known fact that the Boylston Professor of Rhetoric and Oratory, the poet Robert Hillyer, would leave the room if someone mentioned T. S. Eliot or Ezra Pound. So Laughlin applied for leave—he became a pioneer of the multiyear B.A., taking his degree in 1939 at the age of twenty-five—and went to Paris, where he consorted with Gertrude Stein and Alice B. Toklas; he was found useful for changing tires. Then he wrote Ezra Pound in Rapallo, presuming upon the Fitts connection, hoping to visit—and received a wire in return: "Visibility high."

Laughlin attended the Ezuversity in Rapallo for six months, studying Italian with an old lady Pound procured for him, Signorina Canessa—"about a hundred, stooped over like a barrel-hoop"—and studying everything else with the Ezuversity's sole professor. Tuition was free, books were loaned, examination took place over meals, or whenever the master paused in his labors. Italian lessons continued in the evening at the cinema, where Pound relaxed after his day's work, feet propped on the balcony rail, in a cowboy hat and a velvet coat, eating peanuts and roaring with laughter at bad indigenous comedies.

When Laughlin showed Pound poems and stories he was working on, Pound cut and cut and cut. Finally, as Laughlin tells it, Pound suggested that instead of becoming a writer he should make himself useful to others by becoming a publisher. Never has advice been better followed.

It should be said, however, that Laughlin has continued to write poems in the interstices of his publishing career. Lawrence Ferlinghetti's City Lights published "In Another Country" in 1978, Laughlin's poems 1935-1975 selected by Robert Fitzgerald—a short book, the poems mostly brief, the accomplishment modest but solid: observations, notes, poems of love and tenderness. Normally easy-going in speech, Laughlin becomes tersely self-deprecating when he speaks of his writing: "It's very light; it's sentimental, it deals with no great subjects, no great thoughts. . . ." Perhaps, if the poet pretends that he does not take his work seriously, he is free to continue it.

Coming back to Harvard from Italy, Laughlin founded ND with his own money. When he started college his father gave him $100,000, which he invested and which sustained him until the fifties, when he began to inherit more substantial sums. During the first twenty years of ND, Laughlin acquired the reputation of a skinflint. When he hired assistants he paid low wages; when the cupboard was bare he delayed royalty payments. "Like other rich men patronizing the arts," says an old friend, "he makes a point of playing the hard-boiled pro rather than the dilettantish easy mark." But even the assistants he underpaid were witnesses to generosity. He published and promoted Delmore Schwartz, hired him to help edit, and later—when Schwartz in his paranoia attacked Laughlin to everyone who would listen, claiming that Laughlin collaborated with Nelson Rockefeller to cuckold him—paid Schwartz's psychiatrist behind Schwartz's back. "He had been so sweet, so funny! He just got loopy. I wanted to see if anybody could fix him up." When Kenneth Patchen and his wife were broke, Laughlin installed them in the cottage at Norfolk, attached to the end of the offices, where they would work and write and survive. (One time, when Laughlin was away skiing, Aunt Leila discovered that the Patchens were dumping refuse in the woods behind the cottage. "She blew her top and they were gone.")

In later years, when John Hawkes needed time away from teaching to work on a novel, Laughlin made him interest-free loans. "Thanks to him," Hawkes says, "I was able to spend essential years writing in Europe and the West Indies." But the money was not the most important thing to Hawkes: "The main thing was his support, his steadfast encouragement in the face of vitriolic reviews or no reviews at all, the constant strength he lent me when fiction writing, or my kind of it, seemed nearly impossible." The books remained and still remain in print. For the most part Laughlin has done little line-editing for his writers, because they would not stand for it. "Henry Miller would not let you change a word. Bill Williams didn't want to change a line."

Not all relationships with writers were easy. Readers of Edmund Wilson's letters to Vladimir Nabokov will remember Wilson's continual hostility toward Laughlin. Perhaps the most difficult of all writers was Edward Dahlberg, who was once discovered in the ND offices ripping bookjackets from the walls, enraged because his own were unrepresented.

In the forties ND began to issue books in series. Volumes called "Five Young American Poets" appeared for three years, providing the first lengthy publication of Jarrell, Berryman, Karl Shapiro, Tennessee Williams, Paul Goodman, Jean Garrigue, John Frederick Nims, and Eve Merriam. "The Poet of the Month," twelve pamphlets available for $4.50 a year, ran for forty-two issues from 1941 to 1944. (When the Book-of-the-Month Club threatened a lawsuit, the series became "Poets of the Year.") The series began with William Carlos Williams, followed by F. T. Prince, Delmore Schwartz, Josephine Miles, Robert Penn Warren, Richmond Lattimore, John Wheelwright, Richard Eberhart, John Berryman, Vladimir Nabokov, and Yvor Winters, among others.

There was also the New Classics series of reprints—Waugh, Fitzgerald, Forster, Stein, etc.—and the critical Makers of Modern Literature, which sponsored Trilling on Forster, Levin on Joyce, and Winters on Robinson. In the old annuals are notices of the ones that got away—books planned and never done. If only one could read those "forthcoming books" advertised in the 1941 annual. Henry James by R. P. Blackmur, Franz Kafka by Harry Levin, Baudelaire by Allen Tate, T. S. Eliot by Delmore Schwartz, and Emily Dickinson by John Crowe Ransom. Critical books actually published include John Crowe Ransom's "The New Criticism," Yvor Winters's "Maule's Curse," and William Empson's "Seven Types of Ambiguity."

In one memorable summer of the forties Vladimir Nabokov and family spent time with Laughlin at Alta, Utah, where the novelist-lepidopterist pursued butterflies and moths. Nabokov's fiction has never been praised for its compassion; he was singleminded if nothing else. One evening at dusk he returned from his day's excursion saying that during hot pursuit over Grizzly Gulch he had heard someone groaning most piteously down by the stream. "Did you stop?" Laughlin asked him. "No, I had to get the butterfly." The next day the corpse of an aged prospector was discovered in what has been renamed, in Nabokov's honor, Dead Man's Gulch.

Laughlin did some assistant-butterflying. "We nearly got killed once. At the end of the range there is a mountain called Lone Peak, about 13,000 feet high. He had the idea that at the top of this mountain there would be a certain very rare butterfly that would live only a day or two. We set off to try and get it. We drove at first by car through a canyon and then climbed up through the damndest jungle, about eight hours of climbing. . . . and there sure enough on the top was this butterfly!

"But we had made the mistake of going in summer clothes, in shorts and sneakers. As we started down this snowfield below the peak, we lost our footing and began to slide. We were sliding faster and faster down this snowfield, toward a terrible bunch of rocks, but Nabokov had his butterfly net. . . . He managed somehow to hook his butterfly net onto a piece of rock that was sticking through the snow. I grabbed his foot and held onto him. Then he crawled back to the rock, and somehow figured out a way. . . . If it hadn't been for that butterfly net. . . ."

There are a thousand stories. With Dylan Thomas there was a three-day London binge which ended when the two men, with several unidentified companions, woke on the floor of a female stranger's flat. With Thomas there was also the desperate loan of a hundred pounds, on the ground that his eldest son had been committed to a tuberculosis sanitarium, an event elsewhere unrecorded. With Elizabeth

Bishop there was a polite tea party at a Key West brothel called The Square Roof, of which Bishop had befriended the proprietor and her employees.

Many publishers have approached Laughlin for his memoirs, which will never be written. "When they ask ya to do yar meemoirs"—Laughlin imitates Pound—"ya know ya're finished." But the documents of ND, available to scholars, are protected in Norfolk in a fireproof room together with thousands of rare books and magazines. A resident archivist keeps them in order. Most of them will go to Harvard.

At this age Laughlin does not work so many hours as he once did. In winter he likes to cross-country, in summer to play golf and swim in Toby Pond. And he does his own investing. Still, he reads manuscripts six or seven hours a day, usually until one or two in the morning. Still, he comes to New York once a week—Ann Laughlin drives the two and a half hours while her husband reads manuscripts beside her—staying overnight at their Bank Street apartment and working with the ND staff nearby on Eighth Avenue. When Laughlin worked for the Ford Foundation in the fifties, editing the international magazine Perspectives among other things, Robert MacGregor handled the bulk of ND work. MacGregor died four years ago. Now Frederick Martin heads a staff of seven, and manuscripts are accepted by discussion and consensus.

Beginning with the sales of "Siddhartha"; helped by the million-copy sale of Lawrence Ferlinghetti's "Coney Island of the Mind"; by the academic acceptance of Pound, Williams and other old authors; by the amazing sales of younger poets like Gary Snyder and Denise Levertov; and by the growing backlist sales of John Hawkes and other discoveries, the firm has been in the black for two decades. In some of these years, however, the black was thin.

Laughlin could sell ND if he wished, but he does not choose to. (Only recently a rich friend offered to buy the firm for his child, who had just graduated summa cum laude and was interested in publishing.) Instead, planning for a future without the publisher, Laughlin has set up a trust fund to insure that ND will survive his death for at least a decade—time, as he supposes, for his authors to find other publishers. If they succeed, most will need to find publishers that resemble ND, which will not be easy. These are publishers of the middle way—larger than the one-owner small press, smaller than dinosaurs ponderously sustained by Big Books only—who by low overhead, by infusions of capital from the responsible rich, by wit, or most likely by all three—can choose with taste, publish with economy and keep a good book in print.

Robert Frost Corrupted

(1982)

In 1974 it was discovered that works by the American sculptor David Smith had been altered after the artist's death. One of the executors of his estate, acting on his own initiative, changed the patina on some of Smith's metal work. A friend of Smith's reported that the sculptor had "painted 'Primo Piano III' with a yellow undercoat something like twenty times. Then he painted it three times with white paint. Then he died." An artcritic-executor stripped the paint from "Primo Piano III" and varnished it brown.

The Poetry of Robert Frost, edited by Edward Connery Lathem, is the only full collection of Frost's poems in print—but the text is corrupt; the editor has altered the rhythm of Frost's poems by re-punctuating them throughout. Although several of Frost's critics have complained of these alterations, no one has noted their full extent and nature; most anthologists and many critics now reprint the corrupt text. Lathem has removed commas, added commas, removed hyphens, added hyphens, made words compound, added question marks, and altered dashes. Besides regularizing quotation marks—double quotes for single seems a tolerable change—the editor makes by my count 1,364 emendations, of which his notes justify 247 by reference to earlier printings. Thus he makes 1,117 changes for which he offers no textual sources, an average of 3.39 for each poem.

Frost wrote the line:

> The woods are lovely, dark and deep

We do not find this line in *The Poetry of Robert Frost*; instead we find:

> The woods are lovely, dark, and deep

To say that the woods are 1) lovely, 2) dark, and 3) deep differs considerably from claiming that they are lovely *in that* they are dark and deep. In Frost's line, the general adjective *lovely* is explained by the more particular modifiers *dark* and *deep*. In the editor's line, the egalitarian threesome is non-parallel—as if we proclaimed that a farmer grew apples, McIntoshes, and Northern Spies.

Before *The Poetry of Robert Frost* our texts were the books that Frost saw into print during his lifetime, individual volumes added serially to a collected volume. Most of these poems were reprinted without change while the poet lived, and at his death in 1963 were available in *Complete Poems of Robert Frost* and the 1962 collection *In the Clearing*. In 1969 Lathem published his edition with Holt, Rinehart and Winston; it is now available in paperback. (Two volumes of selections use Lathem's text; there remains a Pocket Books selection edited by Louis Untermeyer with Frost's punctuation.) In England Jonathan Cape published Lathem's Frost in 1971, and Ian Hamilton edited a *Selected Poems* for Penguin in 1973 that uses the corrupt text.

It would seem axiomatic that an editor's task is to represent the author's intent insofar as the editor can establish it. When the author is long dead, when manuscript or printed sources are absent, when a variety of evidence lacks single authority, an editor must rely on historical scholarship to inspire guesses of authenticity and to mediate a readable, probable text. The matter of Robert Frost, however, differs from the matter of Shakespeare or Keats. Frost lived long and spoke his poems aloud on thousands of occasions, reading from one of his printed texts. If he had wished to sprinkle his lines with new commas, as one might salt a roast, he could have pencilled them into his reading copy. If he wished to add a question mark, or to delete a hyphen, it would have been simple to do. In the absence of alterations, his repeatedly-printed texts suggest intention—almost as clearly as twenty undercoats of yellow.

Frost's inconsistencies in punctuation and his deviations from standard practice bother a tidy mind. A tidy mind will find relief in Lathem's revision, which insists on consistency to the exclusion of other criteria. But poets are notoriously innovative in punctuation, inventing combinations like "—:" and ";—?". E. E. Cummings would make an extreme example, but we need not go so far. William Butler Yeats arranged colons and dashes and semicolons among his lines, not according to the conventions of prose but as notation for pause and pitch; T. S. Eliot's punctuation and capitalization were eccentric and expressive; among Frost's American contemporaries, Wallace Stevens most nearly abided by conventions of punctuation, but was partial to an unorthodox colon; Marianne Moore was both scrupulous and inventive. Even E. A. Robinson, the one contemporary whom Frost praised, was given to coinages like ",—".

We await a history of punctuation in modern poetry. In the meantime we may suggest that eccentric punctuation has been purposeful. Possibly some punctuation fails its purpose, but deliberate intent remains clear—to serve as notation to sound, the pale cousin of musical notation. There is a story about E. A. Robinson at the MacDowell Colony, who became annoyed when a novelist at his dinner table boasted of writing five-thousand words in a day. Robinson responded: "This morning I deleted the hyphen from 'hellhound' and made it one word: this afternoon I redivided it and restored the hyphen."

(Frost's editor has removed one hundred and one of Robert Frost's hyphens, usually compounding two words into one, sometimes dividing them into two separate words. And in other places he added eighty-one hyphens to word-pairs Frost left uncoupled. On one hundred and eighty-two occasions he has done to Robert Frost's text what Robinson took a day to do and undo.)

Poetic practice supports the notion of expressive improvisation in punctuation, rather than consistency of editorial rule. Most magazines, the better newspapers, and some publishers have house rules by which copy-editors try to standardize practice, but these rules tend to change every few years as one party or the other gets the upper hand. For instance there is the habit sometimes called the Harvard comma. Should it be "Holt, Rinehart and Winston," or "Holt, Rinehart, and Winston"? The publishing company uses the first formula. American academic practice frequently follows the second. Frost usually omits it, but not always. For a careful stylist, this comma has become optional, depending on pace and meaning. If commas be our servants not our masters, we vary them to represent the sounds of speech; by commas we may control pitch and the groupings of words. Or by omitting punctuation an author may leave much to his readers, controlling pace and pitch by word-choice alone. Hemingway was a master of the omitted comma. In his letters and in much of his prose, Frost punctuates like Hemingway. When someone wrote Frost in 1930, criticizing details of a book, his reply included the boast: "One of my prides is that I can write a fifty word telegram without having to use a single 'Stop' for the sense." (He refers to the old requirement of telegraphy; the word "stop" indicated a period or full-stop.) He prided himself on so arranging words, on so mastering spoken syntax, that he needed few marks of punctuation to indicate relationships among words, or to fix pace and pitch. Frost admired self-reliance even in sentences.

Frost cared for the sound of verse. He went so far as to claim that words existed in order to make noises: "Words are only valuable in writing as they serve to indicate particular sentence sounds. . . ." Frost seems not to have cared much for assonance, lush vowels rubbing against each other. He cared most for the cadence of talk, with the nudge and thrust of intelligence in pace and pitch. Continually he refers to a semantics of noise. "Remember," he tells us, "that the sentence sound often says more than the words. . . ." "There are tones of voice that mean more than words." Another phrase he likes is "the sound of sense," the way cadence makes sense and sense makes cadence: ". . . if one is to be a poet he must learn to get cadences by skillfully breaking the sounds of sense with all their irregularity of accent across the regular beat of the metre."

Anyone who has read Frost's letters and essays becomes familiar with the theme of "sentence sounds" and "the sound of sense," Frost's contribution to modern poetics. Doubtless both critical idea and poetic practice derive from Wordsworth, an extension of the desire to write with the material of the spoken idiom. And in his best poems Frost exemplifies again and again the miraculous wedding of speech and metrical line. If ever one feels puzzled by a phrase like "breaking the sounds of sense . . . across the regular beat . . . ," one can refresh one's understanding by listening to a stanza like this one, from "A Patch of Old Snow":

> There's a patch of old snow in the corner
>   That I should have guessed
> Was a blow-away paper the rain
>   Had brought to rest.

Frost listens to speech and repeats it like a mimic. With a line break the poet expects some voice-indication (almost always a slight pause; often pitch-change) to match the line-structure visible on the printed page. Set as prose Frost's lines make a sentence without tension: "There's a patch of old snow in the corner that I should have guessed was a blow-away paper the wind had brought to rest." Breaking the sounds of sense across the regular beat, Frost gives us "the wind / Had brought," making a pause both unnatural and wonderful, raising pitch on "wind" and hesitating between subject and verb.

With this poem, Mr. Lathem was largely merciful; but he

puts a comma at the end of the first line, after "corner," where the line-ending pause is all the pause Frost wanted. (The added comma is of course grammatically incorrect.) Put a comma after "corner" and you pile Pelion-pause on Ossa-pause, slowing the poem down, making Frost's cadence sluggish.

I cite this alteration not because it destroys the poem but because it is typical. Unlike the comma in "lovely, dark, and deep," it is not confusing; it does not alter Frost's thought. Lathem adds punctuation that Frost omitted, and by so doing he slows things down. In the second line of "Stopping by Woods," Lathem changes Frost's "His house is in the village though" into "His house is in the village, though." Besides adding pause Lathem adds pitch variety because we drop our voices when the comma isolates "though." It is no calamity, perhaps, to drop the voice—but we have Frost's word for it that "The living part of a poem is the intonation entangled somehow in the syntax idiom and meaning of a sentence." By intonation we may know character. Maybe the speaker who runs over the pause—"His house is in the village though"—tosses away his notion more lightly than the speaker who pauses and lowers pitch: "His house is in the village, though." This latter fellow seems more calculating.

Doubtless many readers will find these objections quibbles, as if they resembled the discomfort of the princess troubled by a single pea under a dozen mattresses. Many readers find a poem's identity in its paraphrase or summary, "what the poet is trying to say," instead of its articulate body, its bulk and its shapely dance, its speech and color and tone and resolution, its wholeness of which meaning is part. But a poem resembles a Henry Moore Reclining Figure at least as much as it resembles philosophical disquisition. Frost defined poetry as what gets lost in translation; meaning, in the vulgar sense, is what gets translated. When you change the movement of a poem by adding pause, you alter the Reclining Figure's dimensions or you use paint-remover on David Smith's metalwork. The 1,364 peas under these mattresses add much pause: Lathem adds 443 commas to Robert Frost's poems, thirteen colons, 156 long dashes some replacing short dashes, and twenty-two semi-colons. He adds three parentheses; he adds ellipses three times and deletes them twice. In most categories he deletes some occasions of the punctuation mark; but when he deletes one mark he often adds another which indicates greater pause—and a semi-colon or a long dash replaces a comma.

Lathem also adds twelve question marks, altering not time but pitch and meaning. On many occasions, especially in narrative poems, Frost wrote sentences in the grammatical form of questions, but concluded with periods instead of question marks. If we assume that Frost is aware of this mark of punctuation, we may suspect that he omitted it on purpose. In "Home Burial" the wife gazes out a window from which she can see her son's grave; Frost has the husband say:

> "What is it you see
> From up there always—for I want to know."

The idiom, grammar, and pacing embody the husband's state of mind. He feels his wife estranged and he wants the sensitivity he lacks. As Frost punctuated it, the husband began the speech as a question which he interrupts with a demand: "—for I want to know." Lathem alters and diminishes Frost's characterization of the husband by supplying the question mark:

> "What is it you see
> From up there always?—for I want to know."

Of course if a reader charges through "Home Burial" as if it were *Newsweek*, Lathem's question mark does little harm; but if the reader hears the poem in the mind's ear, then the question mark raises the pitch of "From up there always," sentence-sound is altered, and the husband's voice becomes gentler and less demanding.

Later in the poem the wife remembers that her husband, after digging their child's grave, remarked casually how little time it took a birch fence to rot. She cannot forgive "talk like that at such a time!"

> What had how long it takes a birch to rot
> To do with what was in the darkened parlor.

Her sentence is not a question inviting an answer but a statement of outrage. Lathem's question mark raises pitch and diffuses anger:

> What had how long it takes a birch to rot
> To do with what was in the darkened parlor?

Correctness makes politeness. For one more example, "The Witch of Coös" cackles at her son, "We'll never let them, will we, son! We'll never!" For Frost the exclamation is the thing. Lathem has the witch inquire: "We'll never let them, will we, son?"

Elsewhere, Lathem adds 81 hyphens and deletes 101. These alterations are as destructive as added commas and question marks, but the changes are more various and more difficult to describe. Of E. A. Robinson's "hell hound" there would be three possible forms, not only his alternative "hell-hound" but the further possibility "hellhound." When Lathem removes a hyphen he usually makes a single compound word out of it; but sometimes he turns it into two words and sometimes he takes two separate words and makes a compound; more rarely he takes a compound word and divides it again, either into a hyphenated pair or into two separate words.

In our language, the compounding of words is variable and practice changes rapidly. As Theodore Bernstein puts it, "The world of the hyphen is anarchic." The current Chicago *Manual of Style* advocates compounds; it usually favors omitting hyphens and running any two words together, with the result that we find monstrosities like "antiintellectual." Perhaps this contemporary fashion influences Lathem. I question the editorial practice which imposes new habits on old poems; I would not expect Yeats's editor to change the line into

> That dolphintorn, that gongtormented sea.

Let me assert that there are three possible ways to spell this place or direction: uphill, up hill, and up-hill; each is permissible; each differs to the eye; each can be pronounced so that audible difference represents visual difference: therefore, each spelling affects the sound of the sentence that contains it. In "uphill" the first syllable is louder than the second; in "up hill" the volume of the two syllables is virtually identical; in "up-hill" (less common) the relationship of loud and soft falls between the other two; and its eccentricity calls attention to the linkage.

When Lathem emends "lower chamber" in "Storm Fear" into "lower-chamber" he alters the rhythm of the line because "low-" becomes louder than "chamb-". In "The Trial by Existence," Lathem turns "cliff-top" into "cliff top," slowing the line down by adding the percussion of equal volume. When Lathem changes "sun-burned" into "sunburned" ("Pan With Us") and "tip-toe" into "tiptoe" ("The Death of the Hired Man") he follows modern usage but he does not represent the sentence-sounds of *A Boy's Will* and *North of Boston*. In the "Hired Man," "barn-door" becomes "barn door" and "harp-like" becomes "harplike"—and on the other hand, "college boy" becomes "college-boy." For Frost's "pocket-money" we have Lathem's "pocket money." Frost's "up hill" becomes Lathem's "uphill" and Frost's "down-hill" becomes Lathem's "downhill." In "A Lone Striker," "many, many eyed" travels a long distance to become "many-many-eyed," and Frost's pace is considerably quickened. In "Birches," Lathem removes five hyphens from Frost's fifty-nine lines. "Ice-storm" and "ice-storms" become "ice storm" and "ice storms," and "snow-crust" becomes "snow crust." One line loses three hyphens; "With all her matter-of-fact about the ice-storm" becomes "With all her matter of fact about the ice storm," with considerable change to the sentence sound; "matter-of-fact" speeded the line up. In "The Last Mowing" Frost wrote the touching lines,

> There's a place called Far-away Meadow
> We never shall mow in again . . .

which are destroyed in this edition. Surely that hesitation, that mini-mini-pause of the hyphen in "Far-away," makes delicate mimickry of emotion. Lathem's "Faraway Meadow" sounds like a real estate agent's name for a subdivision.

Often Lathem has changed dashes, commas, and hyphens within the same few lines. It is most upsetting, of course, when alterations hurt the best poems. In "To Earthward" there is a new comma which extends the pause at the end of a line—and which, as it happens, destroys the paralleling of syntax and therefore the sense of the stanza. Frost wrote:

> Now no joy but lacks salt
> That is not dashed with pain
> And weariness and fault . . .

Frost hurtles passionately from line to line, making this poem as overtly emotional as anything in his work. Feeling is diminished by Lathem's comma after "salt"—and the sense vanishes:

> Now no joy but lacks salt,
> That is not dashed with pain
> And weariness and fault . . .

Frank Bidart wrote in the *Partisan Review*: "Suddenly 'is' becomes parallel to 'lacks,' and the lines say that *every* joy is 'dashed with pain.' This is not only wrong, but self-contradictory: if every joy *'lacks* salt' it cannot also be 'dashed with pain.' . . . in the name of 'textual clarity' Lathem has ruined a crucial stanza." Almost as bad, in this wonderful poem, is an earlier editorial revision. Frost wrote this swooping cadence:

> The flow of—was it musk
> From hidden grapevine springs
> Down hill at dusk?

Here the enjambed swoop of the question—Frost employed a question mark when he wanted to—hurtles over two lines into the two monosyllables beginning the last line—two equally-loud words with a slight pause between them. But you will not find this effect in *The Poetry of Robert Frost*, where the last line begins with the single trochaic word, "Downhill."

For one more example let me cite a small change in a poem which some critics consider Frost's best work. "The Most of It" does not escape revision. "And then in the far distant water splashed" finds itself changed into "And then in the far-distant water splashed." Doubtless this addition of a hyphen is a small matter; its alteration of sound is slight. But if the hyphen does *not* change the sound of the line, why bother to add it? If it *does* change the sound of the line, how dare we alter Frost's sentence-sound?

I mean to argue with a two headed coin.

Edward Connery Lathem was graduated from Dartmouth College in 1951, took a D. Phil. at Oxford in 1961, and was Librarian of Dartmouth College from 1968-1978. A friend of Robert Frost's for many years, he is author or co-author of several publications connected with Frost, beginning with *Robert Frost: Farm-Poultry-Man*, edited with Lawrance Thompson in 1963. With Frost's biographer Thompson he also edited *Robert Frost and the Lawrence, Mass. High School Bulletin*, in 1966. Also in 1966 he and Hyde Coxe edited the useful *Selected Prose of Robert Frost*; Frost's frequent omission of the expected comma goes uncorrected in his prose. In the same year Lathem collected *Interviews with Robert Frost* and in 1969 the edition under discussion.

It should be acknowledged that Lathem's notes, at the back of the text, record his emendations. And of course some of them are justified. Lathem discovers that broken type in an old edition deleted a comma, a deletion scrupulously followed in subsequent editions; he restores this comma clearly intended by the author. Lathem replaces English spelling with American; evidently Frost had expressed annoyance at the English spellings surviving in some of his poems. Also Lathem standardizes practice in the use of double and single quotation marks. Although I cannot say that the old inconsistency bothered me, I find this alteration innocuous because it is silent. These alterations are the editor's proper business.

In 1971, two years after his edition was greeted with some criticism, Lathem defended himself in an introduction to the Imprint Society's reprint of *The Poetry of Robert Frost*. He began with the statement that Frost requested Lathem's help toward a new collected edition which the poet did not live to make. "Following the appearance of *In the Clearing* in 1962," Lathem tells us, "Mr. Frost spoke with the current editor about such an undertaking and requested his assistance with parts of the overall task." When Frost died early in 1963, "the responsibility [for the undertaking] devolved upon his publishers and estate." (Executor of the Frost estate is Alfred Edwards, who was Frost's publisher at Holt, Rinehart and Winston; he came to Holt from the National City Bank of New York. It is understood that Lathem will succeed him as Executor.) Chosen to be editor, Lathem arrived at the decision that "the general reader would oftentimes be helpfully served by some degree of editorial attention to the poems. . . . Thus, the desired objective could be attained of editorially enhancing textual clarity. . . ."

It would be difficult to object to the motives acknowledged in these passive sentences; but looking back from the perspective of the completed text, "enhancing textual clarity" seems understatement and "some degree of editorial attention" gross euphemism. Lathem nowhere alleges that Frost authorized him to change the punctuation of his poetry. He quotes from the letter I cited earlier, in which Frost spoke of his pride in omitting punctuation. As Lathem puts it: "[Frost] replied disarmingly [to the correspondent who complained about the 1930 *Collected Poems*]: 'I indulge a sort of indifference to punctuation. I don't mean I despise it. I value it. But I seem rather willing to let other people look after it for me.'" At first glance these sentences seem almost the permission Lathem requires. But the whole letter is not so much disarming as enraged. Leonidas W. Payne, Jr., Chairman of the English Department at the University of Texas, had sent Frost a list of "errors" in the 1930 volume. After speaking of his indifference, Frost makes his boast about being able to write a telegram without using the word "stop," and continues: "I'll have these commas and hyphens tended to though, if only for your peace of mind." Enjoying his sarcasm he goes on: "You must remember I am not writing schoolgirl English"; defending an inversion he says, ". . . the order should remind you of a very ancient figure of speech. Your friends of the Classical Department will tell you about it." If I had received this letter, I would not have characterized it as "disarming."

Although Frost appears to give way to Payne on punctuation—"Fortunately it turned out you were wrong in all your findings of errors except the punctuational."—it is noteworthy that he lived thirty-three years after writing this letter without "[having] those commas and hyphens tended to. . . ."

Acknowledging that Frost hated to be corrected, Lathem tells of three occasions on which Frost accepted correction during his lifetime; two of the suggestions were offered by Lathem himself. These corrections add commas to remove ambiguity. Because of George Whicher's puzzlement, Frost altered "To err is human, not to animal" into "To err is human, not to, animal." Lathem's two suggestions are similar—but if Lathem, after years of association with Robert Frost, has only two corrected commas to tell us about, how can we accept his addition of 441 others? If we cannot accept these revisions we may at least understand why Lathem hesitated to propose them to the living poet. As Lathem puts it, ". . . Frost did not actually relish having individuals challenge him regarding the punctuation of his verse. . . ."

Of course the great majority of Lathem's changes do not

remove ambiguity. Lathem's unauthorized repunctuations exist for the purpose of consistency—and they impose a consistency on Frost's poems that Frost gave no evidence of desiring. "Mr. Frost was," says Lathem, "in many ways, a very inconsistent person—as Emerson proclaims great souls are wont to be. (It was, withal, one of the myriad fascinating aspects of his personality.)" Fascinating as Lathem found Frost, surely the two men differed in character as thoroughly as they differed in prose style. One observes that Mr. Lathem is, in many ways, a very consistent person—one for whom consistency, order, and regularity are primary virtues. Perhaps they are—but I regret that a consistent editor should enforce his passion on an inconsistent poet.

For Lathem is passionate on the subject of the consistency which his friend lacked. Consistency is *his* pride, as Frost's pride was self-reliance. Although Lathem acknowledges that "Diverse spellings and irregularity of practice in punctuation" are not "apt to render a text unintelligible . . ." he insists that "they can distract, puzzle, and indeed annoy readers, undesirably intruding upon an assimilation of what the author has wished to communicate."

Here I must object. The inconsistency of omitting question marks in "Home Burial" was itself communicative; the inconsistency of grouping "dark and deep" together rather than separating them by a comma was itself communicative. The poet who argued that sentence-sounds carried the thrust of meaning would not agree that altering these sounds facilitated communication: *these sentence-sounds were themselves the communication.*

We need no proof that Frost was inconsistent. When Lathem defends the comma added to "His house is in the village though," he quotes six lines in which Frost used the comma that he omitted here.

It's seldom I get down except for meals, though.

That's always the way with the blueberries, though:

You can see what is troubling Granny, though.

I tell them they can't get through the door, though:

This is not sorrow, though; [. . .]

Unfortunately all of one kind, though.

In these lines Frost used the comma because he heard the pause. But when he did not hear the pause he omitted the comma—and not only in "Stopping by Woods." In "Death of the Hired Man," when the husband claims that the hired man had a rich brother, the wife responds, "He never told us that"; quick as a wink the husband returns, "We know it though." It is a snappy reply, and Lathem's "We know it, though," with its pause and lowered pitch, falsifies Frost's "sound of sense." Again, in "The Witch of Coos," the witch speaking of the ghost hisses, "It's with us in the room though." Be-Lathem'd, she says, "It's with us in the room, though." "What the author wished to communicate," with its observant notation of speech, is what the editor removes.

Lathem's defense has another component. As evidence supporting his revision of Frost's punctuation, Lathem cites Frost's performance of the poems preserved on records and tapes. He uses this device to support only "lovely, dark, and deep": ". . . literally scores of voice recordings exist of Frost saying his poems. Over and over again he is heard to give the three adjectives approximately equal stress, with no vocal suggestion that punctuation [might be otherwise]." Well, I also have listened to Frost and I do not agree; perhaps we hear what we expect to hear. As a reader of his poems, Frost was as inconsistent as he was in other matters, and often hurried through them as if he wanted to get the reading done with. He kept to the meter, usually kept to the line break—but he would sometimes rush through the pauses his punctuation indicated; if we were to punctuate according to Frost's performance we would find ourselves omitting many commas in his true text—and omitting periods as well. His performance recalls another Frost comment on punctuation, quoted by Lathem: "I hate to depend on punctuation at all. I hate to end with a word in one sentence that might well belong to the next sentence."

But editors must not punctuate by performance. In "Ash Wednesday" Eliot's text omits expected commas in "my legs my heart my liver . . ." But in performance he paused where we would expect commas in ordinary punctuation; perhaps the unaided ear needs help the eye does not require. Should Eliot's future editor add commas to "Ash Wednesday"? Wallace Stevens has the most consistently beautiful ear among modern poets, equally skilled in meter and free verse; but if his editor relied on his ghastly poetry readings, we could find periods between words in a single phrase, or the lines broken after every word, to represent the rhythm-destroying pauses of his speaking voice.

Of course I raise an old question, never to be answered: what *is* a text? If a text is the product of consistent copy-editing designated as official by the poet's estate, then Lathem's Frost is Frost's text. But I would rather a poet's text represented a poet's *probable intentions*, even if these intentions are inconsistent. My editor's task is picayune, difficult, and humble; it serves the poet and the poetry. I would have my editor repair broken letters, study manuscripts to discover proofhacks and printer's unauthorized emendations, and study the poet's own texts and correspondence for clues to intended revision. Perhaps I would have him perform mechanical (preferably mandated) changes like making English spelling American, or regularizing double and single quotes. Perhaps I would have him repair the spellings of proper names, and footnote the original misspellings. To discover an author's intentions is often difficult, the evidence contradictory; we are grateful to editors who serve reader and poet in the cause of authenticity.

Editors of other modern poets make contrast with Lathem's practice. There is the *Variorum Edition* of Yeats, which includes all printed versions of Yeats's poems, monumentally useful for readers of this poet who revised so frequently. The editors print the poet's latest known version at the top of each page and footnote earlier variants. This poet's punctuation was eccentric and inconsistent. The editors note that ". . . in later years W. B. had become very irate several times with a publisher who had taken it upon himself to change the poet's punctuation." Acknowledging Yeats's irregularities, the editors "decided it was not their concern to resolve this matter . . ." but to discern and follow the latest intention.

Perhaps the 1981 edition of Marianne Moore's *Complete Poems* is even closer to the point. Superficially it resembles her collection of 1967; but that volume was a mess: Miss Moore was alive at the time, ill, and could not pay her usual scrupulous attention. Clive E. Driver edited the 1981 volume, with Patricia C. Willis as his consultant. Driver's "Note" on the text reports that

> The text conforms as closely as is now possible to the author's final intention. Late authorized corrections, and earlier corrections authorized but not made, have been incorporated. Punctuation, hyphens, and line arrangements silently changed by editor, proofreader, or typesetter have been restored.

Ms. Willis adds in a letter:

> We worked from proofs, MS, corrected books, correspondence, searching for MM's intent until we were satisfied that the text met her standards. The cleaning up meant about five hundred changes in the text . . . [someone] had failed to query changes, and had failed in several cases to follow instructions from the poet.

In the case of Moore, a variorum edition like Yeats's will be useful because she revised her poems throughout her lifetime, and because many readers prefer early versions of some poems. But the careful editors of the current volume are bound to her latest intentions only.

It seems strange that there has not been more complaint about Lathem's Frost. However, some voices have been raised. Richard Poirier is perhaps Frost's best critic; in *Robert Frost: A Way of Knowing*, Oxford University Press, 1977, he complains of Lathem. He cites examples from "Home Burial" and "Stopping by Woods" which I have used. ("Without the question mark [in 'Home Burial'], there is the implication that the husband has learned, after many trying experiences, not to expect an answer to his questions.") William Pritchard, who teaches at Amherst and was acquainted with Frost, has spoken out on several occasions. ("Aside from what seems to me the needless and presumptuous fiddling involved in such emendations, what happens when the amusing line from 'Fireflies in the Garden' about how though the fireflies aren't stars they 'Achieve at times a very star-like start' now becomes 'starlike'?") Gerald Burns in the *Southwest Review* complained of "Lathem's hyperconservative commas, largely unnecessary in a poet who prided himself on writing lines you *couldn't* misread. . . ." The most outraged commentary on this edition was published by Frank Bidart in *The Partisan Review*. Bidart is a poet whose control of speech tempo depends on ingenious, expressive, and eccentric punctuation. (See *The Book of the Body*, Farrar, Straus, and Giroux, 1977; Faber, 1979.) "Lathem has re-punctuated about half of Frost's poems," Bidart complains, as he calls this edition "a grotesquely corrupt text" and a "betrayal of Frost." His small prose ode to punctuation deserves quotation: "Lathem . . .

> doesn't understand the way punctuation works in poetry. Basically, I think, a poet punctuates not simply for "meaning" or some notion of grammatical "correctness," but for rhythm and dramatic accent. Confronted with Lathem's "regularizing" of Frost's punctuation, one realizes how genuinely strange and adventuresome Frost often is. . . . Obviously, "punctuation" doesn't exist in isolation: it is only part of the difficult process of trying to put the poem on the page, of trying to make written lines correspond to the complex rhythms and accents in the poet's head. When it succeeds

usually it is invisible; one doesn't notice commas and semi-colons, but hears pauses and accents.

Richard Wilbur writes poems as different from Frank Bidart's as may be, but shows the same attitude toward punctuation. He writes in a letter:

> We all know that poets punctuate—or leave out punctuation—in deliberate personal ways, and not only for meaning but for timing. . . . If memory doesn't deceive me, Frost once said to me, "The less punctuation the better." If he did say that, and I think he did, he was saying that the right words can govern one's tone and pacing well enough to make full standard punctuation redundant. Or inauthentic, a finical obscuration.

In Lathem's defensive "Introduction," cited earlier, he quotes a line from John Benbow's *Manuscript and Proof* (Oxford University Press, 1937) evidently in mockery: "Poets, however, are to spell, capitalize, and punctuate (or not) as fancy moves them." There is little doubt of Frost's opinion on the question: he wished to do his own work. As an old friend of the poet says in a letter: "He was stubborn and adamant about leaving the poems as writ." Another writes: "He would be much disturbed if any of the sounds of his poems were altered." It is ironic that this editing-revision should happen to Robert Frost, of all modern poets; for of all the modern *genus irritabile vatum*, he was the most determinedly self-reliant.

This corrupted text of Robert Frost is increasingly taken as the true text. When a critic or anthologist writes Holt for permission now, permission is granted to reprint from Lathem's edition. Not everyone does as he is told. Poirier quoted the old text, as did Pritchard in *The Lives of the Modern Poets*, and Robert Pinsky in *The Situation of Poetry*. The first volume of Thompson's biography, published in 1966, uses Frost's punctuation; the second volume (dedicated to Lathem) and the third use Lathem's punctuation. Anthologists by and large do poorly. William Harmon's *Oxford Book of American Light Verse* preserves the corrupt Lathem text. Richard Ellmann's *New Oxford Book of American Verse* prints thirty-three poems, almost thirty pages, and uses Lathem's versions every time. These books seem especially regrettable, because Oxford books have the half-life of Strontium 90; it is as if the historian, not of Dada but of the Renaissance, illustrated the Mona Lisa complete with moustache. Ellmann's *Norton Anthology of Modern Poetry* (edited in collaboration with Robert O'Clare) is possibly worse: here the text follows Lathem most of the time but occasionally follows both, as when "Stopping by Woods" has the "though" comma but not the "dark and deep" comma, and occasionally it provides punctuation that neither Frost nor Lathem anticipated. In time, if we do nothing, the sounds which are not Frost's sounds will be the only sounds one can hear—and Frost's own punctuation, when it turns up in an eccentric edition, will look like a misprint.

Lathem's edition should be allowed to go out of print. Holt should commission a responsible literary scholar to edit a variorum edition of Frost's poems. It would not be nearly such an undertaking as the Yeats volume, for Frost revised little and there are few uncollected poems. A variorum Frost should re-establish Frost's intended punctuation, while a sub-text records variations—including broken letters, English spellings, single or double quotes, and even Lathem's corruptions for all I care. But the poet's sentence sounds should return to the poet's page. If David Smith's "Primo Piano III" were repainted with twenty coats of yellow, we would never be sure we had it quite the way the sculptor wanted it. It is easier to ascertain the authentic Robert Frost.

II

Celebration

Richard Eberhart
*The Internal Cape**

(1980)

When Geoffrey Hill was a young poet, living in the Worcestershire village of Bromsgrove, his father brought him a present returning from Bristol: Oscar Williams's anthology, *A Little Treasury of Modern Poetry*. The earth shook: *Geoffrey Hill had discovered Richard Eberhart*. When Hill and I became friends at Oxford, I was older than he—a condition long since rectified—and he deferred to my antiquity; especially, he deferred because in my years at Harvard I had seen Eberhart plain. One day I asked him: "What do you think he looks like?" Hill knew *exactly* what Eberhart looked like, and he poured forth a description: Richard Eberhart was lean, tall, bony-faced, with deep sunken burning eyes; he walked the city streets at night, a lone and haunted figure wearing a cape.

In haste, without mercy or tenderness, I disembarrassed Hill of his images. The real Eberhart did not resemble a starved El Greco martyr; the real figure looked more like a Toby jug: red-cheeked, plump, shortish, gregarious, and cheerful. I met the real figure first at Gordon Cairnie's Grolier Book Shop, where everybody met everybody. Poets, critics, writers of all sorts dropped by all day to talk literature,

---

* Each of these notes appeared in a special issue of a magazine celebrating the poet.

and also to meet literature, as literature visited in the shapes of Conrad Aiken, Mr. Eliot once a year, John Hawkes, Alison Lurie, Richard Wilbur . . . and Richard Eberhart.

He was in business then, working for Butcher's Wax. I seem to recall a brown suit with a fine-figured necktie. I certainly recall his enthusiasm over poetry and poets, and his generosity toward the young; I recall the founding of The Poet's Theatre in the Eberharts' living room. A little later it was Eberhart, of all the Eastern sorts, who drew attention to Allen Ginsberg, to *Howl*, and to the Beat Generation in San Francisco—phenomena which many of us hoped to ignore out of existence, protecting our castles. Eberhart was past fifty at the time, and trumpeted a poetry that appeared to threaten his kind of poetry.

It did not really threaten it. If Eberhart traveled in Harvard Square circles, he was not what was called an academic poet. His poems were always individual, Romantic, unlike anyone else's—and while he sold wax his soul waxed. Everything about him blazed with the fire of contradiction. By enantiodromia opposites turn into each other, and factual errors become final truths. Thus the Eberhart imagined by Geoffrey Hill was more genuine than the Eberhart I described: and within the poetry of Richard Eberhart something prowls the night streets, caped, with eyes like coals.

Robert Francis
"His Running My Running"

(1982)

His Running My Running

Mid-autumn late autumn
At dayfall in leaf-fall
A runner comes running.

How easy his striding
How light his footfall
His bare legs gleaming.

Alone he emerges
Emerges and passes
Alone, sufficient.

When autumn was early
Two runners came running
Striding together

Shoulder to shoulder
Pacing each other
A perfect pairing.

Out of leaves falling
Over leaves fallen
A runner comes running

> Aware of no watcher
> His loneness my loneness
> His running my running.

The rhythm does it. The rhythm fixes it, as the acid bath fixes the photograph. The most common line is c/cc/c, for which there is doubtless a Greek name in Saintsbury—irrelevant because Francis's lines are variant and non-quantitative. Two loud noises a line, that does not vary; usually two unaccented syllables mid-line; *always*—and this is the most important item of description—the falling rhythm's soft final syllable, so that the rhythmic signature, no matter whether the line begins loud or soft, remains its gentle falling-off at the end.

Yet prosodic description though accurate may give the lie. This meter was never counted out on fingers; it is a short enough line that the poet's ear could never deceive itself into irregularity; instead this ear or this tapping foot *improvises* metric integrity. It is not making free verse, but it finds a variety of procedures for arriving at the same arithmetic sum and rhythmic resolution.

The sound compels. As for the sense? Well, Robert Francis (one could have said the "I of the poem," if one were given to such things, and if there were an I in the poem; even "my" waits for the last two lines) or the eye of the poem sees a jogger in autumn twilight, remembers that earlier it had watched two joggers together, and returns to the observant present by feeling itself into the runner outside.

(Paraphrase reminds me of Public Television.)

The poem is its rhythm. If it is also an enactment of loneliness, and a cure for loneliness, it is reticent about its purposes. There is something attractive about those "bare legs gleaming;" the watcher's furtiveness comments on the attractiveness. The watcher's memory of two joggers, which is literal enough, makes reference to past companionship *outside* which must refer to past companionship or lost companionship *inside*—or behind the glass; as Whitman's lament for the widowed bird is his lament for everything lost. The loss lessens itself by empathy, the power of the eye to imagine, as watcher becomes runner and therefore companion. Eye met two runners; eye lost a runner; eye joins a runner.

So it is with the repetitions of rhythm, which establish, depart, and re-establish.

John Heath-Stubbs
The Smoldering Fire

(1978)

I met John at Oxford in the early fifties. I got to know him a year or two later when he came to Harvard.

Someone from a newspaper was interviewing him in a bar. The interviewer asked for the names of his books. John had just given the name of the first volume when I butted in. I decided that the interviewer should take not only the titles from John. "Dates, too," I interjected. John's face crumpled for a moment, then he smiled gingerly, "Yes, I suppose it does."

Let other people talk about John Heath-Stubbs's poetry. I will discuss his incendiarism.

Heath-Stubbs and I were summoned one day to Detroit to be interviewed together on a television program. For the trip I borrowed a car from the University of Michigan—where both of us were teaching.

We chatted in the car, heading for Detroit. John smoked continually, lighting one cigarette from the butt of another. After half an hour I realized the smoke was hurting my eyes. I found it difficult to drive. I was about to ask John to open the window beside him when I glanced in the rear-view mirror and saw that the back seat was on fire. Smoke was pouring from the plastic seats. Flames were reaching the seat-tops.

John opened the window. He surmised that by throwing cigarettes out a closed window he might have caused the conflagration.

Finally we came to an exit. I pulled off, and immediately found a garage. I jumped from the car—parking some distance from the gas pumps—and ran to the garage owner. I looked back to see flames crawling over the back windows—and to see John still sitting in the front seat, lighting up a cigarette.

Donald Davie
The Mixture

(1980)

Writing a poem is an impure act, mixing consciousness and unconsciousness, reason and imagination, inspiration and analysis—wild poet and sober critic, wild critic and sober poet. As a poem is let the poet be!—a creature thoroughly mixed and composite, gathering scholarship and inspiration together, prosodical learning and the gifts of dream. Not all poets allow themselves the extension of impurity; some insist on being poets alone, and we are poorer for it. I suppose there are poets who are *unable* to edit, criticize, or adjudicate—a mental or temperamental disability—but there are others who cultivate a purity which evades the rigors and harshness of judgment: the freeloaders of the poetic community, who avoid making enemies by never committing a book review or an anthology.

Donald Davie—poet, critic, man of letters—is a marvel of impure responsibility. In poems, scholarship, theory, pedagogy, and criticism, he has served literature and therefore all of us for thirty-five years. The scope of his stewardship has been limitless: he has translated, lectured, and edited; he has kept the transatlantic lines open more steadily than anyone else, demonstrating that one reader can become sophisticated enough to read Yukon Jake and Lord Mountroyal—or at least Ed Dorn and C. H. Sisson.

Extensiveness is what I praise. Now he co-edits the best

poetry magazine in our language, the *PN Review*. His criticism began long ago with *Articulate Energy* and *Purity of Diction*, theoretical analyses which have influenced not only subsequent criticism but the possibilities of new poetry. His two books on Ezra Pound remain the best introductions to that poet. His *Thomas Hardy and English Poetry*—together with two recent collections of periodical pieces—show Davie in dedicated fierce combat over the poetry of his own time.

Of course we honor the poet most. He began almost neoclassical, an expert metrist with a fund of wit, a young man's irony combined with mature skepticism. In recent years his poetry has become more ambitious, more inclusive and extensive, more varied in form and feeling. (See pages 80–81 for an example.)

William Stafford
Eight Notions

(1979)

1. One needn't write about *Stories That Could be True* as if it were cast in bronze. One can pick it up and read in it for an hour or two, as one expects to do with prose. Few good poets are subject to the accusation of readability. To admirers of poetry at its most ambiguous and enigmatic, "readability" may imply triviality or minority: Eliot is wonderful, but neither he nor Hopkins is "readable." Anyone whose preconceptions exclude Stafford on account of his accessibility loses too much.

2. Stafford is a poet of ordinary life. His collected poems are the journal of a man recording daily concerns. That is why his daily method of writing is relevant to his life's work. You could say that his poetry is truly quotidian: he writes it every day; it comes out of every day. And the poet of the quotidian did not find it necessary to become *maudit,* to follow Hart Crane to the waterfront or Baudelaire to the whorehouse or even Lowell to McLean's. He got up at six in the morning in a suburb of Portland and drained the sump.

3. If we attend to chronology, William Stafford is a member of the tragic generation of American poets. Stafford was born in 1914, the same year as Weldon Kees and Randall Jarrell and John Berryman, three suicides; Delmore Schwartz was born in 1913, and Robert Lowell in 1917. How wonderfully the survivor contrasts. What makes him so dif-

ferent? Like Lowell, Stafford was a C.O. during the Second War. Like Berryman and Kees he came from the midwest. But Stafford is a low-church Christian far from the rhetorical Catholicism that Lowell and Berryman entertained. I suspect that his survival is related not merely to his Christianity but to his membership in a small, embattled, pacifist sect.

4. The poetic surface is often ordinary (not always: Stafford salutes a lost Cree inside a knife . . .) with famous dead deer in roads, with remembered loves, with fancies about wind and weather. This ordinariness doth tease us out of thought; while we are thoughtless, the second language of poetry speaks to us. Stafford has referred to an unspoken tongue that lives underneath the words of poetry. This second language is beyond the poet's control, but we can define a poet as someone who speaks it. English teachers afflicted with students who lack control over their own language— ignorant, illiterate, wordless—often assume that the best language is the most controlled and the most conscious. Not so, or not always so: poets are literate, poets control, poets command syntax and lexicon—but the best poets *also* write without knowing everything that they are up to, trusting in the second language's continual present hum of implication.

5. For years, Stafford has built a reputation for modesty, while accumulating 263 pages of poems. This "modesty" is steel plate twelve inches thick which allows penetration into enemy territory (I pick this analogy for a pacifist), there to plant not mines but tough flowers that endure.

6. Looking at photographs of poets, printed on jackets and in magazines, one continually discovers that the photographer of the best portraits is William Stafford: close-ups, characteristic in expression, inward and meditative. Is it far-fetched to find the poet in the photographer, the photographer in the poet? These photographs allow no fantasy; they are inquiries into reality directed by intelligent, watchful, patient *attention*. Most photographs make a glossy surface. Stafford's speak from a level of the second language.

7. English poets and critics have a hard time judging

American poetry, as Americans do with English. Sometimes mistakes illuminate. It is a mistake to place Stafford, as I have seen English critics do, with the Black Mountain inheritors of William Carlos Williams. Yet it is an observant mistake, because Stafford writes a plain American which from a distance looks like any other endeavor at plain America. Stafford differs because the rhythm of his characteristic speech makes a noise wholly at odds with the noises common to Black Mountain; it is slower, less nervous, more metaphoric and contemplative, just as idiomatic but less concerned to represent or embody idiom. Still, this long distance English view helps to isolate Stafford from other Americans, for instance from the rhetoricians of his tragic generation.

8. I mentioned his Christianity earlier, to begin to name a quality. It need not follow, but Stafford's poems show forth goodness and compassion. These qualities together with affection and shrewd reticence make him unusual in the great zoo of contemporary American poetry. Torture, pain, cruelty, egotism, and selfishness, madness, and lust are common to human existence. Much poetry will—must—represent cruelty, pain, torture, lust, madness, egotism, and selfishness. But there is an unexamined and neurotic notion that only these qualities equal seriousness; Stafford gives the lie to this currency.

Robert Bly
Poetry Food

(1981)

These occasions allow the expression of gratitude. I met Robert Bly in February of 1948, when I tried out for *The Harvard Advocate* of which he was already an editor. We have remained closest friends over the decades—through many disagreements and even quarrels, our friendship based on the bewildered but unflagging affection that opposites sometimes feel for each other. We have bickered so much—I have made many essays out of these bickerings!—that he may find it outrageous that I recommend him as a model of behavior.

As vain as anyone, and as avaricious of praise—yet among my acquaintances of poets he is the most nearly disinterested. (I refer to Keats's favorite moral idea, a word which alas loses meaning every day as people use it to mean "uninterested.") A thousand times, I have observed with amazement Bly's cordial response to negative criticism: if there is an *idea* lurking in the denunciation, he lifts the idea up to the light, examines it like a dog a bone, remarks it, wonders at it, sniffs learnedly, and then chews on it—for nourishment and to keep his teeth sharp.

Of course such behavior is only sensible—what use are the complaints against us unless we learn from them?—but most people respond to blame not with curiosity but with plots of murder Many artists as they grow older become expert at defending themselves against taking criticism seriously. They build castles out of the praise they get from younger writers, from old students, from sycophants, and from editors seeking their names. They build moats of exclusiveness; they surround themselves with dragons and princesses. Bly on the other hand seems to look for blame, as if he were daring himself to improve.

Writers who will grow and improve through their fifties and sixties, even into their seventies and eighties, are writers who best develop dissatisfaction with themselves. Only from disappointment with one's old work can one possibly move ahead. Lately Bly has become aware that much of his work lacks sound, and lacks variety of syntax. Therefore he has tried to begin again, to hear vowel and consonant sound as if for the first time.

It takes a doughty temperament. It means of course that one will never be satisfied. (To be a satisfied poet, to believe what the flatterers say . . . this is to be dead.) So one goes to the grave in labor. But the labor's end, if one is serious and persistent, is not the gratification of one's ego but a stewardship. Not long ago, when I felt discouraged, I wrote Bly a long letter; I whined to him as I would to no one else. He answered me with these words: "That the poems are useful to other people, that they are bread, that they can be eaten, and strengthen strangers, that is precisely our goal, our reward, and our vocation. . . ."

III

Reviewing

Adrienne Rich[*]

(1978)

When she was young her masters were men: Auden, Frost, Robinson, Lowell. To whom was a woman to turn for a model? Emily Dickinson and Marianne Moore, although superb poets, were models of stylistic idiosyncracy. Men could look everywhere for a master; a woman, unless she would submerge her femininity to a masculine model, contended with the astounding (socially inevitable) paucity of women poets; there are bleak centuries between Sappho and Dickinson. Yet by the late seventies, anyone who reads American poetry must be struck by the preponderance of young women: Carolyn Forché, Olga Broumas, AI, Laura Jensen, Kathleen Fraser, Carol Muske . . . one could go on and on. The survival, endurance, and gathering excellence of Adrienne Rich has provided a model for young women poets, provided a female resource to sponsor female poetry.

These new poems are Rich's best—poems of ambition, dignity, and wisdom—and they derive from scrutiny of a particular life. As with her prose work, *Of Woman Born*, she writes best when she writes directly out of her life. In the beginning her poetry used to sound like other people's; one

---

[*] Adrienne Rich, *The Dream of a Common Language: Poems 1974-1977* (New York: W. W. Norton, 1978)

could guess, reading her work, the subject of her latest enthusiasm. Over the years, her poetry has progressed toward intimacy without sacrificing intelligence. She has a gift for being herself, much the way certain film actors possess the rare and difficult genius—which looks easy—of always seeming *natural*.

Rich's dream is the dream of intimacy; *the dream of a common language*. Much poetry enacts the pursuit of unrealizable desires. Yeats rhymed out his dream of being's unity; Walt Whitman's America is as imagined as Blake's—or Blake's Albion. Rich defines "the true nature of poetry" as "the drive / to connect"—the desire to connect wholly, nakedly, with a nakedness profounder than the skin's, without reserve or protection, past ambiguity and ambivalence—with another human being.

> It's simple to wake from sleep with a stranger,
> dress, go out, drink coffee,
> enter a life again. It isn't simple
> to wake from sleep into the neighborhood
> of one neither strange nor familiar
> whom we have chosen to trust.

Then the dream of a common language reaches beyond the personal:

> But I can't call it life until we start to move
> beyond this secret circle of fire
> where our bodies are giant shadows flung on a wall
> where the night becomes our inner darkness, and sleeps
> like a dumb beast, head on her paws, in the corner.

The desire for total intimacy may be as unattainable as the desire for unity of being, or it may be glimpsed not steadily but only in a moment's transport. But without the dream of a common language we are speechless.

We can say: only the impossible is worth attempting—yet if one affirms the *achievement* of the impossible, one is a liar. Therefore a poet must continually seek and fail, discovering the negative of the dream, the reverse of the vision. In "Cartographies of Silence," Rich finds bare rock, yet concludes with praise for the word as the only instrument possibly complex enough to measure human feeling:

If from time to time I envy
the pure annunciations to the eye

the *visio beatifica*
if from time to time I long to turn

like the Eleusinian hierophant
holding up a simple ear of grain

for return to the concrete and everlasting world
what in fact I keep choosing

are these words, these whispers, conversations
from which time after time the truth breaks moist and green.

The "Twenty-One Love Poems" make an especially beautiful section of this book, an exploration of intimacy as we might hope to find it. In their honesty they again find bare rock, but they find also joy and understanding. So many writers imply that to feel passion you must forego intelligence. Tenderness here has room for wisdom. And there is dignity in plain statement: "We were two lovers of one gender, / we were two women of one generation."

Plain statement is not always a friend, and there are bad patches in this book. ". . . The failure to want our freedom passionately enough" is language *about* emotion, which embodies *no* emotion. It is commonplace that political or didactic poetry—poetry committed to ideas and principles—will often fail through an excess of abstraction. The dream will only connect by bodied language—idiom, image, metaphor—to the long body of the human moment. And the image must be new, and it must connect with other images. Where poetry suffers disconnection—dead metaphors spoil a few of these poems, as in the failed work of many poets—we sense that the poem is inauthentic; when Rich will use the adverb "blindly" like a journalist, to indicate obtuseness, she is unsure of her *ideas*.

But if lines fail, the book is a victory. With *The Dream of a Common Language* Rich has taken the step she has looked to take since her first book appeared in 1951 when she was a twenty-year-old senior at Radcliffe. She has fought through facility, obeisance to elders, glibness, *style*—and has become a superb American poet.

You wouldn't know it from the reviewers, who have remained virtually silent, and this bears considering. *Of Woman Born*, a courageous and moving book, was vilified and misrepresented by reviewers. Rich grew up as the token female poet of the fifties until she became a feminist. Now she is a token of something else, or a symbol—but she has in the meantime become a far better poet: as she writes her best work the people who used to praise her have turned away.

Look at the poem, "Natural Resources," for instance, which includes a quiet and resourceful observation of Vermont things which must please anyone who loves the motions of assured language:

> The enormity of the simplest things:
> in this cold barn tables are spread
>
> with china saucers, shoehorns
> of german silver, a gilt-edged book
>
> that opens into a picture-frame—
> a biscuit-tin of the thirties.
>
> Outside, the north lies vast
> with unshed snow, everything is
>
> at once remote and familiar
> each house contains what it must

The best of this book happens when ideas and observations come together, abstraction and statement wedded and complicit with observation, with *seeing through*: "A whole new poetry beginning here." Here is the last stanza of the poem ("Transcendental Etude") which ends the book:

> Vision begins to happen in such a life
> as if a woman quietly walked away
> from the argument and jargon in a
>   room
> and sitting down in the kitchen, began
>   turning in her lap
> bits of yarn, calico and velvet scraps,
> laying them out absently on the
>   scrubbed boards
> in the lamplight, with small rainbow-
>   colored shells
> sent in cotton-wool from somewhere
>   far away,
> and skeins of milkweed from the
>   nearest meadow—
> original domestic silk, the finest find-
>   ings—
> and the darkblue petal of the petunia,
> and the dry darkbrown lace of seaweed;
> not forgotten either, the shed silver
> whisker of the cat,
> the spiral of paper-wasp-nest curling
> beside the finch's yellow feather.
> Such a composition has nothing to do
>   with eternity,
> the striving for greatness, brilliance—
> only with the musing of a mind
> one with her body, experienced fingers
>   quietly pushing
> dark against bright, silk against rough-
>   ness,
> pulling the tenets of a life together

with no mere will to mastery,
only care for the many-lived, unending
forms in which she finds herself,
becoming now the shred of broken
    glass
slicing light in a corner, dangerous
to flesh, now the plentiful, soft leaf
that wrapped around the throbbing
    finger, soothes the wound;
and now the stone foundation, rock
    shelf further
forming underneath everything that
    grows.

Glass, leaf, and stone make an emblem for Adrienne Rich and her poems. Yet we will have more, for the dream is unsatisfied: "I look at my hands," she tells us elsewhere, "and see they are still unfinished."

Thom Gunn, Seamus Heaney[*]

(1979)

Eliot wrote of James that he was "difficult for English readers because he is an American; and . . . for Americans, because he is European. . . ." Thom Gunn reverses the direction. An English poet who has lived in California for most of the last twenty-five years, Gunn is largely ignored in America because he is English, which is to say we tend not to read poets we call Englishmen. In England Gunn is still read, but he is no longer automatically paired with Ted Hughes, or grouped with Philip Larkin in the elite—lately swelled by the arrival of Seamus Heaney and the recognition of Geoffrey Hill; he is not ignored but bypassed as no longer a local chap. There is about his name the slight flavor of exoticism, attributable not only to his residence but to a subject matter of motorcycle gangs and tattoo parlors.

Some poets who suffer their reputations have positively constructed them. Gunn's willful exile or assumed estrangement takes up certain burdens in exchange for certain liberties. I have the sense that his situation—nationless, speechless, placeless, almost a name without an address—suits him exactly, and makes for him the kind of island Yeats

---

[*] Thom Gunn, *Selected Poems 1950-1975* (New York: Farrar, Straus & Giroux, 1979). Seamus Heaney, *Field Work* (New York: Farrar, Straus & Giroux, 1979).

was always imagining: a vantage point, a place to write poems out of. If I call him speechless I refer only to the accent that would pin him down, for his poems make compelling speech, constructing in their language a place for the placeless, ". . . the large gesture of solitary man, / Resisting, by embracing, nothingness." This language is perhaps described, though not in the poem's overt intention, by the beginning of "Vox Humana":

> Being without quality
> I appear to you at first
> as an unkempt smudge, a blur,
> an indefinite haze, mere-
> ly pricking the eyes, almost
> nothing. Yet you perceive me.

For Gunn's is a voice that wishes to fly any nets that would entrap it, nets of family or nation or doctrine; he has cherished silence, exile and cunning in an American city. If his exile is a vantage point, it is also a vision: life pared down to its nakedness. "Confessions of the Life Artist" ends with the Rilkean death of the sun:

> The art of designing life
> is no excuse for that life.
>
> People will forget Shakespeare.
> He will lie with George Formby
> and me, here where the swine root.
> Later, the solar system
> will flare up and fall into
> space, irretrievably lost.
>
> For the loss, as for the life,
> there will be no excuse, there
> is no justification.

Because there is nothing, therefore he will embrace it.

This is a remarkable book, consistent in its bleak detachment, varied in style and manner, an anthology of changing voices chanting the same song. It starts with the young poet, a Cambridge undergraduate, writing vigorous stanzas of pentameter, poems constructed of large conceits inventively fleshed out.

> The huge wound in my head began to heal
> About the beginning of the seventh week.
> Its valleys darkened, its villages became still:
> For joy I did not move and dared not speak,
> Not doctors would cure it, but time,
> > its patient skill.

The language begins as English and progresses toward American. The iambic pentameter of the early "On the Move" ends a line "always toward, toward." If the last words are pronounced as the American monosyllable, "tord," the line will not scan and collapses on the page; pronounced as the English "to-*ward*, to-*ward*," the meter picks itself up after the medial inversion of "always" and strides to its appropriate conclusion.

Along the way Gunn writes the best syllabic verse of his generation, notably in the title poem of an earlier volume, *My Sad Captains*:

> One by one they appear in
> the darkness: a few friends, and
> a few with historical
> names. How late they start to shine!
> but before they fade they stand
> perfectly embodied, all
>
> the past lapping them like a
> cloak of chaos. They were men
> who, I thought, lived only to
> renew the wasteful force they
> spent with each hot convulsion.
> They remind me, distant now.
>
> True, they are not at rest yet,
> but now that they are indeed

apart, winnowed from failures,
they withdraw to an orbit
and turn with disinterested
hard energy, like the stars.

No one has used so well the strange but defined shape of the syllabic stanza; he makes it seem as if it had been created to contain his own paradoxical detachment and willed connection.

In later works, some conviction departs from his metrical poems. English metrical writing at its best (Larkin, Hill) uses the line as a structural connection to 500 years, and in early Gunn this confidence is unquestioned. More recent poems show metrical wit and trickery which remind me more of American practitioners (Hecht) for whom meter seems less structure and allusion than ornament or decoration. "In the Tank" contains this *faux naïf* final rhyming phrase:

A man sat in the felon's tank, alone,
Fearful, ungrateful, in a cell for two.
And from his metal bunk, the lower one,
He studied where he was, as felons do.

But by the end of this volume Gunn has assimilated the short-lined free-verse movement of American poetry that descends from William Carlos Williams to the rest of us:

What did that
mean? Anyway next day
he was gone, with
all the money and dope
of the people he'd lived with.

The book ends with two poems in which Gunn becomes a dog and a cherry tree, creatures embraced as convincingly as nothingness.

Seamus Heaney's new volume is *Field Work,* containing poems written since *North* in 1976. *North* was a superb volume; I suppose *Field Work* is even better, though it is possible that I merely hear more of his voice as I come to know him better. Heaney is as located as Gunn is placeless. But with an Irish poet nothing is ever so simple. Heaney's land is Ireland, heaven knows; but what Ireland? He is a northerner who lives in the south; he writes the English inherited from centuries of oppression, sweetened by the excellence of earlier Anglo-Irish poetry. These conflicts make for energy, I suspect. If Heaney is the best Irish poet since Yeats, a sentiment often expressed, it is less known that there are half a dozen other living Irishmen who could run for the title without fear of disgrace.

Heaney's subjects in *Field Work* range from troubles in Ireland to skunks in California, but his geographical spread never suggests the tourist. The voice speaks of love with an astonishing and wholly captivating tenderness. It speaks as well of violence, desire and memory, and it speaks with deliberate intelligence—willful, diligent, and playful. For all the qualities I list, the most important is *song*, the tune Heaney sings which is poetry's tune, resolutions of cherished language. This is the first section of the title poem:

> Where the sally tree went pale in every breeze,
> where the perfect eye of the nesting
>   blackbird watched,
> where one fern was always green
>
> I was standing watching you
> take the pad from the gatehouse at the crossing
> and reach to lift a white wash off the whins.
>
> I could see the vaccination mark
> stretched on your upper arm, and smell the coal smell
> of the train that comes between us, a slow goods,
>
> waggon after waggon full of big-eyed
>   cattle.

American poets seem *shy* of making lines like the last one

here, as if it were pretentious to lay out a line like a gift. American poets, all eye and imagination, lack song which is poetry's body. If they can journey to an alien place for it, they should arise and go to Ireland and to Seamus Heaney. Here is a small whole poem:

Song

A rowan like a lipsticked girl.
Between the by-road and the main road
Alder trees at a wet and dripping distance
Stand off among the rushes.

There are the mud-flowers of dialect
And the immortelles of perfect pitch
And that moment when the bird sings very close
To the music of what happens.

To sing "the music of what happens" is an ambition appropriate not only to birds.

Two Poets Named Robert

(1977)

In 1976 Robert Lowell published his *Selected Poems*, two hundred and thirty-eight pages taken from *Lord Weary's Castle*, *The Mills of the Kavanaghs*, *Life Studies*, *For the Union Dead*, *Near the Ocean*, *Notebooks*, *Notebook*, *History*, *For Lizzie and Harriet*, and *Dolphin*. Four of the last five volumes involve duplication, because Lowell kept revising the fourteen-line poems first collected in the plural *Notebooks* of 1966. *Selected Poems* include nothing from *Imitations* or the plays. I believe that a few of the early poems first appeared in different form in *Land of Unlikeness* (1944) but I have been unable to check that volume. Lowell was born in 1917, and turned sixty this year.

Also in 1976, Robert Francis—born in 1901, seventy-six this year—published his *Collected Poems*, filling out two hundred and eighty-four pages. Francis published his first volume in 1936, *Stand With Me Here*, and a second in 1938, *Valhalla and Other Poems*. In 1944, he published *The Sound I Listened For*. There were long gaps in publication, though not in writing; in 1950, finding no publisher at all, he printed *The Face Against Glass* at his own expense. Ten years later the Wesleyan University Press printed *The Orb Weaver*; and the University of Massachusetts Press published *Come Out into the Sun* in 1965, *Like Ghosts of Eagles* in 1974, and now the *Collected Poems*.

Comparisons stop with the similar number of pages in the two volumes, and with the first names. The styles of the two poets do not resemble each other. Neither do the shapes of their lives, or the public's response to their poems. It is pure perversity to review them together. I do it here, not because there's justice in the juxtaposition, but in order to talk about the perversity of literary reputations—or perhaps the injustice.

For Francis is an excellent poet, and although he is published, now, and available for reading should anyone be curious, and although a few anthologies print him—the *Norton Abomination of Modern Poetry* omits him, while it prints Judith Johnson Sherwin, Daryl Hine, Irving Feldman, Edwin Honig, Lawrence Ferlinghetti, Theodore Weiss, and Lincoln Kirstein—he is largely unread and unknown. Readers of the *New York Review of Books* will not run into his name on those pages; neither will readers of the *New York Times*. (Nor will *Vogue* tell us that people are talking about him, or *Time* about his capacity for whiskey.) But when Robert Lowell publishes a slack, dishonest, careless, time-serving collection—something he has been wont to do in recent years—the predictable reviewers clap their predictable hands. Not a voice is raised in protest.

Lord Weary's Castle is one of the great books; it established Lowell in 1947 as a bright moment of American literature. It did not, I think, grant him deity, or place his subsequent work beyond criticism—yet that is just what has happened. There is an unorganized conspiracy—please grant me my adjective as well as my noun; I am not Richard Kostelanetz—which I call the Literature Industry. The conspiratorial elements of the Industry derive not from greed—"As for literature / It gives no man a sinecure"—but only from fear and laziness. A consensus of wise and sensible intellectuals produces a list of writers one may *not* dislike; or one dislikes them at the risk of revealing oneself as out of touch and beyond the pale. The function of such consensus is simple; it allows us *not* to read, *not* to judge, *not* to assume the burden of skeptical intelligence. Some years back, the Board Chairman of the Literature Industry, Edmund Wilson (a worthy man, maker of many essays; also routinely poor in judging poetry; also routinely deified, beyond criticism) interviewed himself in the *New Yorker*, and asked himself what was happening in contemporary poetry; no sweat—he answered himself in effect—Lowell is it, and there is no reason to bother yourself with anyone else.

In *Selected Poems*, the verses from *Lord Weary* look as good as they ever looked, and that is very good. For starters, let me say that their quality is greater than the quality available in the collected work of Hart Crane, Allen Tate, and John Crowe Ransom—and that's a sum of quality. *Lord Weary* is as good a book as *Harmonium*, as good as Eliot's shorter poems, and nearly as good as Pound's *Personae*. Lowell's dramatic monologues—the best of the early poems are dramatic monologues—make it new, for all their obvious derivation by way of Tate from the English seventeenth century. No American has written with greater force—as a mind made energetic by rebellion struggled with its culture in a decosyllabic line as dense as Milton's; and as a Calvinist Catholicism raged at the bars of its self-constructed cage. My only complaint, as I read the first section of this *Selected Poems*, is that any *Lord Weary* poems were omitted; for instance, the omitted "New Years Day":

> Again and then again . . . the year is born
> To ice and death, and it will never do
> To skulk behind storm-windows by the stove
> To hear the postgirl sounding her French horn
> When the thin tidal ice is wearing through.
> Here is the understanding not to love
> Each other, or tomorrow that will sieve
> Our resolutions. While we live, we live
>
> To snuff the smoke of victims. In the snow
> The kitten heaved its hindlegs, as if fouled,
> And died. We bent it in a Christmas box
> And scattered blazing weeds to scare the crow

Until the snake-tailed sea-winds coughed and howled
For alms outside the church whose double locks
Wait for St. Peter, the distorted key.
Under St. Peter's bell the parish sea

Swells with its smelt into the burlap shack
Where Joseph plucks his hand-lines like a harp,
And hears the fearful *Puer natus est*
Of Circumcision, and relives the wrack
And howls of Jesus whom he holds. How sharp
The burden of the Law before the beast;
Time and the grindstone and the knife of God.
The Child is born in blood, O child of blood.

Even an omitted poem can serve to remind a reader of the early Lowell's cruel and vital power.

Lowell's second collection was thinner than his first, which is typical; poets grow older for ten years while they make a first book; it's a time when they quarrel about poetry with their poet-friends, and contrive collaboration by quarrelling. Then the second volume comes too quickly, with less critical collaboration, in a burst of joy over being *known* to be a poet. Although *The Mills of the Kavanaghs* is thinner than *Lord Weary*, it contains one monologue which is arguably the best of all his poems, "Mother Marie Therese," a reverie of a nun over her dead Mother Superior which ends with these lines:

Mother, we must give ground,
Little by little; but it does no good.
Tonight, while I am piling on more driftwood,
And stooping with the poker, you are here,
Telling your beads; and breathing in my ear,
You watch your orphan swording at her fears.
I feel you twitch my shoulder. No one hears
Us mock the sisters, as we used to, years
And years behind us, when we heard the spheres
Whirring *venite*; and we held our ears.
My mother's hollow sockets fill with tears.

This volume also contains the brilliant "Falling Asleep over the Aeneid" and "Her Dead Brother."

I suppose that *Life Studies* is Lowell's best known volume, possibly his most popular. One must strain to remember what a shock this volume was, for it was from shock more than from excellence that this book acquired its initial reputation. I can remember staring at a page of the *Partisan Review*, at a poem signed with Lowell's name, that began "Tamed by *Miltown*, we lie on Mother's bed. . . ." (That dazzlement seems innocent now—after "Menstruation at Forty," after "Lady Lazarus.") Lowell was not the first poet to undertake great change in mid-career, but he was the *best* poet to change so *much*. It took great and essential courage to change as Lowell changed; one must grant him this courage, but one must not value his poems merely because he had this courage, or merely because he changed—just as one must not blame another poet for not changing, the way people tend to blame Richard Wilbur.

Lowell's change abandoned syllabic tightness and formal diction for idiom, improvisation, surprise, and for details of the American scene. In the new style he wrote several excellent poems, almost as fine as "After the Surprising Conversions" and "Between the Porch and the Altar." If they were not quite equal to the excellence of the older poems, they were excellent enough to make discrimination *nice*. I speak of many poems reprinted here: "Ford Madox Ford," "Waking in the Blue," "Memories of West Street and Lepke," and above all the wonderful "Skunk Hour."

Many of the other poems—it went largely unnoticed—were flat, narcissistic, and self-indulgent. Formerly rebellious against the Lowell background, Lowell began in *Life Studies* to boast of it, endlessly dragging his relations into flat anecdotes:

> Family gossip says Aunt Sarah
> tilted her archaic Athenean nose
> and jilted an Astor.

Is this "confessional"? It seems more gossip than confession—a poetic equivalent of *People*.

I have heard Lowell praised because he always retains a consistent *voice*. I don't think the voice of *Lord Weary* resembles the voice from *Life Studies* on; it's true that for twenty years after *Life Studies* the voice has remained recognizable. But what if the voice is merely a manner? What if it can be summed up in a few tricks? There is use of multiple adjectives, for instance: ". . . your enlarged, hardly recognizable photograph . . ." makes a Lowell-ish sound because the syntax is jammed, *Time*-style, with modifiers which might have been subsidiary clauses in a more relaxed and wordy style: ". . . the sensitive, pale concavities of your forehead. . . ."

There is also the askew ending; instead of ending with a summary, or at the height of a progressive rhetoric, or trailing off, the Lowell poem suddenly takes a violent zig, or possibly a zag, to another place; then it stops. It is most startling, and effective—once or twice. Then it becomes his "voice" or manner.

These mannerisms begin with some energy in *Life Studies*, and a decade later become bad habits. In between, Lowell flounders, rewriting foreign poets in his own image, and making *For the Union Dead*. In this volume, the title poem is excellent, and there are three other good poems, but in most of the book the emperor wears progressively fewer clothes; and the poetry becomes nothing but style, lacking substance, feeling, and intelligence. It reminds me of the careful eccentricity affected by an Oxford undergraduate—who contrives a stammer; or who with his cane and palsy contrives at the age of nineteen to resemble a man of ninety. Then the one discovers that his stammer is unavoidable, and the other that he has developed gout.

Near the Ocean was an attempt to break away from the manner, and to do something different—late seventeenth century, even early eighteenth century—but the poems fail. They do not fail by being meretricious, like the worst of *Union Dead* and the best of *History*; they are lifeless, lacking either real or fake vitality.

It is with the first *Notebook* that fakery becomes constant. Creating a fourteen line receptacle—out of Berryman-envy—Lowell fills it with everything to hand. Commonplaces out of history books, elegies over his sad generation, anecdotes about an earlier and nobler set of poets, predictable elegies on King and Kennedy, souvenirs from the headlines, flagellations of memory about his father. Again and again, the poems exhibit a *New York Review of Books* knowingness, intellectual hip, certitude of implication implying nothing. Last lines make formulas: "Coleridge, / the one poet who blamed his failure on himself." He imitates his old poems. We hear, "he was a good man, and he prayed with reason," which is inferior to the finely cadenced ending of his Ford Madox Ford poem, "You were a good man, and you died in want." In one of the Jarrell poems, he writes, "Randall, the scene still plunges at the windshield, / apples redden to ripeness on the whiplash bough"—which is good writing, until you revisit the conclusion of "After the Surprising Conversions." Writing of Jarrell—Lowell is so promiscuous with his old friendships; is there room anywhere for a private man? The poet becomes a creature of *celebrity*—he calls his generation of poets, "old buffs of death." I note the cant "buffs;" I note the melancholy accuracy.

Most of the time, these poems are shapeless, pointless, and heartless. The morals are as blunt as the metaphors are dead. In a protest poem, he calls policemen "the Martian, the ape"—using that political sophistication which begins by denying the humanity of your enemies. "I want words meat-hooked from the living steer," he writes—with dishonesty, fake ferocity, and genuine insensitivity.

Obviously I should try to prove my point, not just by sputtering with indignation (it is something like indignation which I feel, when I see what the poet has done to himself; when I see the Industry's boneheaded rote response) but by talking about a particular poem. To be fair, I will pick one which Lowell apparently likes, because he has chosen it for the *Selected Poems*; to be fairer still, I will choose one which has the approval of the Industry, as indicated by its presence in the *Abominable Norton*.

Robert Frost at midnight, the audience gone
to vapor, the great act laid on the shelf in mothballs,
his voice is musical and raw—he writes in the flyleaf:
For Robert from Robert, his friend in the art.
"Sometimes I feel too full of myself," I say.
And he, misunderstanding, "When I am low,
I stray away. My son wasn't your kind. The night
we told him Merrill Moore would come to treat him,
he said, 'I'll kill him first.' One of my daughters thought
     things,
thought every male she met was out to make her;
the way she dressed, she couldn't make a whorehouse."
And I, "Sometimes I'm so happy I can't stand myself."
And he, "When I am too full of joy, I think
how little good my health did anyone near me."

What does it mean to say that the audience has gone "to
vapor"? Does this compare Frost to a wizard? Or to some-
body in command of a hydrogen bomb? Does Lowell mean
that Frost wished to annihilate the audience? Perhaps. But
nothing in the rest of the poem explains or gives solidity to
this murderous metaphor; the metaphor is irresponsible.
Now "the great act" compares Frost to a performer, possibly
to a magician—which is close enough to a wizard—but then
the line goes on, immediately, to compare the act itself to
something else, perhaps to a tool, something which at any
rate can be put away "on a shelf" when it is not in use; a poet
becomes a magician becomes a power drill—which is then
suddenly made of wool. If you strive to make the image
work, you can try to think of the "act" as compared to a
magician's woolen cape; but such striving is too energetic.
The point is that Lowell does not begin to *invent* metaphor
when he writes this poem. Merely, he staggers from cliché to
cliché, dead metaphor to dead metaphor, and his loyal
reader is asked to strain considerably, if he wishes to invent
coherence.

And Lowell makes irresponsible and incoherent syntax;

he multiplies simple sentences but fakes the coherence of hasty speech by run-on commas: "his voice is musical and raw." Here sounds are first compared to song or to instrument, and then to meat or to a sore; then by means of a disjunctive dash, he leaps to a wholly new subject: "—he writes in the flyleaf . . ." and repeats Frost's conventional, commonplace inscription. There's *no point* to it; but then, there was no point to the trite comparison of Frost to a magician either, or to the murderous disposal of the audience, or to the disposition of "the act," or to the condition of Frost's voice: the poem is a junk-heap of particulars, a jumble of mere recollection.

In the fifth line, for no apparent reason, Lowell starts talking about himself, and repeats a sentiment which might be interesting if it were developed. But the sentiment only serves for Frost to misunderstand it. Frost was deaf, and misheard much; but here, what's the point of being told that Frost "misunderstood," when it's not clear how or what he misunderstood? It is *mere* particularity. Lowell's assumption is unmistakable: at the meeting of these two men, *anything* that happens is worth recording, no matter how trivial or boring.

Now Frost brings up the subject of Lowell's madness. Frost speaks of his suicidal son Carroll, and of his mad daughter Irma. (Lowell obviously feels that suicide and madness are subjects inherently interesting; after all, it is a premise of confessional verse.) Carroll threatened homicide, Irma's sexual fears were inappropriate. Then Lowell answers these anecdotes with an irrelevant, even insensitive response—if it's a response; it is at least sequent, and if it is not a response, then what is it? Possibly Lowell intends to answer Frost's implicit reference to his insanity. We cannot tell; the line functions as a Lowell mannerism—Askew Leap #24.

Frost's final sentence, directly responding this time, is the poem's *good bit*, when the old poet cannot sustain his flippancy about his mad children, and instead flies the flag of his guilt. It is touching; because Frost performed this scene thousands of times, in letters and conversations, it is a touching moment we have encountered elsewhere. And touching moments do not make poems. Great language, disciplined and honest feeling, creative intelligence make poems. By the time he writes this poem, Robert Lowell has descended to slack name-dropping self-imitation, in his pursuit of Stockholm.

Elsewhere, his language is often slacker still. The author of "Colloquy at Black Rock" now speaks of "gaping jaws," and makes other trite metaphors: ". . . our eyes glued to the window," and ". . . blinds us with surprise . . ."; he speaks of "heartache" and "life-enhancement."

In another poem, he quotes a painter: "Kokoschka at eighty, saying, "If you last, / you'll see your reputation die three times. . . ." I don't decry Lowell's concern with his reputation, but I blame him for publishing bad work. I think he should have sought out tough critics and listened to their harshness. I blame people around Lowell—friends, publishers—for letting him publish garbage. I blame the Literature Industry for its routine assurance that everything Lowell writes is golden. In the latest work, *Dolphin*, (at this writing a new book is imminent) the best lines were apparently lifted from letters written to him by a wife he left for a younger woman. These lines have the strange effect of showing up all the lines around them, for they are spoken with passion and anguish.

What happened to Robert Lowell? People suggest ambition; people suggest his move to New York—which was perhaps ambition, for that matter, because New York is the power and the prize. Certainly he began to campaign for the Nobel Prize, writing topical poems which I have called postcards to Stockholm. Certainly he became jealous of his old friend John Berryman, and in *Notebooks*' fourteen-line stanza contrived to outdo Berryman at the Dream Song game. There is at least one possible source for the decline which would disarm criticism: everyone knows that Lowell has been psychotic on a number of occasions; one hears that chemotherapy has stabilized his mind and that he no longer suffers from these episodes. Could the pills—schizophrenia is controlled by massive doses of tranquilizers—account for the growing slackness, carelessness, complacency, vanity, and general debility of Lowell's poems? In a late poem, Lowell describes himself: "Cured, I am fizzled, stale, and small." (I do *not* suggest that he ought to prefer madness to sanity, for the sake of his poems. I raise the question in order to drop it, because I know nothing.)

Then there's Robert Francis. In 1971 the University of Massachusetts Press published his autobiography, *The Trouble with Francis*. The title came from somebody's comment in the *Chicago Review*, "The trouble with Francis is not that he's too happy as that his happiness seems to lack weight." The poetry *does* lack a heavy misery, I suppose; mid-century literary culture demanded these qualities of its poets, and Francis was unwilling or unable to supply them. Instead, his poems are typically shapely, witty, and short. Here's one from his second book:

Mountain Blueberries

These blueberries belong to birds
If they belong to anyone.
Who could have planted them but birds
Three thousand feet up toward the sun?

They live on sunshine, dust of granite,
A little rain, a little dew.
In shape a miniature moon or planet,
In color distant-mountain blue.

To cherish this poem, you must love qualities not often cherished in the last twenty years, which include (besides shape, wit, and brevity) close observation of things of the world, and the willingness to take pleasure in them. The blueberries are as real as the rhymes are, and the dance of resolution resonates far beyond what four lines could seem to hold. The new word for blueberry color rhymes with the place where they live, as remote almost as outer space. But the poem's not merely a dance among real things. It's also a poem about making do on little, on reticence, on the opposite of greed—and this is a major theme of Francis's, in poems and in the autobiography, where he tells us his own diet, his own economy, and writes a letter to Thoreau about the pleasures and virtues of eating soybeans. This poem is also about loneliness, separateness—more bragging than complaining; there's no whining here, no more than the blueberries whine.

There's also, heaven knows, for all the pleasures taken in language and rhythm, a harshness in Francis which is available when you read for what a poem leaves out, as much as for what it leaves in:

Four Men

I

Old age without a wife has made a wife
Of him. He cooks for one, sews on buttons,
And on Monday mornings hangs out his wash.
After supper he and his cat stroll out
To superintend the growing of the flowers—
Scarlet salvia, magenta coxcomb,
Side by side in peace. So he gets along
Talking to his cat or to himself.

II

If it is hard to die before your time
With strength still in your hands and knees, it is harder
To die by wearing out, to die by days.
Once I planned to climb the Rockies. Now
I'm here. I can't take the first flight of stairs.
It is hard to be a baby twice and weep
At the memory of anything or nothing.

III

Laughter is easier for him now than talking.
Three meals a day and a pipe after each meal.
What's that? He doesn't hear what you are saying.
He forgets what he was saying. So he laughs

At whatever it was, and laughs again to think
He can't think what it was he's laughing at.

IV
He died at eighty. Out in the fields that summer
He had picked a stalk of Queen Anne's Lace
And held it up to see the blue sky through
For the first time. While he stood there looking
There were three whites over the field that morning:
His white head, the white flower, and a cloud.

This poem also shows another reason why people over-looked Francis for so long. At the end of the third stanza, Francis breaks the idiomatic American sentence across the English iambic line—the way he learned from Robert Frost. When he says, ". . . at last again to think / He can't think what it was he's laughing at"—repeating "think" and "laugh," using the clause "what it was" in the middle of a regular pentameter line which is almost monosyllabic—this is to "sound like" another poet. There are moments when it almost seems as if Francis thought that there would never be enough Robert Frost in the world to go around, so he'd make some more.

> Sometimes a boy on such a blueberry day
> Little by little will wander up so far
> That before he knows it he is near the cow,
> The one white cow . . .

When Francis "sounds like" Frost, it is only the one trick of cadence that he copies—not the rest of Frost's many repeated tricks of voice.

And then Francis stopped doing it. The lines just quoted are from his one long poem, the narrative *Valhalla*, and in *Valhalla* he wrote his way past Robert Frost. (The last third of this poem is deeply moving, by the way, as it chronicles the end of a family that lived in a cherished place.) But it's lyric poems that, one after one in quiet triumphs like Thomas Hardy's, number the days of the poet and his works:

Three Woodchoppers

Three woodchoppers walk up the road.
Day after day it is the same.
The short man always takes the lead
Limping like one a trifle lame.

And number two leans as he goes
And number three walks very straight.
I do not time them but I know
They're never early, never late.

So I have seen them for a week,
Have seen them but have heard no sound.
I never saw one turn to speak.
I never saw one look around.

Out of a window to the south
I watch them come against the light.
I cross the room and to the north
I watch till they are out of sight.

Note again the solitude, the *strangeness* of this poet. He's invisible—one would *not* consider him confessional—yet the imprint of an idiosyncratic vision gives these poems their textured particularity, an idiosyncracy again like Hardy's. With Hardy it's the diction that carries the strangeness; Francis's diction on the other hand is *decorous*—but his vision is as eccentric as Emily Dickinson's. I do not make this a virtue; it is only a fact, it is here. And it is not a mannerism, it is not a trick of "voice."

Here are two of his baseball poems:

Pitcher

His art is eccentricity, his aim
How not to hit the mark he seems to aim at,

His passion how to avoid the obvious,
His technique how to vary the avoidance.

The others throw to be comprehended. He
Throws to be a moment misunderstood.

Yet not too much. Not errant, arrant, wild,
But every seeming aberration willed.

Not to, yet still, still to communicate
Making the batter understand too late.

The Base Stealer

Poised between going on and back, pulled
Both ways taut like a tightrope-walker,
Fingertips pointing the opposites,
Now bouncing tiptoe like a dropped ball
Or a kid skipping rope, come on, come on,
Running a scattering of steps sidewise,
How he teeters, skitters, tingles, teases,
Taunts them, hovers like an ecstatic bird,
He's only flirting, crowd him, crowd him,
Delicate, delicate, delicate, delicate—now!

Francis is not one to care about baseball much. But he
observes it. (He may not like blueberries, for all I know.)
Baseball is a diamond to begin with, and on this diamond
the young ballplayers perform their ritual shapes, as if con-
spiring to place a grid over the chaos of experience. And this
is what, by his shapely resolutions, Francis does with his
poems.

The result frequently is the "timeless poem." In recent
decades we have decided in America that we don't like
timeless poems, and we write poems (like Lowell self-
consciously in *History*) overtly connected with events of the
moment. Reading Hardie St. Martin's glorious anthology of
modern Spanish poetry in translation, *Roots and Branches*, I
was struck by how Guillen, Jimenez, Lorca, Unamuno and
others look as if they might have written most of their poems
at any time in history. (I am aware that history prints itself on
our lives, whether we know it or not; I am talking about

conscious, *engagé* references to current affairs.) Neither the one prejudice nor the other, of course, takes any kind of precedence. And for that matter, poets are nicely inconsistent; just to make generalizations impossible, Francis's response to the Republic's adventures in Vietnam was unpredictably strong and overt:

The Righteous

After the saturation bombing divine
worship after the fragmentation shells
the organ prelude the robed choir after
defoliation Easter morning the white
gloves the white lilies after the napalm
Father Son and Holy Ghost Amen.

(He may omit punctuation and rhyme, but look closer; nothing goes unresolved.) The effect is strangely like the Simon and Garfunkel song, with "Silent Night" sung against the news broadcast. I call this poem unpredictable, because his rage is usually covert; but the values are resonant in all the poems which call forth this exact rage.

Other poems celebrate language, like the poem on the word "hogwash," or this one:

Like Ghosts of Eagles

The Indians have mostly gone
but not before they named the rivers
the rivers flow on
and the names of the rivers flow with them
　　Susquehanna　Shenandoah

The rivers are now polluted plundered
but not the names of the rivers
cool and inviolate as ever
pure as on the morning of creation
　　Tennessee　Tombigbee

If the rivers themselves should ever perish

> I think the names will somehow somewhere hover
> like ghosts of eagles
> those mighty whisperers
>   Missouri   Mississippi.

But the most continual effect is an alienation, sometimes amused, sometimes lonely, sometimes amused and lonely at the same time:

> *Comedian Body*
>
> Forgive comedian body
> For featuring the bawdy.
>
> For instance the poor fanny
> So basic and so funny.
>
> Forgive the penis pun
> That perfect two-in-one.
>
> Forgive the blowing nose.
> Forgive the ten clown toes
>
> And all the Noah's zoo
> Of two by two by two.
>
> Forgive a joke wherein
> All love and art begin.
>
> Forgive the incarnate word
> Divine, obscene, absurd.

Well, I said that it was a silly comparison. I do not claim that any single poem of Francis's equals the best early Lowell for grandeur and intensity. I do claim that Francis is a modern American classic, better (say) than almost anyone who has been gifted with a Pulitzer or a National Book Award in recent decades. I claim him as better (say) than John Berryman or Robert Penn Warren or Delmore Schwartz or A. R. Ammons, and these people have written beautiful poems.

As with Hardy, as with Frost, as with Richard Wilbur who has learned from him, Francis must be read in bulk. He does not write big poems. The accrual of small triumphs—told in the same skeptical, tender, funny, and reticent language—make a big poem out of this *Collected Poems*.

What do we make of the Industry's neglect of him?

First, let us admit that the Industry is us. Let us admit that all of us are sometimes lazy in not-reading poets, and lazy when we do read them—lacking the stubbornness to stay open-minded, reading instead according to the slogans of what's fashionable; if for a while in the fifties we cared for elegance and ceremony, we left these terms behind for confession, for extremity, for openness, for nakedness, and for vulnerability. When poetry did not conform to its latest requirements, we allowed ourselves not to take it seriously. We rode the waves of doctrine, little literary Vicars of Bray, table-hopping from Andrew Marvel to Pablo Neruda, from Emily Dickinson to Charles Bukowski—and every time we joined a new group, we put down the old one.

So Francis went unpublished in middle life, and has gone largely unread and without public reward. For him, perhaps it has been just as well. A man of solitude, he has been able to preserve his solitude without setting up a machine gun nest at Fort Juniper. Given his pacifism, and vegetarianism, it would have been difficult for him to defend his privacy with a gun, as Gary Snyder has learned to do. Although the neglect he suffered for a decade—no books, books rejected—depressed and embittered him, he has survived intact, unflattered by fools. He is perhaps luckier than Robert Lowell.

Robert Lowell and the Literature Industry

(1978)

When Theodore Roethke died at fifty-five in 1963, he left in galley *The Far Field*, his best work. When Yeats died, his posthumous *Last Poems* revealed that he had regained, between the ages of seventy and seventy-four, the powers he had appeared to lose in his middle sixties. I had hoped that Robert Lowell, after the disastrous collections of recent years, would emerge into old age with energy and genius as Yeats had done. But when Lowell died last September, he had just published *Day by Day*, a volume as slack and meretricious as *Notebook* and *History* which preceded it. The great poet died thirteen years earlier, with the publication of *For the Union Dead*.

One would not know it, from the book reviews or from the academy. The Literature Industry manufactures truisms like slogans. For years, as we have known that Ford had a better idea, or that Winston tastes good like a cigarette should, we have known that Robert Lowell was our greatest living poet. No matter how self-indulgent his latest self-imitation, the *New York Times Book Review* would agree to its genius. I suspect that this inflation—made windier now by his death— helped precipitate the appalling decline in Lowell's achievement.

Inflation is the Literature Industry's product. If the Faulkner dies, the Industry shouts: *Long live the Faulkner—*

and Saul Bellow becomes a major novelist. To speak of an Industry is to risk suggestions of paranoia. I do not see a network of Smersh agents bent on world literary conquest; I see a network of incompetence, diffidence, and laziness. We ourselves are the Industry, when we proclaim truisms of excellence and no longer read, judge, or discriminate. The slogans are designed by R and D in Manhattan, stamped out at critical assembly plants on campuses across the country. Consumers are first of all the Industry's own directors and employees—editors, reviewers, teachers—and then book-buyers in Los Angeles, BOMC subscribers in Florida, former English majors in Massachusetts who read the *Saturday Review*. These truisms are fixed like stars in the old astronomy, and woe to the heretic who denies them.

The Literature Industry's attention fixes itself mainly on prose. When it attends to poetry, it feels less secure; it canonizes two or three poets in a generation, defers to them with exaggerated reverence on Saints' days, and excuses itself thereafter from reading or judging contemporary poetry. In Bennett Cerf's *At Random*, that editor summed up an Industry attitude toward poetry with customary elegance; referring to Random House's acquisition of Robinson Jeffers, he said: "There are always a few poets that people think it's smart to have around."

It started to be smart to have Lowell around in 1946, when he published *Lord Weary's Castle*. After I read *Day by Day*, depressed by its trashiness, I looked back at *Lord Weary's Castle* again; it is great poetry, and with *The Mills of the Kavanaghs*, *Life Studies*, and *For the Union Dead* adds a strong poet to American literature. But our literature—it is customary to observe—is characterized by writers who do not grow old in their art, but who fly high and explode and crash. We do not deny the height if we deplore the crash. Lowell's downfall began earlier, but was confirmed by *Notebook 1967-1968* in 1969, and by the frantic revisions and new poems—seven volumes in nine years—that followed. The original *Notebook* assembled hundreds of blank verse fourteen-liners—diffuse and self-serving gossip, slovenly clichés assembled with a zeal like Roget's. And the *New York Times*, in a front page review, declared it a masterpiece.

As did the *New York Times* with *Day by Day*, which is no better. If one had spent the years since *Life Studies* in Antarctica, let us say, and visited one's local book store on one's 1977 return to check up on Lowell—one would have discovered . . . *cliché*. Not ironic cliché, not arguable cliché—just good old Edwin Newman cliché, the sort of cinderblock that publicity releases are built with: "I blushed to acknowledge . . ." / ". . . His heart is swallowed in his throat. . . ." For hyperbole one would have found: "a limb that weighed a ton." For a clever way to describe restoring a house, one would have found, "putting the place on its feet."

Twice Lowell tells us about anticipation in the word "heralded," the way a newspaper will tell us that a robin heralds spring. "Heralded" is a dead metaphor; neither in the newspaper nor in the poems does anyone blow a trumpet. *Day by Day* has more dead metaphors than it has live ones. These dead metaphors—"lost in the clouds" / "brink of adolescence"—carry no lively sense of idiom, as one might hope— "Why have I twisted your kind words . . ." / "cardinals . . . dart" / "children dart like minnows . . ."—but reveal a poet no longer custodian of the language of the tribe—"in sharper focus" / "promise has lost its bloom."

One result of dead metaphor is mixed metaphor. When Lowell has children "dart," he turns them into swift objects ejected from blow-guns by pygmies (or into feathered toys hurled in English pubs); then he turns the children instantly into tiny fish; because of the deadness of both metaphors, we take neither image seriously, so the dart's feathers do not metamorphose into fins—at the precise expense of image, of intensity, of concentration. In another place, Lowell gives us "the sun" as "bonfire" which is fair enough; but the Lord giveth, and the Lord taketh away, for immediately he has this bonfire-sun "rattle" like a child's toy, and then "eat like a locust." "Her speech is spiced," Lowell tells us elsewhere, "with the faded slang. . . ." The cliché of the kitchen mixes badly with the drapes in the south window. And one of the matters heralded is "heralded . . . by corkscrews . . . of snow. . . ." Poetry should be at least as well-written as newspapers.

Day by Day is as loose in grammatical connections as it is loose in metaphorical coherence; lines wander down the page, unconnected with each other:

> Dreams, they've had their vogue,
> so alike in their modernist invention,
> so dangerously distracted by commonplace,
> their literal insistence on the letter,
> trivia indistinguishable from tragedy—
> his monstrous melodrama terminating
> at a playhouse . . . dreaming, overhearing
> his own voice,
> the colloquial sibilance of the circuit-court,
> once freedom, the law and home to Lincoln—
> shot while sleeping through the final act.

All these end-stopped parallel lines—rhythm gone slack— leave us no sinew or syntax to hold the one perception to the other.

If the language of *Day by Day* is trite, and its connections unfixed, its overall tone proclaims the lassitude and despondency of self-imitation. Again and again, Lowell heaps adjectives before a noun, collapsing clauses into modifiers, a mannerism which once carried energy and invention. Again and again, Lowell fakes cloture with a little leap to one side, away from his poem's apparent thrust—a routine that was new in *Life Studies*. Self-imitation—the famous "voice" for which critics praise Lowell—appears adjunct to self-regard. A weary narcissism pervades these poems, whining its complaints. Frank O'Hara said years ago that Lowell's "confessional manner" lets him "get away with things that are plain bad but you're supposed to be interested because he's supposed to be so upset." *Day by Day* proclaims a celebrity life lived in public, and lived to be written about. One marries, one leaves one's wife, one marries again, one prints one's old wife's protests chopped into lines. . . . And the reviewers namedrop writing their reviews.

On the front page of the *New York Times Book Review* last August, a reviewer known for applying rigorous standards to beginning poets exercised vacuous praise of *Day by Day* as "altogether remarkable." "Accuracy and fidelity to perception have rarely received such a desperate pledge of faith. . . ." She spoke of ". . . the newest and the most imperial [mode], comprehending, as it does in Horace, the pains of age, loss and experience. . . ." Horace in his *Ars Poetica* advised that a poet keep his poems around for nine years before publishing them. One of the lines in *Day by Day* reads, "January 10, 1976."

Then *Time's* book department joined its praise, speaking of the poet's "unique genius and lasting accomplishments" in nervous prose. Showing us how *knowing* he was, the *Time* reviewer referred to Lowell's old poetry, with his "ear unmatched among his contemporaries for the off-rhythms that can be made to rattle in the sonorities of a line of blank verse." (Prizes for the best description of "off-rhythms." Prizes doubled for examples of "off-rhythms that can be made to rattle." Prizes tripled for one example of blank verse in the early poetry of Robert Lowell.) One could multiply examples of fatuous reviews and fatuous obituaries. They all say the same things, share the same platitudes or truisms. All exemplify the Literature Industry. They are not in themselves interesting, but it is interesting that they exist, interesting that they are the same—and perhaps that they helped to produce the outrageous decline they deny.

Poets need external criticism to bolster internal criticism. As poets get older, they often need it more and more. At the same time, if they have made their mark, they are surrounded by toadies who applaud everything they write. Their editors have studied them in school. Vatileptics gather at their poetry readings, dazzled by celebrity. If the poet asks, "Please pass the salt," poetry-groupies exalt the wit and brevity of the phrase. For most aging poets, the only useful critics are the same old friends, if they are still alive, who told them what was wrong with their poems when they were young.

I don't know whether Lowell sought criticism in his last decade. If he found good criticism, he paid it no heed. His own sad generation of poets died off. Replacing it—or what it might have been—was the uncritical and automatic paean of the Literature Industry, which allowed no thought that Homer, flattered and celebrated and growing old, might nod into imbecility.

In twenty years, no one will praise *Day by Day*. There will be reaction against Lowell, and it will be severe, unfair, and sheep-like. Sheep-critics will throw *Lord Weary's Castle* and *Life Studies* out with *Notebook* and *For Lizzie and Harriet*. In the longer run, of course, the *poetry* will endure: as long as there are libraries, as long as there is an American language, "After the Surprising Conversions," "Mother Marie Thérèse," and "Skunk Hour" will sing out their lines to the ears of people who love poems. *Day by Day* will remain a sad footnote to the corruption of a great poet, and to the corruption of the Literature Industry in the latter third of our century.

Wendell Berry[*]

(1977)

As I look out the window I see wasted land. My great-grandfather bought this farm in 1865. After he died in 1913, my grandfather continued to farm it: he grew vegetables and raised pigs and chickens to feed a family, and milked seven Holsteins and sent the milk to Boston. When I hayed with him in the summers of the 1940s—as late as 1950—he met me at the depot with horse and buggy. As we drove the slow mile back to the farm, I looked to left and right at working farms. Stone walls at road's edge reminded you that these fields had not always been clear; not only had they been littered with the glacier's rubble, they had been thick with trees. Thirty years later they are thick with bushes, and the stone walls no longer pen sheep—or even field corn. Walls keep weed trees from escaping into ditches. The farmers have gone from their hilly New Hampshire land, and their husbanded land grows slack and slovenly.

Wendell Berry's Kentucky differs considerably from this New Hampshire. It is better farmland, for one thing, with a longer growing season. But much of Kentucky is hilly like New Hampshire, and much has gone to waste. All over this country, good farmland lies abandoned, and grows up to

---

[*] Wendell Berry, *The Unsettling of America: Culture and Agriculture* (San Francisco: Sierra Club Books, 1977).

bush; other farmland, badly plowed for greed's sake, washes itself away in mud. Farmers and farmhands, displaced, become urban poor.

For many years, I thought the small farm was doomed, as if by some impersonal fate, by forces as uncontrollable as God or the weather. In Wendell Berry's "The Unsettling of America," he documents the claim that powerful men have wasted the land for reasons of profit; and he argues with careful logic for the recovery of lost land, for the return of the small farmer to the countryside, the small farmer expropriated by the army of agribusiness. This repulsive neologism describes a conspiracy of big manufacturers (that make farm equipment and chemical fertilizers), big banks (that finance the capital required for equipment), big university professors (supported by manufacturers' grants), big landowners (who sacrifice land for profit), and the Department of Agriculture (recruited from the ranks of bigness). Corporate capitalism, collectivized in this country, overthrows American independence; our huge farms are more efficient collectives than the Soviets can manage, because we are better at suppressing individualism. In a phrase of Berry's we are "the imperialist invaders of our own land."

Wendell Berry is poet, novelist, essayist; he teaches at the University of Kentucky; he farms his own acreage in the country where he grew up, using draft animals instead of tractors. Of his many identities, farmer is the most recent, slowest growing, and most profound. As a young man he left Kentucky for New York City, where he was another promising young writer and teacher. Returning to the country he grew up in, he first approached farming tentatively, with hesitation—and gradually granted more of himself to the ground, and gradually worked out a systematic worldview that derives its premises from the experience of working on the land.

Finally his system has become as integrated as a religion, but its character speaks its slow, earthy derivation; he is no bourgeois pursuing scenery like many a contemporary celebrator of land. This book is published by the Sierra Club, and contains excellent and appropriate criticism of the Sierra Club's occasional scenic elitism. Places aren't for exploiting, even to look at: places are for working and caring; the only moral connection to earth is one of "kindly use."

Connections are what matters. Berry writes: "The modern urban-industrial society is based on a series of radical disconnections between body and soul, husband and wife, marriage and community, community and the earth. At each of these points of disconnection the collaboration of corporation, government, and experts sets up a profit-making enterprise that results in the further dismemberment and impoverishment of the Creation. . . . Only by restoring the broken connections can we be healed."

Berry is a prophet of our healing, a utopian poet-legislator like William Blake; Blake's words turn up in this book almost as frequently as former Secretary of Agriculture Earl Butz's, to somewhat different effect. In his passion for social change, Berry resembles several other poets roughly of his own generation, who have developed systems of value—based on love of what poetry starts from—which sponsor criticism of the world as it is; I think of Gary Snyder, like Berry a passionate defender of the earth household; of Adrienne Rich, whose *Of Woman Born* made her a foremost feminist theorist; of Robert Bly, who led protests during the Vietnam War. Perhaps contemporary poetry begins by seeming to isolate poets from the mass of humanity; I think poetry's values join poets up again.

Berry speaks from a *vision of work*, the hard work of the cyclical farm, where the farmer uses animal and human waste to grow crops for animals and humans, where the wheel of seasons rolls its round, human and animal muscles behind it. On the other hand, contemporary agribusiness, always *specializing*, uses animals or plants as protein-sheaths, as molecule-processors—and turns good manure into a pollutant; creates poison, rather than conserves energy.

When did Americans lose their taste for work? It happened before Henry Ford paid five dollars a day to workers on his line. The notion that work is evil sponsors waste leisure, the religion of weekends, of holidays, of retirement; it sponsors pollutant hedonism like the Playboy philosophy. At the end of work-hatred, common to intellectuals as to factory workers, lies the destructiveness of drugs and alcohol. When Americans after the Civil War decided that service was silly—to others, to God, to land; decided that Number One and Number One's comforts were all that mattered, the patio became our promised land, our manna potato chips, and Robert Ringer our Moses. In place of the Kingdom of Heaven, we created lung cancer, cirrhosis—and a sick dread of death which in turn led to a general denial of death. It is not too much to say that these diseases derive from the expropriation of most Americans from their old connections; the cyclical farm accepts both birth and death, decay and growth as sources of energy.

Everyone reading this review descends from cyclical farmers. For many Americans, our ancestors' landwork shows forth in our tending of suburban lawns, as if care for the land—attention, time, love—was a survival-oriented characteristic, not yet wholly bred out.

Berry's newest book of poems, *Clearing*, (New York: Harcourt Brace Javonovich) prints seven longish poems, all of them testimony which could be interleaved among the chapters of "The Unsettling of America." In "Vision"—part of a longer poem called "Work Song"—Berry allows himself to articulate the good world his work serves toward:

> The river will run
> clear, as we will never know it,
> and over it, birdsong like a canopy.
> On the levels of the hills will be
> green meadows, stock bells in noon shade.
> On the steeps where greed and ignorance cut down
> the old forest, an old forest will stand,
> its rich leaf-fall drifting on its roots.
> The veins of forgotten springs will have opened.
> Families will be singing in the fields.
> In their voices they will hear a music
> risen out of the ground.

Occasionally these poems turn flat and prosey as they attempt to carry the all-important ideas—but it is then that they betray these ideas, because they are no longer as well made as a bull rake. At their sonorous best, the poems embody the passion for excellent honesty that derives from Berry's duty to soil and season.

David Wagoner*

(1979)

Here is the first stanza of "For a Woman Who Dreamed All the Horses Were Dying," one of sixty-three new poems in David Wagoner's tenth poetry collection, *In Broken Country*:

> You saw them falling in fields beyond barbed wire,
> Their forelegs buckling, the horses kneeling
> In the dead grass, then falling awkwardly
> On their flanks to finish breathing
> Where stems give way to roots under the earth
> That will let no hoofprints last for a whole season,
> Their eyes still staring, but sightless now, their withers
> > Still, their long tails still.

Good writing! I admire the stanza's one long elegant sentence; I enjoy the last lines as they mimic lamentation by means of repetition and line-break. But after a second stanza which emphasizes the emptiness of "distances" and "open plain. . . ," the poem ends:

> And they were dead then, all of them
> > everywhere,
> You told me, dead and never to return.

---

* David Wagoner, *In Broken Country* (Boston: Little, Brown—an Atlantic Monthly Press Book, 1979).

Love, I offer my own brief dream: together
We wait in an unfenced field, and slowly
Shying along the hillside, the small wild horses
Come walking toward us, their unshod hooves
Tentative on the ground. Warily they stretch
                    To muzzle our trembling hands.

I am let down: so what? The horses die, the place is empty:
predictably, "I offer my own brief dream. . . ." What is this
"brief dream" in service of? What does it represent in
thought or feeling? I fear it represents nothing at all except a
way to end a poem. The poem has taken us on a pleasurable
journey through attractive scenery, and when the journey
has ended, we realize that we have gone nowhere, discovered
nothing, retained only the light pleasure of remembered
landscape.

If I describe the poem correctly, I may seem to call it
worthless; but I am not at all certain that it is worthless.
Writing poems over a lifetime, most poets must aggregate
years of work at the desk. In those years of diligence, how
much time has been spent in the making of new metaphor or
the discovery of the final poem? Even for Wallace Stevens or
Robert Frost or Robert Lowell, I suppose that a long lifetime
may have yielded something like one hour and thirty-seven
minutes of true *invention*—where the dazzled eye watched
the inspirited hand in amazement. The rest was, well, just
good writing (along with some writing we might as well
forget). Reading David Wagoner, I note much good writing,
and I am grateful for it. Later in this volume, we find a whole,
short poem which embodies in its fantasy something like the
third stanza of the poem just quoted:

The Orchard of the Dreaming Pigs

As rosy as sunsets over their cloudy hocks, the
    pigs come flying
Evening by evening to light in the fruit trees,
Their trotters firm on the bent boughs, their
    wings

All folding down for the dark as they eat and
     drowse,
Their snouts snuffling a comfortable music.

At dawn, as easily as the light, they lift
Their still blessed souse and chitlings through
     the warming air,
Not wedging their way like geese, but
     straggling
And curling in the sunrise, rising, then
     soaring downward
To the bloody sties, their breath turned sweet
     as apples.

These airborne pigs do not merely answer a formal need, as
the envisioned horses do; and if they embody or express a
human desire to fly, coupled with a sense of the absurdity of
that dream, I do not think that the discovery compares with
Columbus's. Yet these lines make a small artifact, not ex-
pressive of anything profound, as delightful to touch and to
hold as a particular carved stone. It is not, I think, the
dazzled eye and the inspirited hand; it is a lucky moment of
making.

What I most often need and want as a reader is this lucky
moment. If there are hours when we are capable of reading
genius, when we need it and are adequate to it, there are also
hours when we take pleasure and instruction from lesser
work. Although we may love someone very much, a state of
continual orgasm would be intolerable. In between the mo-
ments of highest intensity, we read the paper, we play bridge,
we walk, we eat grapes, we talk together. . . .

Much of the discussion of poetry, over the last twenty or
twenty-five years, has assumed that only intensity is tolerable.
This opinion has a number of unfortunate corollaries: if
poetry is only moments of the greatest intensity, it follows
that poetry cannot argue a point (we will allow prose to do
the arguing) or tell a long story (we will allow prose to tell
long stories) or be conversational or amusing like witty
speech (we will leave that to prose). Fifteen or twenty years

ago, it followed that poetry could embody only extreme states of emotion—and then the poets killed themselves.

By such standards, David Wagoner is no poet. I suggest we chuck the standards instead of chucking David Wagoner. His poems are actually readable. For more than a century, we have learned to scorn the readable poem; if it tastes good it must be bad for you. Victorian Americans and Britons actually read Whittier, Tennyson, Longfellow, Browning and even Whitman, poets who wrote in bulk and at length and with varying intensity. Apparently these readers were interested not only in phrases or stanzas which could serve as touchstones, but in books to read for continuing pleasure. It is seldom noticed or attended to that William Carlos Williams is eminently readable, as are Robert Creeley and Denise Levertov, Gary Snyder and Philip Whalen.

William Stafford is another poet who comes to mind as I read Wagoner's often prosy and ruminative poems; both write poems "of the second intensity," which is the level on which we live much of our lives. Wagoner also reminds me of a voice which is common in England, the tone of David Wright or John Heath-Stubbs, which talks in measure and metaphor about anything at all, to make a shape of irony, wit, and pleasure—like good conversation determined to be honest and to please.

Our critical standards must learn to tolerate this tone. If we become irritated at what seems complacency—thinking in contrast of Sylvia Plath or Robert Lowell—and wish to shout that this tone of voice has "never in its life lost itself," we might remember poets as varied as Richard Wilbur and Marianne Moore, Ben Jonson and Robert Herrick. There is perhaps a fine tradition which asserts that poetry is precisely a way of not losing yourself.

Reading the readable, I indeed find moments of formal pleasure mild enough to suggest disappointment. However, in the work of a good poet, there are other moments too, approaching the hour and thirty-seven minutes of a lifetime's genius. In his title poem, "Walking in Broken Country," Wagoner transcends his normal competence:

Long after the blossoming of mile-wide, fire-
    breathing roses
In this garden of dead gods when Apache tears
Burst out of lava
And after the crosshatched lightning and
    streambeds cracking
Their sideslips through mid-rock, after
    burnishing wind,
Your feet are small surprises:
Lurching down clumps of cinders, unpredictably
    slipshod,
And gaining your footholds by the sheerest
    guesswork,
You make yourself at home
By crouching, by holding still and squinting
    to puzzle out
How to weave through all this rubble to where
    you're going
Without a disaster:
One dislocation, one green-stick fracture, and
    all your bones
May fall apart out of sympathy forever.
In this broken country
The shortest distance between two points
    doesn't exist.
Here, straight lines are an abstraction, an ideal
Not even to be hoped for
(As a crow flies, sometimes) except on the
    briefest of terms:
Half a step on legs, after which you slump,
Swivel, or stagger.
You cling to surfaces feebly in a maze without
    a ceiling,
A whole clutch of directions to choose among
From giddy to earthbound,
Where backtracking from dead-ends is an end
    in itself.
Through this clear air, your eyes put two and
    two
Together, take them apart,
And put them together again and again in

                baffling pieces,
        Seeing the matter of all your sensible facts
        Jumbled to the horizon.

Here everything that is best about David Wagoner falls into
place at once.

C. H. Sisson*

(1977)

Something new is happening in English poetry. In the magazines *Agenda* and *PN (Poetry Nation) Review,* we find poems ambitious in scope, precise in rhythm, strict in thought, polished in technique, often conservative in politics. Nothing could be further from most English verse of recent decades: modest, humanitarian, inept.

Something new derives from much that is old. Appropriately, the best of the new English poets is a man in his sixties. C. H. Sisson was born in 1914, and began to publish when he was almost fifty. *Anchises,* just issued in this country, is his fifth volume, and his best. Sisson is a strange figure of a poet: Most of his life he has been a public servant, rising in the Civil Service to become Under Secretary in the Ministry of Labour before his retirement. A collection of his literary and political essays—he writes a noble English prose—is called *Art and Action.* His poetry is also frequently political, concerned with national spirit and with the mystery of nationhood.

A monarchist, Sisson does not accept Parliament as his nation; nor is his nation democratic. For him "governance" is

---

*C. H. Sisson, *Anchises* (Carcanet New Press. Distributed by Dufour Editions, Chester Springs, Pa., 1977).

continuous, whether the ruling party be labeled Conservative or Labour, Tudor or Stuart. Governance would continue under a Communist regime, or a Fascist one. Although Sisson is by no means a Fascist, his intellectual affinities bring him into compromised company. Sisson admires Charles Maurras of *L'Action Française*, monarchist and intellectual activist put in jail with Pétain for wartime collaboration with the Germans.

After the regicide of Charles I, Sisson says, "The intelligence of England deteriorated." In *Anchises,* Sisson writes a long, amusing poem at the expense of the French Revolution—a subject generally retired from the area of debate. Although he is a man of the present world in his professional life, he nevertheless detests the present world. Sisson's mind works by moving *backward:* "In the Trojan Ditch," his collected poems (also distributed here by Dufour) begins with his most recent work and moves in orderly fashion backward to the first poem he has preserved; and in his one novel, *Christopher Homm,* the narrative proceeds from the protagonist's death backwards to his imminent birth.

In Sisson's early poetry, one heard at times echoes of the seventeenth century, especially the devotional poems of George Herbert. But as he has grown older, his idiom has become more modern—a strange direction for C. H. Sisson. He has progressed as a poet chiefly by translating Latin poets into contemporary English. The endeavor to render Catullus, Virgil, Horace, and Lucretius into contemporary idiom—highly successful—has freed his line, loosened his syntax and enlarged the range of his diction; he retains firm control through diction and rhythm.

Sisson's language is the common speech of an educated Englishman: dry, ironic, Latinate, harsh, eloquent, especially strong in denunciation. This is the speech of thousands of people in England, and yet it has rarely become the source of poetry. His greatest resource is the rhythm that organizes this diction, rhythm that compels attention and belief. In the foreword to his collected poems, he wrote, "The proof of the poem—any poem—is in its rhythm and that is why critical determination has in the end to await that un-arguable perception." In "Cotignac," his lines pass his own stern test:

> River, deep as death, deeper, Avernus,
> Red water of ox-hide, oxblood, clouded,
> Drawn across these caverns like a taut sheet,
> What is down there, under the cliff edge,
> Deeper than hell? Village
> Lost to all time, under the sick archway,
> The lost steps lead there, the life
> Stirs like a movement of moss.

Sisson's mind is large and supple, his European experience varied, his ideas religious and moral as well as political. He is full of the emotion of self-accusation. Bitter sarcasm—directed in his prose toward the *idea* of the individual—in his poems is often self-directed. This self-accusation may seem to resemble confessional verse; but Sisson's lines do not confess; they *accuse*, and in their accusations they assume an objective morality. For instance, there is a short poem called, "Virtue:"

> Virtue instead of failure, a fine choice,
> Virtue is its own damnation. I, who see man
> In his external shape, acting and bowing,
> Take no account of his inner movements
> Which are lies only, must admit
> Myself virtuous although my heart is a sink
> Where ambition swills round with lost lust
> And even the last words are spoken with envy.

Sisson's work contains small sense of possibility, small sense of possible change except for the worse; no rhetoric of betterment, no liberal hope, no Christian euphoria—but a conservative sense of limitation and a Christian sense of sin. Yet we read this dour, reactionary retired civil servant with joy—because of his passion and his love. His poems move in service to the loved landscapes of England and France; they sing (and growl) in love of argument, in love of *seeing through*, in love of the firm descriptions of moral self-disgust; they move in love of the old lost life by which the new life is condemned.

Basil Bunting*

(1978)

It is public knowledge that the greatest poets of any age go undiscovered until they are dead. Like most items of public knowledge, this one is almost perfectly untrue, but literary reputation *is* erratic enough to provide examples for any saw; good poets *do* get overlooked. One common phenomenon is the poet who, in the language of a former President, "peaks too soon," and by early success creates an expectation he lives to disappoint. James Atlas's biography of Delmore Schwartz gives melancholy testimony to such a life. Other poets sweep into prominence with one literary mode—confessional poetry, perhaps, or witwork—and are swept away, the best and the worst together, when fashion changes.

For critics and academics are as herdlike as television watchers, and today's "Laverne and Shirley" is tomorrow's "Life of Riley." Thus a number of excellent poets who surfaced in the twenties and thirties—modernists and objectivists who developed their poetics out of Pound, Eliot, and Williams—went largely unread during the forties and fifties,

---

* Basil Bunting, *Collected Poems* (New York: Oxford University Press, 1978).

230

only to be rediscovered in the last decade or so. These American poets include George Oppen, Charles Reznikoff, Louis Zukofsky and Carl Rakosi. Their equivalent in England is Basil Bunting.

For many years it was impossible to get hold of Bunting's poems. He was so far from fashion as to go unprinted. His name was tainted with suspicions of discipleship. Ezra Pound's "Guide to Kulchur" was dedicated to Bunting and Zukofsky, and for decades Pound's notorious generosity promoted Bunting with tireless zeal. Alas, at the same time, Pound was promoting social credit and Mussolini (about whom Bunting tried to offer Pound correction), and Pound's promotion only served to warn people away from Bunting.

Meantime, Bunting had begun a literary life, and then moved away from it. In the twenties he lived in Paris, friend to Ford Madox Ford, and assisted in editing the *Transatlantic Review*. Visiting Rapallo in the thirties, he was pressed into service to witness W. B. Yeats's will. After World War II, however, he spent many years in Persia as a journalist, correspondent for the *Times* of London. He disappeared from the literary scene, metamorphosed into a footnote. In 1950 a press in Texas printed a collection of Bunting's poems— nothing had been in print for years—that remained obscure. (I found a copy in a used-book store in Oxford in 1963. It seemed typical of the *luck* associated with Bunting that I quickly lost it on a London bus.) But in the sixties the Fulcrum Press in London brought Bunting out of the rare-book room, reprinting old work, issuing the major work *Briggflatts* in 1966 and a *Collected Poems* two years later. Now Bunting has retired from journalism to his native Northumberland, and at the age of seventy-eight his *Collected Poems* (corrected and slightly expanded) comes to us from the Oxford University Press. Now we are able to do homage to the last minor master of the modernist mode.

Bunting's poems are not easy to read, unless you take Bunting's advice and read them as pure sound. It is tempting to follow his advice, because the sound is pleasing:

A mason times his mallet
to a lark's twitter,
listening while the marble rests,
lays his rule
at the letter's edge,
fingertips checking,
till the stone spells a name. . . .

These lines come near the beginning of *Briggflatts,* which
gives us in its Coda:

A strong song tows
us, long earsick.
Blind, we follow
rain slant, spray flick
to fields we do not know.

Night, float us.
Offshore wind, shout,
ask the sea
what's lost, what's left,
what horn sunk,
what crown adrift.

Where we are who knows
of kings who sup
while day fails? Who,
swinging his axe
to fell kings, guesses
where we go?

The sound, vowel and dance, is gorgeous—but emotion
rises not only from the sound of "what's lost" and "day fails"
but from the meanings the words gather. We must look
askance at Bunting's advice not to inquire into meanings:
"The attempt to find any meaning in it would be manifestly
absurd." The poet barks to warn us from digging for content
in this poem, which he calls autobiographical only to deny
the word. He tells us elsewhere how the poem began when
he intuited a visual shape, a diagram of peaks and valleys;

then it was merely a matter of writing: "Once I had got the thing clear in my head as a diagram, I simply set to work and wrote it, writing when I could, three lines in the train on the way to work, three lines on the way home. . . ." He reckons he wrote 20,000 lines to find the 700 lines of the finished poem.

Literary history is full of poets who strip themselves naked for us and then describe the robes that they are wearing. Robert Frost's public performance was a denial of what his poems revealed. Eliot's doctrine of impersonality attempted to disguise poems supremely personal. Bunting hands us his life—Briggflatts is the place where he spent his holidays as a child—and tells us that we are hearing birdsong. When he speaks in a prose reminiscence of Yeats, he says that the Irishman spoke of poetic technique rarely, perhaps because he felt "technique . . . too intimate a matter for public discussion." The wily Bunting, questioned about his own poems, reduces them to themes and variations, possibly because they are too intimate a matter for public discussion.

As for the old suspicions of discipleship, we need not worry. There are poems here that bare the relationships to Pound or Browning. There are others that resemble Pound not at all. Writing about Herbert Read, Bunting once said that he had ". . . used Pound's tools . . . to engrave experiences not like Pound's." True enough, for Bunting himself—and there is also the matter of national and regional speech to separate the two poets. The flavor of Bunting's diction is un-American; it is English, and I gather it is more specifically Northumbrian. Of all the traditions that inform a poet's work, the tradition of national or regional speech is often strongest, and often overlooked. And William Wordsworth is Bunting's poetic master, along with Pound.

These *Collected Poems* gather fewer than 150 pages, poems dated as early as 1924, as late as 1975. Fifty-one years of diligence, of searching for "an origin that poetry and music share, in the dance. . . ." From the early "Villon," to the late "Overdrafts"—versions and reversions of other people's

233

poems, which remind me of Asger Jorn painting pictures on top of old pictures bought in a flea market—the long life dances forth in a living voice. Like this:

> Fifty years a letter unanswered;
> a visit postponed for fifty years.

> She has been with me fifty years.

> Starlight quivers. I had day enough.
> For love uninterrupted night.

Ted Hughes*

(1977)

In *Gaudete* the English poet Ted Hughes has made something new. I do not mean merely that the book is original, for in the modern tradition we demand originality as a matter of course—too much as a matter of course. *Gaudete* creates a *new form* within the possibilities of poetry. More innovative than *Crow*, thorough and unrelenting, *Gaudete* is Ted Hughes's best work after *Lupercal*.

Like any new form, Hughes's poem touches back on old ones: The most ancient surviving poems are stories, and *Gaudete* is largely narrative. Hughes tries to bring back to poetry the detail and the muscular drive of strong storytelling, provinces largely abandoned to prose for some centuries. His narrative is prosaic, as it must be, for we lack in modern poetry a heroic or narrative line. Narrative must *refer* to prose. *Gaudete's* line is loose, end-stopped where the sense pauses, and thus lacks implication that the line lives for its own sake, in some brute place where shapeliness sings its song of self-concern.

On the other hand, the diction within these lines is usually tense, intense, complex, violent. Narrative *line* conflicts with lyric *image*, and conflict makes energy. The result is *new*,

---

* Ted Hughes, *Gaudete* (New York: Harper and Row, 1977).

235

and when you have read enough of *Gaudete* to learn the way it speaks, the result is enthralling:

> He stands and tries to run but
>   the thick sludge grips his feet,
> And he falls again, gets up again
> Staggering slowly, losing both
>   shoes in the quag.
> Shapes of men are hunting
>   him across the yard
> Among the plunging beasts
> With cudgels, with intent to kill him.
> The cattle wallow and skid inthe dark,
> Their frightened bellowing magnifies them. From a raw,
>   high lamp
> Broad sweeping strokes of rainy light come and go, wheeling
>   and thrusting.
> He shields his head and tries to
>   see his attackers' faces
> Among the colliding masses
>   and tossing silhouettes.
> Caught in the flashing diagonals
> The faces seem to be all wide-stretched mouth,
>   like lampreys.

But in this narrative line, successful in plunging us forward through sensation and act, language is inconsistent. Slackness invades and hampers. We hear of "the tossing sea of faces"; "Flames leap"; we hear that "a horrible revelation is hurdling towards him." When the poet sleeps, narrative mumbles on. At other moments, it becomes so important to advance the idea, to *explain*, that we enter a simplicity as prosaic as Dick and Jane:

> He is starting Christianity all over again, right
>   from the start.
> He has persuaded all the
>   women in the parish.
> Only women can belong to it.
> They are all in it and he makes

> love to them all, all the time.
> Because a saviour
> Is to be born in this village, and Mr. Lumb is to
> be the earthly father.

I must mention such failures. But I must insist that the volume survives them, that the passion of the poem's conception sweeps us over these deserts into the good forest.

The last lines quoted reveal a center of the poem's argument. I will not attempt to summarize. The plot is mythic. The Reverend Lumb (a tree's limb, the *lamb* of God) has wreaked sexual havoc among the women in his village. Then this English priest becomes a sacrificial animal, sacrificed to notions of violence and sexuality underneath civilization's streets of houses. D. H. Lawrence told realistic stories to embody similar ideas; Hughes with the help of folklore, and with poetry's license to fantasy, invents outrageous metamorphoses of human, plant, and animal by which to enact these ideas, and to grant them savagery and power.

"Gaudete" is Latin, telling us "rejoice," a word in this poem observed cut on a tombstone. Within the suicide, murder, and orgy of this poem, the word has its ironies—but it is also direct, a directive, advice directed at the mass of humans serving civilized doctrines of restraint and caution.

At least: the mass of *English* humans; this poem could only have been written by an Englishman. Of all countries in the world, England has been most successful at civilizing itself, the word used as in the injunction to "Be civilized, my dear." This command is an effective opposite to "gaudete." Everything American Anglophiles love about the English—polite policemen, decency, grace under pressure, perseverance, unflappableness; the clichés of an imperial race that practices its first imperialism upon its own emotions; a race which learned to conquer the inner "savages" before subjugating the outer ones—all of these qualities inhabit the background of *Gaudete's* village, and are overwhelmed. Women gather like a coven of witches—dressed as animals, writhing and chanting—at the Women's Institute to await impregnation by their minister. (The plot has its comedy!) Outraged husbands and fathers, types of the English countryside from poachers to retired military men, gather at the Pub before they set out as a murderous posse.

As French *clarté* made Surrealism a necessity for France, English gentility creates *Gaudete's* murderous eroticism.

Edson, Bidart, Broumas, Creeley

(1977)

Sometimes on an airplane a man next to me closes his briefcase and asks, "What are *you* in?" When I tell him I write poems, he may be nervous (I guess I'd better watch my grammar) or tolerant (my wife, she likes that sort of thing). Whatever his initial reaction, within ten minutes he'll remark sadly on the decline in poetry's fortunes. Belief is universal that sometime in the distant past, before television, people used to read poetry all the time. They didn't—not in the United States; not in England either. If we go back to pre-literate cultures, poetry as epic or theater was common property. But the lyric poem—short, intense, emotional, often irrational and dreamlike—has never been popular; not like fiction or prose theater or circuses or baseball or churches or movies or politics or war or good works. In fact, the *present* American audience for poetry is larger than it has ever been. Poetry books—which in 1940 were issued in editions of 750, in 1950 in editions of 1000—now appear in editions of 4000 and 5000 copies.*

---

* Because one keeps on running into this chap, and one has run into him over and over again for the last thirty years, one continues to write this paragraph. I have extended the argument, not to mention the rhetoric, in "Poetry, Popularity, and the Golden Age," pages 313–18.)

Nor are book sales the main story. When I say that the audience for poetry has increased, I emphasize the "audio" part of the word. Thirty years ago poetry readings were rare as blue snow; now poetry reading publishes—"makes public"—poems in the ears of listeners from coast to coast every moment of the day. And listeners become readers; where there are most readings, booksellers sell most books. In the San Francisco area there are 2000 readings a year. In Ann Arbor, there were one or two readings a year in the fifties; by 1975 there were almost a hundred.

For poets, this phenomenon is confirmation that someone is *out there*; a middle-aged poet can read poems to 5000 young faces every year. Critics have noticed a vast change in the poetry of a generation—in the work of James Wright, for instance; Galway Kinnell, Louis Simpson, W. S. Merwin, Robert Bly—from iambic stanzas in the fifties to free verse and fantasy a decade later; the biggest source of change has been the poetry reading, where contact is immediate, intimate, and sensuous. One's body enters the poem, as it needn't with a print poem. American poetry has become more emotional as it has become more physical. And the change is also social, making a poetry that is more gregarious, more public; the poet, who used to live in a tower and speak to the moon only, now speaks to thousands of faces, mostly young.

Yet for all the increase in audience, poetry remains a minority art. Three thousand copies spread thin over 200 million people. It remains so not because it is obscure but because of its nature: because a poem must be honest—because a poem reveals a psyche most of us would keep out of sight—it will often be painful. And much of the time, lyric poetry tells us to *let go*, to abandon ourselves to the west wind, or whatever wind blows through us. By evading ego's controls, poetry lets images and insights, forbidden to reason, surface in reason's light, which is language. Plato expelled poets from his Republic because they admitted the irrational; most of civilization is Platonic, and finds poetry crazy and intolerable.

Reading Russell Edson, you can see civilization's point. Edson writes tiny short stories, which critics call prose poems mostly to let you know that they are crazy.

The Overlap of Worlds

The furniture is like models of animals. You can see the dining room table as a kind of bull standing with its cows, the chairs. Or the easy chair with its footstool, the cow with its calf . . .

And they live a life, as if a spirit world and this were overlapped, oblivious to the other.

In moonlight these animals soften and resume their lives, browsing the rugs; as we upstairs, asleep in our dreams, resume our lives: overlapping and oblivious to the other . . .

I quote from a book called *The Intuitive Journey*.* I quote a small sample, in order to quote at all. The typical Edson poems runs a page or a page and a half. It's fanciful, it's even funny—but this humor carries discomfort with it, like all serious humor. We may not *wish* to understand the fragility of our psychic borders, or that we partake of things outside ourselves, or that we may lose ourselves if we are not careful. Maybe we control nothing; if we control nothing with our egos, if we *let go*, perhaps we can recover an ancient self otherwise lost, or perceive a world never seen before.

Russell Edson's imagination is revolutionary. He explores a small territory, but it is unmapped land. He does adventurous spirit-work for all of us, recovering portions of the lost infant world for anyone who will follow him.

If all poets are psychic revolutionaries, they dig trenches in different places. Frank Bidart's poems in *The Book of the Body* are not like *anyone* else's.† In a time when fantasy is as com-

---

* Russell Edson, *The Intuitive Journey* (New York: Harper and Row, 1977).
† Frank Bidart, *The Book of the Body* (New York: Farrar, Straus & Giroux, 1977).

mon as bread, metaphor and simile buttering everybody's poem, Bidart writes lines which are plain, flat, and "not poetry." He writes such lines as, "An adult's forgiveness of his parents / born out of increasing age and empathy / which really forgives nothing,— . . ." Usually he is abstract, without images, presenting character through speech and action. And his dramatic monologues are wholly genuine.

When I read poems that are "not poetry," and yet "wholly genuine," I know that I am in the presence of something new. Everything truly new has always begun as "not poetry," be it *The Waste Land* or *Lyrical Ballads*. It is hard to remember that Wordsworth was originally denounced as obscure.

Bidart's subject matter is sordid, I suppose; half a century earlier, in prose, these poems would have been called "realistic"; and they would not have been published. *The Book of the Body* begins with a poem spoken by an amputee, and ends with "Ellen West," a poem derived in part from a case study of a woman who will not eat; institutionalized, with her own notion of body, she says of her husband: "He was a fool. He married / meat, and thought it was a wife." Each poem in the book builds itself around the difficulty of accepting or coping with one's own body, and the solutions are disturbing, neurotic—yet they incorporate feelings potential to anyone. For Bidart is not a confessional poet; he is dramatic and universal, a moral observer of humanity overwhelmed by the suffering he observes and records.

Reading his lines over and over, I begin to understand the art that touches me so, to see how Bidart's extraordinary, almost invisible care transforms ordinary language. He is a virtuoso of punctuation and syntax. As his lines spread down the wide page, his indentations (and capitals and italics and combinations of colon and comma and semicolon and dash) improvise a musical notation for speed, pause, and volume. His notation *bodies* the plainness of his language. We hear the victims speak in their true tones.

It is impossible to quote Bidart in these narrow columns. For that matter, to read Bidart you need to read whole poems, perhaps whole books—for, unlike many contemporaries, Bidart writes whole poems rather than collages of bright lines tenuously connected. I've said of many modern poets—Dylan Thomas, for instance—that they write poetry, not poems; maybe a last word on Bidart should be the opposite: he writes poems, not poetry.

It's possible that twentieth-century American poetry is at a high moment, even a high moment of literature. (Wouldn't *that* surprise a lot of people?) The fecund variety of our poetry astonishes me. The books come tumbling out—little presses, New York, college presses, little *little* presses—and of course most of them are bad; but with astonishing frequency, I run across a gifted new poet whom I had never heard of. Thus when Yale's Younger Poet this year was first-rate, and I had never heard of her, I was not surprised. Olga Broumas was born in Greece, and English is her second language; I know nothing else about her, save what her poems tell me. In her collection, *Beginning With O,* she shows an excellent young poet's joy in words, in gorgeous rhythms, in images fixed on the mind's eye with a printmaker's permanence.

But unlike most young poets, Olga Broumas has a political passion and a political vision—for she is a feminist and a lesbian, or Sapphist. Because of the women's movement, which liberates and energizes, women may well dominate the next decades of American poetry. (Last year's Yale winner was another brilliant young woman, Carolyn Forché.) Some of the best new poetry by women is Sapphic, as the sexual politics of feminism undertakes a reflexive journey, like black pride and concomitant black separatism; Sapphism is feminism's nationalism. In the work of Olga Broumas, it is both erotic and metaphorical. As metaphor, Sapphism is search for female identity; in mother and in lover, the poet seeks and discovers her sources; as Eros, the poetry requires no explanation:

---

*Olga Broumas, *Beginning with O,* (New Haven, Conn.: Yale University Press, 1977)

You wanted to compare, and there
we were, eyes on each eye, the lower
lids
squinting
suddenly awake

though the light was dim. Looking away
some time ago, you'd said
   the eyes are live
   animals, domiciled in our head
but more than the head

is crustacean-like. Marine
eyes, marine
odors. Everything live
(tongue, clitoris, lip and lip)
swells in its moist shell. I remember the light

warped round our bodies finally
crustal, striated with sweat.

Here is metaphor and body together, from a poem called "Amazon Twin." For Olga Broumas, "The Twelve Aspects of God" are all female and Greek, both personal and immemorial. Her psychic revolution takes sexuality as its vehicle, or perhaps as its highway, but the goal is self-exploration; not vehicle or highway but river or mountain is its goal—a universal landscape.

In making this tiny survey of recent poetry, I wanted to talk mostly about new or young poets. But I want also to praise a book that collects parts of a longer life, Robert Creeley's *Selected Poems.** Generally the selection is good; one misses "After Lorca," and "The Hill," but there is *plenty* here to please eye and ear and mind and spirit. Creeley is funny, insightful, domestic, amorous, and moving. He writes a

---

* Robert Creeley, *Selected Poems* (New York: Scribner, 1977).

"not-poetry" like Bidart's (he omits metaphor and simile) but he does not resemble Bidart, because Creeley keeps far from narrative and dramatic monologue. Personal speech is his focus, its own texture and local color taking the place of image, character, or scene. There is the famous "I Know a Man," Creeley's "Lake Isle of Innisfree," which is comic, ominous, and natural:

> As I sd to my
> friend, because I am
> always talking,—John, I
>
> sd, which was not his
> name, the darkness sur-
> rounds us, what
>
> can we do against
> it, or else, shall we &
> why not, buy a goddamn big car,
>
> drive, he sd, for
> christ's sake, look
> out where yr going.

No ideas but in things, said William Carlos Williams; no ideas but in *talk*, says Creeley.

If the object (and the material) is Creeley's exact and particular New England speech, the subject is the "I" as it approaches others, or tries to govern feelings and conduct in relationship to others. The great subject in Creeley is love, and he is a rare modern poet obsessed by the pairing of a man with a woman.

> Love, if you love me,
> lie next to me.
> Be for me, like rain,
> the getting out
>
> of the tiredness, the fatuousness, the semi-

lust of intentional indifference.
Be wet
with a decent happiness.

There's warmth and generosity in many of these poems. In others, Creeley plays word games, almost like blind old Thurber, practicing his footwork as he breaks lines, and pauses, and turns:

The bird
flies
out the
window. She
flies.

The foot moves well, but I love the poems most when the dance represents domestic matters—after hours in the practice room repeating motions in a mirror, the encounter with life and death. My favorite of all Creeley poems is his recent elegy, "For my Mother: Genevieve Jules Creeley," from which I excerpt only a few lines:

Tender, semi-
articulate flickers
of your

presence, all
those years
past

now, eighty-
five, impossible to
count them

one by one,
. . .

. . . They want
to make you

happy when
they remember. Walk
a little, get

up, now, die
safely,
easily, into

singleness, too
tired with it
to keep

on and on. . . .

Such dancing is not easy. Only the work of a lifetime—
including the poems which look like exercises—prepared
him to write the poem.

Reznikoff, Snodgrass, Budbill

(1978)

When Charles Reznikoff observed a handsome woman aging, he made note of it:

> Holding the stem of the
> beauty she had
> as if it were still
> a rose.

His note became poem XXXIV of *Autobiography: New York*, published originally in 1941. Born in Brooklyn, Reznikoff died two years ago at the age of eighty-one in Manhattan, where he had lived most of his life. Black Sparrow Press has brought out his *Collected Poems* in two volumes—and every page is generous, affectionate, compassionate. Reznikoff records natural things and city streets, making his own Lake District from the New York blocks where he loved to walk:

> The avenue of willows leads nowhere;
> it begins at the blank wall of a new
>   apartment house
> and ends in the middle of a lot for sale.
> Papers and cans are thrown about the trees.
> The disorder does not touch the flowing branches;
> but the trees have become small among the
>   new houses

and will be cut down;
their beauty cannot save them.

In language that never calls attention to itself, in poetry almost transparent, Charles Reznikoff for sixty years rendered life as it is—as it passed, as the trees came down. He wrote about people observed in subways, in markets, he wrote about New York faces. Sometimes he told stories out of his reading, delicate and exact selections of story and image, recounting with compassion anecdotes from American labor history, or in a late volume called *Holocaust* tales of the Nazis' victims.

He was little read in his lifetime, routinely pigeonholed as an "Objectivist." Perhaps the transparency of his voice accounts for his obscurity, and perhaps his relative obscurity left him free, unencumbered by the celebrity of the poetic platform, to wander unknown among the things of this world, observing and recording with a tender fidelity.

It is fitting that his work be recovered for us not by a big publisher but by a small press. Black Sparrow Press, of Santa Barbara in California, is small compared to Doubleday and Scribner's, but among private presses it is a backyard Gutenberg, a cottage Caxton. Black Sparrow makes beautiful books, and rides high among small American presses. My copies of Reznikoff are soft-cover, a gray stock printed in red ink with a border that is green for the first volume and blue for the second. Each volume's end papers repeat the border's color.

Other small publishers from coast to coast print much of the best new American poetry. The best is good, and amazingly widespread. More poetry is written and published today than ever before in the United States, and more copies are sold. But if poetry sells, it sells only at a clip that is modest and reliable; no publisher suffers from the illusion that his poetry books may run away with the best-seller list, or become a six-part series on ABC. Big publishers print most of the better-known poets, and to a degree they act as major leagues to the small presses' Triple-A; they draft potential superstars. But small publishers take an increasing part of the whole market. Their distribution is not so good, but their attention is more focused. What poet in history could compete for his publisher's time with the latest *Book of Lists*? Poets may find it preferable to publish with a one-person firm, when that one person puts everything into the book.

In 1960, W. D. Snodgrass won the Pulitzer Prize for *Heart's Needle*, published by Knopf. Last year he published a new collection of poems with BOA Editions of Brockport, New York. *The Führer Bunker* is an audacious book: a series of dramatic monologues spoken by Nazis inhabiting the bunker with Hitler in Berlin just before the end. Snodgrass explores *extremity*: here are ultimates of evil, disloyalty, misplaced loyalty, hypocrisy, banality, desperation, and obscenity. The book is hard to take, to say the least. It provokes anger in many readers—as if it were pro-Nazi to imagine speeches for the Nazi leaders.

Snodgrass speaks from a vision of evil, a vision no longer *out there* among Germans only, but *in here*; this evil resides in the American soul, in the human soul, and not only in the souls of National Socialists. Snodgrass speaks in full consciousness of My Lai, of Attica, of Rhodesia and Cuba, of Gulag and Chile. Perhaps it is this conviction of human depravity that angers some readers. It is unpleasant to share one's humanity with these people: a minor Nazi goes before the firing squad shouting obscenities—until the bullets cut him off; Hitler meditates betrayals; Eva Braun sings *Tea for Two* as she thinks about her Führer in *22 April, 1945*: "I have it all. They are all gone, the others— / The Valkyrie; and the old rich bitch Bechstein; / Geli above all. No, the screaming mobs above all. / They are all gone now; He has left them all. / No one but me and the love-struck secretaries . . ." All the time, as her internal monologue continues its boasting, another part of her brain repeats a tune. Snodgrass shows this simultaneity by indentation and italics, as *"No friends or relations / On weekend vacations"* sings itself in counterpoint to: "That I, I above all, am chosen—even I / Must find that strange. . . ."

The Führer Bunker is "a cycle of poems in progress"; we can look forward—with dreadful pleasure—to an expanded and revised edition.

Many small presses are more modest than Black Sparrow and BOA Editions—small-budget, their books made for the moment, not for the ages. If the ages turn out to admire one of their poets, the ages are welcome to print their own editions—bound in blue cloth with gold lettering, perhaps. I love David Budbill's *The Chain Saw Dance*, modestly printed by Crow's Mark Press in Johnson, Vermont. These poems remind me of Reznikoff's, in their quiet attentiveness to the real world of McCullough and Stihl. And Budbill creates the dance as well as the saw. Looking at the reality closely, he sees parts move in a unison—sometimes graceless, sometimes ugly, always resolved in a human wholeness. Old man Pike ". . . took dinner and supper in the village / then walked home across the mountain in the dark." And:

> The old man could have stayed at home,
> milked cows, like everybody else,
> but he needed an excuse to go and come
> through the mountains, every day,
> all his life, alone.
>
> Old man Pike didn't believe in the local
>   religion of work,
> but out of deference, to his neighbors maybe,
> he bowed to it,
> placed its dullness at the center of his life,
> but he was always sure, because of his excuse,
> to wrap it at the edges of his days
> in the dark and solitary amblings of his
>   pleasure.

Budbill creates a Vermont town called Judevine, where people are poor, and drunk, and dear, and angry, and warm—and wholly real. In his own town he has suffered the fate of so many people who have described their neighbors: petitions against him, death threats, snubs on the street, local citizens' outrage. He wrote an honest book, and nothing makes people angrier. Someday they will name a street after him.

The Chain Saw Dance reads as a book, as an accumulation, in long strides, reminding you a little of *Spoon River*, but with more reality and less romance. Budbill writes out of the real, contemporary New England, not from the past, not from the cellarholes. He speaks from the New England which is Appalachia—poverty, exploitation, and good people; not from the hokey, urbanized "country" of Woodstock and Stowe, but from Judevine with its trailers, its mad widows, its farmers expropriated by agribusiness.

It's hard to quote from David Budbill. Read him—but you'll have to go the small presses to find him, as you will to find much of the best poetry in America.

A bookstore can do it, at least with the proper addresses. Or you can order by mail. Charles Reznikoff's books are *Collected Poems, Vol. I* and *Vol. II; Holocaust*; and there is *Charles Reznikoff: A Critical Essay*, by Milton Hindus: Black Sparrow Press, Box 3993, Santa Barbara, Calif., 93105. W. D. Snodgrass, *The Führer Bunker*, BOA Editions, 92 Park Ave., Brockport, N.Y., 14420. David Budbill, *The Chain Saw Dance*, Crow's Mark Press, Johnson, Vt., 05656. (1981: *From Down to the Village*, by David Budbill, reprints 2nd revises and expands his earlier work.

Robert Penn Warren[*]

(1981)

Robert Penn Warren's *Rumor Verified, Poems 1979-1980* follows last year's *Being Here, Poetry 1977-1978* which followed 1978s *Now and Then, Poems 1976-1978*. Over four years of publication, more than 250 pages of poetry. If you admire the work, as most critics do, it is the magnificent late flowering of a life in letters. A dense page at the end of *Rumor Verified* lists the many honors accorded Warren for poetry and fiction—three Pulitzers, a National Book Award, the Bollingen Prize, the National Medal for Literature, the Emerson-Thoreau Award, the Presidential Medal for Freedom. . . . Decades of work have not gone unrewarded. But for this reader, who may be a minority of one, praise for the late poems is misplaced, testimony to the literary world's habit of celebrating the brand name whatever the product.

Warren's language in *Rumor Verified* seems to me a collage of cliché, mixed metaphor, abstraction, and melodrama. We hear of "fading light," of "blind yearning," of "blind, groping rage toward meaning," and of "fleeting moments." If the "heart" is "more delicate, more / Intricate than" something, it will be "a Swiss watch." For imagery we have "Houses / Shrinking to pin-point white dots in distance." For the ex-

---

[*] Robert Penn Warren, *Rumor Verified, Poems 1979-1980*, (New York: Random House, 1981).

pression of an idea, we have "an empire unwittingly headed for the dump heap / of History." Most of these clichés are dead metaphors, leading to inevitable confusion: in "a river, serpentine / In flame, threads fields . . .", we have water turning into a snake which bursts into fire and is transformed into fiber.

Abstractions proliferate. In one short poem we have "love," "heart," "pastness," "hope," "despair," "doom," "future," "history," "ignorance," and "experience." The capitalized abstraction Time turns up fourteen times, along with Reality, Hope, Eternity, History, Space, and Truth. Cliché and abstraction compete with banality: "Have you ever seen your own child, that first morning, wait / For the school bus?" "This was only a trivial incident of / My middle years." ". . . success, / Particularly of a vulgar order, tends / To breed complacency in the logic of / Your conduct of life."

Failure of language becomes a subplot. Warren uses "wordless," "nameless," and "unnameable." Struggling for powerful speech, the poet falls into archaism: "But even / That last sacrifice availed naught." But Warren's main strategy, in his attempt at vigor, looks for energy in violence. "Going West" takes two pages to tell an anecdote about a pheasant crushed by the windshield of a speeding car. If it is an allegory of American murderousness, I do not think it survives its triviality—"Westward the Great Plains are lifting, as you / Can tell from the slight additional pressure / The accelerator requires"—as it ends in an orgy of sanguinary commonplace: "I have seen blood explode, blotting out sun, blotting / Out land, white ribbon of road, the imagined / Vision of snowcaps."

"I think of blood," says the poet in another poem, and indeed he thinks of blood for page after page. The knife's cutting edge is an obsessive image, with "eye-slashing blue" of sky and "curtain of rain" which immediately sheds fabric for metal to become "like a knife edge"; with "sun stabs the red splash;" with "heart-stab;" with "the scarlet slash;" with "storm knifing through" and "knife-edge of no-Time." Violence of description exceeds violence of action, and we have melodrama. When Warren describes the sound a stream makes, he writes, "In the gorge, like a maniac / In sleep, the stream grinds its teeth."

Elsewhere, not melodrama but awkward complexity of expression disguises the commonplace: bathers are "bare-hided but for / Beach-decency's minimum." Some lines are simply unsayable: "He, in characteristic passionlessness, now stands and /. . . ." Elsewhere, rhyme descends to doggerel, where the second line exists only to provide a rhyme for the first. "Slow to heal," he writes,

> Yellow as piss or orange peel,
>
> From eye-edge to mouth-edge, the slash in
> Flesh defined a man born not to win,
>
> But he plunged across the stream-
> In that instant less real than a dream. . . .

It is typical of Warren's carelessness that he gives us alternate colors—"piss or orange peel"—which are different indeed, unless one's urine is trying to tell one something.

Carelessness. Years back a critic titled a review, "The Careful Poets and the Careless Ones." Warren certainly began as a careful one, and perhaps his career is a history of throwing off his astutely cultivated restraints. Our literature is full of palefaces going redskin: there is something heady about letting go. But for this minority critic, Warren goes too far into the wilderness to return bringing us poems. On his way, he may have stumbled on a method—cliché and abstraction salted with violence—to write the poems his literary culture desires.

Ferris's Thomas*

(1977)

Dylan Thomas owed me two pounds when he died. Ten thousand people could make such a claim—and not a voice would be raised in doubt—who handed the money over, as I did, only pretending that it was a loan. And when Thomas asked for a loan—knowing he would never repay it, knowing you knew—he delighted in the lie, delighting in the poet as con man, pirate, or bad boy. Such play-acting could seem an innocent pleasure, but in his character it connected with pain.

There is as much talk of money—debts, borrowing—in Paul Ferris's excellent biography *Dylan Thomas* as there is talk of poetry; appropriately so, for in Thomas's adult life money loomed larger than poetry. Money in its absence, money abundant at rare moments and quickly squandered, with taxes unpaid on the brief abundance. Poetry became largely an absence also—ten poems written in the last ten years— with most of Thomas's hard writing, in the last seasons of his short life, devoted to begging letters. He drafted these letters over and over again, using Roget's help, as he did for his late poems. The letters resemble the poems, with their adjectival strategies, with their desperate multiplicity.

---

* Paul Ferris, *Dylan Thomas: A Biography* (New York: Dial Press, 1977).

Clearly he desired the debts he loathed. He made himself victim by regarding common sense, or planning ahead, or frugality as enemies of the poet. With money, as with drink, he fought valiantly in his own despite. Ferris's detailed and meticulous research, revealing a thousand things we had not known, makes the necessities of self-destruction as clear as road signs.

Ferris (himself from Wales) is a cool biographer, which befits a man writing about a legend. He shatters many rumors. He reports, he scrutinizes, he weighs, he accepts, he dismisses. He stands aside from his subject, neither advocate nor debunker. He reveals Thomas in his lies, disloyalty, self-deceit—and yet one hear's no edge of malice in Ferris's voice. In the wonderful details he assembles of Thomas's youth, one feels, on the contrary, a warmth; yet the biographer never asks our praise for his indulgence. With modest approaches to psychological analysis, Ferris provides suggestions toward understanding the absurd, demanding, complex figure of Dylan Thomas. The biography is scrupulous, well-made, horrifying and judicious.

Many of the legends Ferris has shattered concerned Thomas's death in November 1953. It is not true that Thomas's coma was diabetic. It is not true that he lay for hours in a rainy gutter outside the White Horse tavern. He slipped into coma while lying abed, feeling terrible, not long after a kindly doctor had injected him with a half grain of morphine.

You do not inject a half grain of morphine into an alcoholic who has trouble breathing.

This information was available before, in medical records, but was overlooked or misunderstood by earlier researchers; it seems possible that other doctors in attendance, although shocked at their colleague's incompetence, or malpractice, were loath to accuse a fellow. The drug-happy doctor—you can find one in any city who will give you the pills you want—died a few years ago. When alive he was questioned about his treatment of Thomas and would not answer questions, which Ferris calls "a wise course."

This new information seems at first to validate the old English notion that the Americans killed him. But it's not true. Dylan Thomas killed himself, as we knew all along, the slow suicide of alcoholism, and finally the begging for oblivion, for surcease of pain, which led to his craving for morphine. Whatever the doctor's competence, he gave the man what he wanted.

Thomas knew that he was going to die, and dreaded death; but hastened toward it. The night before he hit me for two pounds, he joked about wanting to die. It was the end of a long evening in Oxford; we drank beer together, sleepy and mildly drunk. I complained of someone writing about "the death wish" in a facile way, and out of the brutal innocence of youth asked rhetorically, "Who would want to die?" "Oh I would," said Thomas; and added, for softening; "Just for the change."

Tomlinson's House of Memoir[*]

(1980)

Some writers erect monumental autobiographies that detail childhood struggles for identity, failures and achievements, until—600 pages later—a hand describes itself writing a final page. To the side of such pyramids stand the smaller houses of memoir, in which modesty is a method if not a conviction, in which writers concentrate on one area of their lives, or ostensibly on people other than themselves. It is a sneaky form of autobiography, and on the whole I prefer it.

For instance, Charles Tomlinson's *Some Americans, A Personal Record*—in the wonderful series of brief Quantum Books issued by the University of California Press—gathers in its 134 pages a variety of pleasures. A British poet of the first rank, Mr. Tomlinson is more indebted to modern American poetry than are any of his peers. In "Some Americans," he touches on his beginnings as a poet, describes his isolation in England, and records the process by which he educated himself in an alien literature.

A different pleasure is Mr. Tomlinson's sensitivity to landscape. When we read his descriptions of Brooklyn or New Jersey, New Mexico or Italy, we recall that the poet is also a painter. He evokes a drive in New Mexico: "Among the

---

[*] Charles Tomlinson, *Some Americans, A Personal Record* (Berkeley, Calif.: University of California Press, 1980).

259

ghostly greys of the winter cottonwood trees, behind the tin-roofed adobes, along the banks of the snow-filled Rio Chama, everything rekindled, glittered, sending up mica showers, crossing blades of light."

But the best parts of this book are the character sketches of American poets. In the first essay the young Tomlinson visits the United States and meets his generous American elders. The portrait of Marianne Moore is especially vivid, showing forth her affection, her humor and her literary intelligence; no one has captured her as well as Mr. Tomlinson. And he writes engagingly about William Carlos Williams, energetic despite a series of strokes, welcoming, enthusiastic. As the author writes, "It is strange to have met the innovators of one's time only when age had overtaken them." "Some Americans" is about aging as well as about poets, poetry and landscape.

In Mr. Tomlinson's America there is room for a variety of poets, and he interprets them judiciously. Meeting Yvor Winters in California, Mr. Tomlinson praised another poet by using a word Winters was not fond of. "'Original?' said Winters; 'there is no particular virtue in originality, you know.'" Mr. Tomlinson's understanding of Winters is exact: "One could imagine a tone in which that could have sounded crushing, yet it was offered not coldly but rather as advice." When Mr. Tomlinson describes George Oppen and Louis Zukofsky in the book's second essay, he embodies character as well as he judges it; two shadowy figures walk into light as the author relates with melancholy scrupulosity the quarrel that developed between them late in their careers.

The last two chapters of the book are less coherent as essays. A visit to Georgia O'Keeffe in New Mexico is brief and enigmatic; but Mr. Tomlinson's admiration for her work (and for the landscape of her paintings) makes the prose a pleasure. The last chapter, about his experiences in Italy, portrays the by-then silent Ezra Pound and praises the old Italy while lamenting its prosperous self-destruction. Mr. Tomlinson's feeling for Italy helps us to remember how English a figure he is—one who exists in Britain mostly at the edges of literary favor, still charged by some with the treason of modernism.

Of course, Mr. Tomlinson is not alone among British poets in his relationship to American modernist poetry. His tutor at Cambridge was Donald Davie, who showed the young Tomlinson a Williams poem in a pub outside Cambridge in 1946. The student's eyes fell not so much on the Williams poem as on another in the same anthology, Wallace Stevens's "Thirteen Ways of Looking at a Blackbird." It was a few years before he added plain Williams to dazzling Stevens.

Charles Tomlinson, Donald Davie and a few younger English poets have learned from the American modernists; few contemporary Americans have learned from any British poet but Auden, whose influence has been largely disastrous. The two poetries, sharing a common origin, have become separate. Such widely different English poets as Geoffrey Hill and Philip Larkin are equally un-American; such widely different Americans as Robert Creeley and Galway Kinnell are equally un-English. Yet it will be a pity if we can no longer learn from each other, as Charles Tomlinson has learned from some Americans.

The Long Foreground of Walt Whitman*

(1980)

As Justin Kaplan says of *Leaves of Grass*, "There is nothing quite like it in literature." Yet when Whitman mailed Emerson a copy of the first edition, in 1855, the philosopher of transcendence—who knew nothing of Whitman, whose own verse was conventional—responded with a letter of unmatched generosity and insight. Emerson welcomed Whitman "at the start of a great career" and spoke of "the long foreground" that must have preceded such a collection.

In this delicate, calm, and painstaking biography (*Walt Whitman: A Life*, Kaplan attempts ". . . to look for the biographically rational line of development that led from the journalist-loafer to the incomparable poet. . . ." The question has persisted: what made this man a great poet? Emerson's "long foreground" grows more puzzling as we first learn of Whitman's background—his family, his childhood and youth, the education which ended when he was eleven, his alternate work as desultory journalist and unhappy schoolteacher. . . .

The common answers beg more questions. If Whitman was Emersonian, Emerson's package of ideas is commonly available in the nineteenth century, not only in Emerson but

---

* Justin Kaplan, *Walt Whitman: A Life* (New York: Simon & Schuster, 1980).

in Thomas Carlyle and in romantic German philosophers. His nationalist or democratic dogmas, reduced to prose, sound like a thousand newspapers of his time. Other poets prophesied American epics—and wrote *Hiawatha*. It is the poetry itself, and only the poetry itself, which is new. Still, no amount of reference to Hebrew parallelism, to the King James Bible, or to the Bible-bathed oratory of the day will account for the mighty line Whitman invented. No record of his reading explains the virtual surrealism of "The Sleepers," or the monumental innovative construction of "Song of Myself." Kaplan summarizes: ". . . for all such parallels, resemblances, echoes, borrowings, or influences, whether direct or reflective of the spirit of the age, it is useless to look outside Whitman himself. . . ."

Yet not quite useless: by his orchestration of detail, Kaplan shows us not one or two sources for Whitman's images and innovations but a thousand sources, amounting to a foreground. His method is not to analyze a poem for its origins, as Lowes did with "Kubla Khan," but to recount the dense days of a life, the incidents of a busy Manhattan—and then to juxtapose a relevant line from a poem; let the reader note and judge the connection. Others have suggested the importance of photography to Whitman's vision; Kaplan juxtaposes Whitman's emblem of the mind—"In a little house picture I keep"—with both "Plumbe's daguerrotype gallery on Broadway" and the cover illustration of a magazine devoted to phrenology. Others have noted Whitman's use of the language of contemporary pseudoscience, animal magnetism as well as phrenology; Kaplan quotes widely from this esoterica, adds Whitman's reading in the Egyptian religion of Osiris, documents his addiction to grand opera. . . . The accumulation of ingredients considerably reduces, while it does not dispel, the mystery of the long foreground.

Whitman may or may not have *believed* in these pseudosciences. In Kaplan's words, they "supplied him with a structure of belief, the underpinnings of a personal mythology." He used them as Yeats used his gyres and phases of the moon. Whitman reminds us also of Yeats's doctrine of self and anti-self, for Whitman shows a familiar doubleness—the man who is his own opposite. In an example which Kaplan beautifully delineates, Whitman proclaims himself the prophet of molecular survival, compost-heap immortality, who will become the grass we walk upon; and on the other hand, Whitman becomes the architect-Pharoah of his own gross and impregnable tomb. This contradiion—it cannot be called hypocrisy—repeats itself throughout his life. The author of *Mr. Clemens and Mark Twain* is alert to every occasion of paradox.

Kaplan begins his narrative toward the end of Whitman's life, with Traubel's well-documented Whitman of Mickle Street in Camden: the old man who wonderfully described himself as "crafty and furtive like an old hen." Kaplan is not so nervous as earlier writers on the subject of Whitman's sexuality—that subject about which we know little and all we need to know. The general direction of Whitman's sexual feelings is clear, and it is clear that his homoerotic feelings underlie—and supply images for—egalitarian ideas.

After Whitman's death, Kaplan returns to the beginning. He was a family man, close to his mother, to his sisters, and to several brothers, notably to Jeff the youngest, to Eddy who was feeble-minded, and to practical George, who put him up in Camden when he suffered his first strokes. Father Walter is a difficult character, apparently a drunkard and certainly unlucky, who embodies a strain of the American character that has received too little attention. Walter was enlightened and grumpy, free-thinking, populist, anti-capitalist, a village atheist-socialist before his time. . . . I think of all the little pamphlets which sold for a nickel, as recently as the 1930s, featuring speeches by Ingersoll and Darrow, fearless denunciations of Popery, imperialism, railroads, and intolerance. . . . Uneducated, self-educated, inferior to no one, this yeoman-class contributed its intractable spunk to the first hundred and fifty years of the United States . . . and it has disappeared in our society of technology, bureaus, and narcissism.

Kaplan is a superb biographer, a master of the forms of factuality, who understands the poignancy of exactness: the names of the opera singers Whitman thrilled to, their voices gone forever. He excels in relating physical details: "He weighed two hundred pounds and was about six feet tall, had big hands and feet. . . . His body was rosy and soft, like a child's, and his skin . . ."—how wonderful the word "rosy". . . . We hear of Whitman's annual lecture on Lincoln, which even Charles Eliot Norton and James Russell Lowell attended—not to mention Mark Twain, José Marti, and the American French symbolist poet Stuart Merrill. We learn that Whitman as a child attended Lafayette's return, that he saw John Jacob Astor plain, and that he watched Junius Brutus Booth play Richard III on June 8th, 1835, when he was sixteen years old. As a young newspaperman, before *Leaves of Grass*, he knew Edgar Allan Poe (who published his journalism); he knew William Cullen Bryant; he saw Charles Dickens on his first American tour. . . .

We delight to discover Pfaff's beer cellar, and the wits who gathered there, men and women, including the great Adah Isaacs Menken, who "attempted a liason with Swinburne but failed to earn the ten-pound reward that Dante Gabriel Rossetti offered if she got Swinburne into bed. . . ." Pfaff's central figure is Henry Clapp, editor of the *Saturday Press*, as witty as George S. Kaufman. We observe with appropriate compassion Whitman's impossible loves, for Peter Doyle especially, and the impossible love women felt for him—especially Anne Gilchrist.

We learn as well that Whitman pronounced "poem" (in the manner of New York) "pome." In this enunciation he was different—as in all things. Even Whittier, the only non-patrician among the New England poets, had more education than Whitman had. The Bostonians all wore their three names like Phi Beta Kappa keys—while Walt diminished his own name by one syllable. Consciousness of his difference—in money, in education, in sex—helped him to seek out and affirm his difference as a poet.

The most literal, visible, obvious difference in his poetry is his long, asymmetrical line—a line with many pauses in it, which repeats its rhythm unmetrically, and which does not rhyme. The difference is wholly important, because when he tosses it aside—notably in "O Captain My Captain"—he writes conventional junk, less competent than the well-worked verses of the Bostonians. Many poets have attested to the efficacy, even the primacy, of sound or rhythm—have attested that noise comes first and content after. Some poets flounder for years until they find a personal line, then flower with it. A painter like Franz Kline makes a parallel, ordinary until he discovers his own calligraphic "voice."

Only when Whitman discovers Whitman's *line* can he write *Leaves of Grass* and become the greatest of our poets. For if "Out of the Cradle Endlessly Rocking" is not the greatest poem written by an American (as I would call it) then that poem is "Song of Myself" or "Crossing Brooklyn Ferry" or "When Lilacs Last in the Dooryard Bloom" or "The Sleepers."

Justin Kaplan is a biographer worthy of his subject, not least because he can *write*. He ends the book, taking us back to the time of the book's beginning, with this sentence: "An old man who never married and had no heart's companion now except his book, he rode contentedly at anchor on the waters of the past."

Hugo*
Like a Man Talking

(1979)

Richard Hugo has the knack of always sounding like himself. *The Triggering Town* consists of "Lectures and Essays on Poetry and Writing," and every page reads like a man talking, a man who celebrates, blames, remembers, argues, praises and reveals. We listen, alternately nodding and shaking our heads, always aware of one man's voice.

The best writing here is reminiscence. In the book's longest essay Mr. Hugo remembers being a bombardier in wartime Italy, then describes a return to that country in 1963. This memoir finds its legitimate place in *The Triggering Town* because Mr. Hugo intersperses his sensuous, sustained prose with poems that derive from the experience described, a doubling that makes for perspective.

In the argumentative and pedagogical essays that make up most of the book, Mr. Hugo's manner is a foxy informality, relaxed to the point where you believe he may fall off the stool, as informal as Perry Como—and whenever we become beguiled, Mr. Hugo makes an apothegm. This book is full of sentences about writing that, if one were talented at cross-stitching, one might stitch into samplers to hang over

---

* Richard Hugo, *The Triggering Town: Lectures and Essays on Poetry and Writing* (New York: W. W. Norton, 1979).

one's desk. "In the world of imagination," he tells us, "all things belong. If you take that on faith, you may be foolish, but foolish like a trout."

He is full of excellent advice for beginning writers: "The subject should serve the words. This may mean violating the facts. For example, if the poem needs the word 'black' at some point and the grain elevator was yellow, the grain elevator may have to be black." "Sometimes the wrong word isn't the one you think it is but another close by . . . look to either side of it and see if that isn't where the trouble is." And he is fine on teaching: "Teachers, like policemen, firemen, and service personnel, should be able to retire after twenty years with full pension. Our risks may be different, but they are real."

Within English departments in the United States, war smolders between the creative writers and the Ph.D's. One of the causes of this war is the division between the teaching of writing and the teaching of literature. I find such a division artificial, but Mr. Hugo thinks of them as different disciplines, and fires some telling shots: "I doubt that academic writing will improve until academics believe Valéry, who said he couldn't think of anything worse than being right. In much academic writing, clarity runs a poor second to invulnerability." I don't know whether Mr. Hugo's conviction that creative writing has little to do with reading is a prideful reaction to academic snubs, but I find it worrisome; where will poetic standards come from if we do not find them in Cowper and Donne, Marvell and Blake, Hardy and Wordsworth? If you measure your own work against your workshop peers, or against your peers in the magazines, you swim in a small, heated swimming pool. The ocean is colder, full of sharks like Keats and Dickinson, but it allows more room for growing.

We part company elsewhere: when Mr. Hugo asks for short sentences, banishes the semicolon as ugly and argues against the conjunction. Demonstrating a revision, he steps back from a newly derived compound sentence and says of his clauses: "Now they are equal. Style and substance may represent a class system. The imagination is a democracy." But the society of simple sentences, or of compounds linking comradely arms with "and" or "or," reminds me of George Orwell's dronelike proles. Faced with this coordinate mass, I must defect to the White Guard of complex, subordinated, even periodic aristocracy.

For all Mr. Hugo's advocacy of this democracy, he writes in his own prose and poetry a mean subordinate clause. The contrast is typical of his manner: relaxation relieved by epigram. It seems to me that American poetry now is afflicted with simplicity, with a tendency toward artificial naïveté, and with the willed transparencies of basic syntax. In this good book, which accuses itself as often as it defends itself, Mr. Hugo makes a wonderful confession: "I confess I'm not nearly as naïve as I sometimes appear. . . . Our vulnerability can also be unhealthy, the social counterpart of the kind of exposure some report to the police." This sentence is naïve the way a fox is dumb, the way a trout is foolish.

Two Critics*
Molesworth, Vernon

(1981)

Criticism is rarer than poetry. It is easy to prove such an assertion, yet I still find it flabbergasting. Great poets in English outnumber great critics five to one, and good poets good critics. If it is depressing to look at *Poetry*'s poetry twenty-five years back, it is five times as depressing to read its book reviews.

Or maybe ten times. If criticism in general is difficult, it is twice as difficult to judge the contemporary. Different sorts of critical ability occur separately. One sort of intelligence performs brilliantly when given a text to perform on, but for heaven's sake never let this intelligence choose its own text: judgment is wholly absent. The analyst of the grandfathers (Eliot, Stevens, Pound) can make a bad reviewer of the grandsons. Thus Hugh Kenner, whose *Pound Era* makes him the best critic of modernist literature, mistakes himself when he reviews James Wright's *Pear Tree*. Thus Helen Vendler, well equipped to scrutinize an agreed-upon text, lacks judgment to discriminate among the new. Judgment begins as intuition before intelligence takes breath to analyze; but people

---

* Charles Molesworth, *The Fierce Embrace: A Study of American Poetry* (Columbia, Mo.: University of Missouri Press, 1981). John Vernon, *Poetry and the Body* (Champaign, Ill.: The University of Illinois Press, 1981).

with judgment are rare—and often lazy about reasoning their intuitions into arguments.

When a critic of the contemporary shows good judgment and good analysis, we are lucky. Charles Molesworth's *The Fierce Embrace*, is excellent criticism of Lowell and Ginsberg, O'Hara and Kinnell and Levine, and above all Robert Bly.

Not everyone will like it. First, Molesworth is afflicted with a vocabulary, and given to words like "catachrestic" and "etiology"; sometimes he falls into academic language when he could speak more simply. I find the habit annoying but finally trivial, because the intelligence is genuine despite its attempt to appear intelligent. Second, Molesworth's literary sensitivity seems to me limited, not balanced among all the qualities of poetry. He seems imbalanced toward responsive understanding, toward paraphrase and summary. He seldom speaks intimately of sounds, rhythm or mouth-sound either; he seldom speaks of the minute collisions of language, the exquisite contrasts and resolutions of language which create the poem's intimate form. He *does* speak of grammar, as few critics do.

His genius is a thorough, capable, inward comprehension of a poem's import, from its social tone to its metaphysical wanderings. Not only a poem's but a poet's, for he is excellent—with a rare excellence—at generalizing about a poet's whole work, taking the long view and being particular about it.

Molesworth also excels at another difficult task, at seeing and describing aspects of the scene of poetry, the social and literary context of it—almost the sociology of poetry. Among the chapters on Roethke and Wright, he poses interchapters on "The Poet and the Poet's Generation," on "Magazines and Magazine Verse."

There is a fierce puritanism in Molesworth, a prophetic denunciation of "the emotional vacuity of public language in America and the insistent psychologizing of a society adrift from purpose and meaningful labor." This sentence comes from a chapter that attacks some poems I love, and *of course* I find Molesworth wrong from time to time. (If I agreed with him all the time he would not be useful to me.) I think he is wrong on late Lowell, on middle Snodgrass. . . . And every time I argue with him I learn from him. So with another contemporary critic whose work I admire and need, Robert Pinsky. Pinsky finds Bly's work almost as loathsome as Molesworth finds it valuable. For that reason Pinsky is especially valuable to anyone who, like me, admires Robert Bly.

It is on Bly that Molesworth excels, in twenty-six pages dense with observation and intelligence. These days, Bly and his work seem to excite either worship or scorn—neither of which tend to inform the brain. Although Molesworth clearly admires Bly, he is no worshipper; he remains shrewd. Molesworth quotes Bly on reason and technique ("What is important is this rebellious energy, not technique. Technique is beside the point . . .") and comments:

> Such a doctrine, in the hands of unskilled enthusiasts (critics as well as poets), might easily spell bathos. But the theories of Eliot and Pound had begun to do the same when Bly wrote this. Few phenomena need a clarifying historical context more than literary theories do; we can identify what past and established theories these words are attacking more easily than we can see, precisely, where they will lead. Thus, Bly's poetics resembles his populist political sentiment: it is rooted in deep feeling, intimately "known" but seldom analyzed, and often more vigorous in its denials than its affirmations.

Alone among Bly's critics Molesworth takes a long view in which oppositions of politics and pastoral reveal their triviality. Alone among the critics, he understands that Bly is a religious poet. . . .

But read the book.

And on the other hand, John Vernon's *Poetry and the Body* is expressionist criticism, urging an attitude toward poetry which also is a way to read poetry—and demonstrating this reading in metaphor and by example:

> The style of a poet is nothing more than the personality expressed in his bodily gestures; since poems themselves are

bodily gestures, they will naturally express this personality as well as the way the poet dresses or lights his cigarette. But since poems are bodies themselves, they will also express their own unique personalities, related to but distinct from the poet's. It is true that the poet speaks the poem, but the poem also speaks itself, and this is because it is a body.

There are antecedents to these ideas in Rémy de Gourmont, in Paul Valéry, in Suzanne Langer; in an essay on Whitman, Galway Kinnell has made similar connections between body and word, vowel, phoneme. Yet Vernon explores the relationship more thoroughly than anyone, in a critical language which is itself bodily and expressive, making criticism which reads like a long prose poem about poetry.

And therefore, I think, he will have few readers among people who need him—American students and critics of poetry. In the last twenty or thirty years, American literary folk have developed a distrust, even a hatred of metaphor. When Eliot wrote about "Tradition and the Individual Talent," he turned his thought on a scientific analogy; when Pound defined the image, he used a metaphor of electricity. But when I read contemporary criticism in the American quarterlies, I find either bland referential language or the jargon of structuralism. Here on the other hand is John Vernon:

> The same is true of Whitman's language. Words in Whitman are never more comfortable than when they occur in large numbers, when they not only signify the democratic plenitude of the world, but also become part of that plenitude. Whitman's poems are not coiled springs, as Donne's and Mallarmé's are. It rarely happens that any one particular word becomes more important than another. The word in Whitman opens rather than closes the poem. In Mallarmé, the poem backs up or becomes lodged in individual words, but in Whitman, the word is the tip of a lash, the mouth of a river. The word, in fact, isn't as important as the energy that gives rise to and passes through words. Often, words tend to dissolve into the line, in the same way letters dissolve into words.

Mallarmé and Whitman are two of the poets chiefly attended to, or cited by way of indicating the range of Vernon's bodily reading. Others are Donne, Blake—and with *great* effect Robert Creeley. The extent of the occasions argues the flexibility of the method.

English departments make bad philosophy departments, as a glance at the "logic" of freshman English makes clear. Today, English departments are haunted by pseudo-positivists who growl at colorful and figurative speech: "Say what you mean." Plain talk is honest—we are given to understand—fancy talk a cover-up. A result of this attitude is textbook anthologies which footnote poets' metaphors, turning them into abstract prose. (The Norton Modern is especially revolting, with its paraphrase of Hart Crane's "Invariably as wine redeems the sight" as "In a state of visionary drunkenness.") Therefore English departments, teaching literature to the young, teach the distrust of metaphor, and occupy themselves with turning poetry into prose—as if that was what the poor idiot poet was "trying to say."

Vernon's *Poetry and the Body*, delighting in a great variety of poets and poems, attends to what is special about poetry. The whole is a hymn to the body and to sexuality, by which the poem is glorified. Paradox is by necessity Vernon's major trope. One can become irritated by its necessity: if A is regarded as moving UP, we soon discover that it must simultaneously move DOWN. But Vernon's vision is the simultaneity of opposites and he must dance his dance among figures of paradox and enantiodromia. Never is a paradox decorative.

Of course Vernon renders what is *said*, but he attends to the saying not by the vulgar use of semantic equivalents, but by calling our attention to the specifically poetic meanings—of syllable and line break, vowel and consonant—by which what is said gets said. It is an antidote—an embodied opposite—to the new dry-as-dusts who dominate the teaching and the criticism of literature today. People will sneer at

274

John Vernon for resembling Walter Pater, people who have not read Pater, and who ought to read Pater.

So Molesworth with energy and passion focuses his intelligence on intellectual summary; Vernon with sensuous vehemence describes the saying and only late arrives at what is said. Myself, I need Molesworth more than I need Vernon; I think most contemporary readers need Vernon more than they need Molesworth. Of course it is clear enough that they need each other—though I denigrate neither of them by saying so; and I am not sure that they can even *read* each other. Put them together, I mean to say, and they make a perfect critic; so do a double reading, add and divide by two.

Hoffman's Slovenly Map[*]

(1980)

The scheme of this book—twelve essays by ten authors—is one of its problems. After essays on "Intellectual Background" and "Literary Criticism," we find chapters on fiction; first comes "Realists, Naturalists, and Novelists of Manners," in effect an elephant's graveyard for novelists not considered under the following subcategories: "Southern Fiction," "Jewish Writers," "Experimental Fiction," "Black Literature" and "Women's Literature." The "Jewish Writers" do not include poets; apparently Jews write fiction. Both "Black Literature" and "Women's Literature" devote some attention to poetry and essay, but largely list and summarize novels. The scheme is nonparallel, awkward, and inefficient. Some novelists turn up several times under different labels. Others turn up not at all; many of the young remain unindexed: Tom McGuane, Larry McMurtry, Craig Nova, Gayl Jones, Laurie Colwin, Jim Harrison. . . .

After "Women's Literature" the *Guide* concludes with "Drama" and three essays on poetry which the editor has assigned to himself. Doubtless the scheme of categories is the editor's attempt to control a multiplicity of detail; it does not work. These categories only reveal that some novelists are Jewish or Southern whom one might otherwise indentify

---

[*] Daniel Hoffman, ed., *Harvard Guide to Contemporary Writing* (Cambridge: Harvard University Press, 1980).

merely as novelists. Sub-categories are implictly belittling; to be "a Southern novelist" is to be a little less than a novelist, as "poetess" functions as a diminutive of "poet."

Of all the categories, Black is the least equivocal, because black culture is separate enough. But of course it is not *simply* separate, nor are the lines of separation clear and distinct. Within black culture and literature, as Nathan Scott acknowledges, there is a struggle between separation and assimilation, between the demotic and the standard. Scott prefers Ralph Ellison and the universities to Don L. Lee and the streets; as I see it, he underrates the best contemporary black poet, Etheridge Knight. If one were to do justice by way of sub-categories, in dealing with the black world alone, one would require further distinction.

Elizabeth Janeway is appropriately restless about the condescension implicit in "Women's Literature," and hazards some suggestions on the nature of her topic, which cannot be "books written by females," any more than Nathan Scott's category can derive from pigmentation alone. Confusion goes unresolved, and good writers go unmentioned. One might reasonably expect attention to Alison Lurie's novels in any survey of recent American fiction; Janeway mentions her in one sentence by way of illustrating a point. Perhaps Janeway omits her because Lurie does not write "women's literature"; perhaps Leo Braudy omits her, among the novelists of manners, because she is a woman.

Authors omitted matter less than whole topics omitted. During the years under discussion, the economics of writing have changed enormously. In 1945 fiction writers could hope to support themselves by writing short stories for magazines. By 1980 the market for short stories has almost disappeared, replaced by a market for nonfiction. Yet the scheme of this book omits separate consideration of essay, biography, or autobiography, which together account for much of the best prose of the period. Nowhere in these six hundred pages do we hear the names of the prose writers Frank Conroy, Peter Matthiessen, Edward Hoagland, or John McPhee.

But if short stories no longer boil pots, the form survives and remains vigorous. For some reason, we hear little about the short story here; Peter Taylor receives eight condescending lines from Lewis P. Simpson. Stanley Elkin's name occurs only in a list of writers identified as Jewish, and the best new practitioner of the form, Raymond Carver, goes entirely unmentioned.

Nor does this *Guide* entertain the subject of publishing; it assumes that "contemporary writing" exists in an economic vacuum. In this period conglomerates have acquired most large publishers, and the independent houses imitate their balance-sheet publishing. Fewer first novelists, short story writers, and poets find themselves published by New York or Boston firms. Instead, small publishers and university presses—the off-Broadway and regional theater of contemporary literature—begin to assume publication of writing that aspires to literature.

In poetry the leading form of publication has become the public reading. Living American poets read their poems thousands of times each year to hundreds of thousands of listeners. Constant public performance has altered the shape of the writing. Some observers—Jack Gilbert is one—feel that the poetry reading has been the ruination of American poetry, accounting for a thin glibness, because nothing complex or serious may be performed successfully to an audience of twenty-year-olds. Others assert that poetry has rediscovered its proper relationship to audience. One might have expected the subject to be explored further in a survey of contemporary American writing.

Even the better contributions omit more than they include. Professor A. Walton Litz conducts a gentle, intelligent summary of literary theory since 1945, full of Frye and Bloom. But the subject of literary criticism is unconnected with the judgment or description of literature. One of this book's ironies is the discrepancy between the theology of literary criticism, as outlined by Litz, and the practical parish work which occupies the rest of the book. Litz regrets that he cannot spend time on criticism that serves texts—on Hugh

Kenner, for instance—and that he must pass "over the great achievements in literary biography, such as Richard Ellmann's *James Joyce* . . . and Leon Edel's *Henry James.* . . ." Nor does he find time to mention literary biographies by Walter Jackson Bate and Justin Kaplan, which surely belong to the literature of the period.

Most inclusive of these essays is Gerald Weales's on "Drama." Not only does the author list and summarize plays, but he speaks of form and innovation, and mentions the conditions under which drama exists: Equity, Broadway, off-Broadway, off-off, regional theater.

If the scheme of the book omits topics and authors, it also sponsors a frantic prose style. Alan Trachtenberg has been known in other contexts to write an elegant prose. In his fifty pages of "Intellectual Background" here, he finds himself writing this sentence:

> Apart from rising protest movements and movements for social justice, notably the women's rights movement, a number of shocking events—the assassination of President Kennedy in 1963, of Malcolm X in 1965, of Martin Luther King in 1967, and of Robert Kennedy in 1968, and the Watergate scandal, which led to the resignation of President Nixon in 1974—fed an undercurrent of doubt, anxiety, instability in the period.

Reading these pages we run out of breath, not alas from outrage but from detail. Sometimes in the lust to list, one of our guides will raise, summarize, and dismiss a baker's dozen of writers in one paragraph. Here Daniel Hoffman disposes of some poets:

> Clarity and strength striate the poems of Charles Edward Eaton. The poems of Robert Fitzgerald and Richmond Lattimore are intensely poised between lyricism of feeling and classical restraint. David Slavitt's work is ironic and forceful.

These poets are not elsewhere described; if David Slavitt is worth only seven words, then he is not worth seven words.

Even when the writing is more competent, we have plot summaries, lists, and generalizations in place of quotation, formal analysis, or inquiry into the use of language. Mark Sheckner tells us the plot of a Malamud story like a ten-year-old summarizing a television cartoon:

> . . . Henry Levin, a young Jewish clerk who is "tired of the past," goes to Italy and, to conceal his identity and play up his readiness for sexual adventure, calls himself Henry Freeman. And on an island in Lake Maggiore he discovers nothing less than the girl of his dreams, Isabella del Dongo, who he takes for Italian nobility and pursues in the full awkwardness of his shlemielhood. . . .

Then after ridiculing the moral of the story, Sheckner disappears in a cloud of blurbtalk: "As imaginatively realized situation, however, the story is potent stuff, rich in conflict and implications. . . ."

Who *needs* this sort of thing? What sort of thing *is* this sort of thing? Leo Braudy compares his task to the cartographer's, making a "preliminary map." But if this book's categories are nonparallel and incomplete, if it omits not only writers but contexts of writing, what does the map guide us to? Not to contemporary American writing. Not to the state of literary criticism. I believe this book guides us to what happens in the American classroom, which is apparently no place for close reading, much less deconstructions or archetypes.

Perhaps the worst essay here is Josephine Hendin's on "Experimental Fiction." Hendin has no grasp of the adjective "experimental." In this passage, "it" seems to refer to her title:

> It may originate in the modernist sense of life as problematic, but unlike the great experimental fiction of the 1920s, it does not lament the brokenness of experience as a sign of the decline of western civilization.

Later she becomes more specific by exclusion: "Innovative in neither style nor form, postwar experimental fiction uses modernist or standard literary devices. . . ." For "experimental," then, we should read "derivative." Here is her final definition of the topic:

> What experimental fiction contributes to us is its perspectives, its faith in possibility. It makes us see in extreme and at times frightening images the impact of the postwar period on our imagination of ourselves at work, in love, and in the recesses of thought.

Surely when we refer to art as "experimental" we make analogy to the scientist's laboratory, and to formal experiment in the service of innovation—new approaches to a medium or to mixing media. Of course a critic may tie innovation to social, psychological, historical, or economic causes—but first the critic must establish the fact of innovation.

Hendin writes about authors who are mostly old-fashioned in literary form, including John Updike, J. D. Salinger, and Flannery O'Connor. She refers nervously to "eccentrics like William Burroughs," and comes closest to talking about form by referring in a parenthesis to his "cut-up method"—which she never exemplifies. She tells the plot of Coover's *The Public Burning* without mentioning its form. At one point in these pages she speaks of the "brief popularity of the non-fiction novel" and refers to Norman Mailer. *The Armies of the Night*, I would suggest, is experimental fiction the way a chicken is an experimental duck.

Nor is Hendin aware of the experimental fiction written and published in the last decade, mostly by small presses like the Fiction Collective and Tuumba. She mentions neither Harry Mathews nor Ronald Sukenick. But then, she would not know an experiment if it burnt like a bush in front of the Administration Building. Richard Kostelanetz, reviewing this *Guide*, has pointed out that Hendin wrote about these authors in an earlier book and made similar observations—except that in her earlier rendition she was not obliged to salt her prose with the word "experimental."

The editor's three essays on poetry comprise a third of this book. Professor Hoffman achieves an appearance of eclecticism and wide reading by the quantity of poets mentioned, but he gets his facts wrong, he makes absurd groupings, he is as conservative as Genghis Khan, and he omits mention of many remarkable poets. He seems unaware of the prominence of women in recent American poetry. He mentions a few women who were publishing in the fifties or sixties, but omits some of the best: Jane Cooper, Ruth Stone, Jean Garrigue, Jean Valentine. And he does not mention recent poets like Louise Glück, Carolyn Forché, Olga Broumas, Kathleen Fraser, Heather McHugh, Laura Jensen, Sandra McPherson, Cynthia MacDonald, Ai, Tess Gallagher, Mary Oliver. . . . Of course he would not wish to mention everyone—but he *does* attend to something like one hundred and seventy-six different poets. Mostly male.

Hoffman's prose is precarious. He tells us, of Marianne Moore, that "her courage and clarity are rock-ribbed by an old-fashioned Protestant ethic." He lets out the purple on Sylvia Plath: "She was living on the very edge, as though breathing a wild intoxicant in the very air. Poems poured out of her in a torrent. . . ." But he does not truly admire Sylvia Plath, and he uses a rhetorical device with which we become familiar in these essays: after summarizing a position which he finds extreme, he shows us a quiet or conservative alternative that accomplishes the same ends, far better, without upsetting anyone. After talking about Plath and suicide, he recommends to us a poet who died of cancer, L. E. Sissman, who is formal, conservative, quiet, Eastern, and male. "These quietly meditative and often wryly humorous poems are the testament of a brave man." One gets the point: Plath was an hysterical woman.

Mentioning visual poetry, Hoffman identifies two poets as "principle American 'concretists'"—using a term which the poets in question have been trying to suppress. Then he goes on:

> More fruitful unions of image and word have been offered by less dogmatic poets. William Jay Smith's playful children's book, *Typewriter Town* (1960), anticipated concretism's avant garde.

There has been considerable activity for the last fifteen years in the use of sound by itself, or sound-text, a movement which goes unmentioned, as does the school of poets associated with a magazine called *L-A-N-G-U-A-G-E*, and numerous other groups attempting to make it new. But doubtless Hoffman would find that they have been anticipated in some children's book or other.

Dealing with one hundred and seventy-odd poets, Hoffman has a problem in sorting them out. His first chapter is "After Modernism," which covers late modernism and continues through the twilight of Roethke, Berryman, Lowell, Warren, and Bishop. Fair enough. But then we have a chapter called "Schools of Dissidents," and another called "Dissidents from Schools," in which the reference to persecuted and exiled writers seems tasteless. The schools include confessional poets, the New York school, Black Mountain poets, and an association of Merwin, Bly, and Wright. The latter are accused of promulgating the Deep Image, a phrase actually used by Jerome Rothenberg and Robert Kelley; and John Logan is incorrectly identified as a Black Mountain poet.

When Hoffman comes to decide who belongs to the Establishment—a label guaranteed to inhibit thought—he must astonish T. Weiss and David Wagoner by revealing that they are bishops . . . and when he lists Dickey, Ammons, Simpson, and Stafford as *outside* the Establishment—prizewinners all, judges of literary contests—he will raise more eyebrows. We are informed that these latter are "Dissidents from Schools"—and they are joined in their dissidence by Anthony Hecht and John Hollander.

Other poets entirely omitted include David Ignatow, who

recently won the Bollingen, and Tom McGrath, Robert Francis, and Charles Reznikoff, and Robert Hass—as well as the many women listed earlier. Yvor Winters is mentioned as teacher, not as poet. And Kenneth Rexroth—whom I would call the best living American poet—is scolded as a polemicist and wholly ignored as a poet.

A somewhat less prominent poet, however, receives brief mention. After acknowledging that "to speak of my own work here would scarcely be appropriate," the editor adds that he "can, however, mention Richard Howard's chapter, 'Daniel Hoffman,' in *Alone With America*, and 'A Major Poet' by Monroe K. Spears (*Southern Review*, 1975)."

Then there is the matter of accuracy. Doubtless libraries have acquired this *Harvard Guide* as a reference work, but anyone who uses it for reference is in trouble. When Alan Trachtenberg speaks of "the moon landing of 1968"—the first man stepped on the moon in 1969—the error is trivial. But when Leo Braudy tells us that John Marquand also wrote under the name of John Phillips—which was actually a name used by Marquand's son when he wrote a novel—the error suggests either that Braudy has not read *The Second Happiest Day* or that he thinks John Marquand wrote it.

There are errors in almost every essay; rivers flow uphill on this map, and mountains are identified as lakes. Henry James was not a Bostonian but a New Yorker; Joyce Carol Oates wrote *them* not *Them*; the *Sot-Weed Factor* was published in 1960 not 1967. . . . Most errors, however, occur in the poetry chapters: Frost was not "past forty" when he published his first book; Pound did not live "with his daughter in Venice until at eighty-seven he died in 1972" but with his mistress Olga Rudge who was mother of his daughter; Yvor Winters did not begin as a "conservator of traditionalist" poetry but as an experimentalist; Apollinaire did not write a poem called "Un Coup de dés"; Charles Olson did not grow up in Gloucester but in Worcester; nor was "Ashbery . . . curator at the Museum of Modern Art and O'Hara an editor on Art News." (It was more like the opposite.) One could go on.

It may be noted that Harvard's connection to this misguided volume is limited to that institution's Press; none of the contributors teaches there. Yet the enterprise appears official: Harvard in the shape of its Press has lent its name, and the contributors teach at prestigious institutions, and the book is a selection of the *Readers' Subscription*, America's middlebrow book club; and Robert Penn Warren tells us on the flap that "The *Harvard Guide* . . . is invaluable. It has no rival." He may be right: this *Harvard Guide* is an unrivalled map to slovenly academic America.

IV

Notation

Letter from New Hampshire

(1978)

It's winter now, after a long cold autumn with little snow. Now the snow has come, and the hills are white, the ground under the bare maples white, the ground white between the snowy pines. The stone walls which we watched emerge from the foliage in the autumn—to mark out hills and fields in staggering squares—disappear under snow.

It's our second winter in this farmhouse, built in 1803. Nobody farms it now. Now it would be an expensive hobby, to farm this small and rocky place, to raise crops or animals in competition with *agribusiness*.

For many years I taught at the University of Michigan, and I am happy to quit for freelance writing, to leave behind what had become tedious—the increasing weight of institutions, *edubusiness*. If it's true that every historical period develops dominant social structures—which all smaller structures emulate, as in the Middle Ages the church dominated, and in the nineteenth century the imperial state—then the dominant structure of American twentieth-century society is the large business, is General Motors or AT&T: USA modelled on IBM. Certainly the universities, with their administrative bureaucracies, and their hierarchies of order, model themselves on big business. For that matter, they are nearly as inefficient. And in their catalogues, the universities boast about the number of citizens they *turn out*, and of the

289

variety suited to society's needs and requirements: some six cylinder, four seated citizens; some roomy big family eight cylinder citizens; not to mention station wagon citizens, pick-up citizens, four wheel drive citizens, and limousine citizens.

It's well to be away from *edubusiness*, but *poëbusiness* follows us everywhere.

There have been a number of outlandish developments in *poëbusiness* lately, not the least of which is its existence. When I use this gross word, I am not initially talking about poems; I'm talking about peripheries—organisations, circuits, schemes, networks, magazines, foundations, grants, and programs; I'm talking about Dial-a-Poem, Associated Writing Programs, Poets in the Schools, Poets and Writers, the Academy of American Poets, COSMEP and CCLM. I'm talking about the systems which have accumulated at the periphery of poetry, largely in the last decade, which collect and administer and distribute small sums of money. Of course these systems take a great deal of time and effort from people who might otherwise be writing poems. I presume that's why they exist; it's a good deal less taxing to administer an organisation than it is to write a poem.

Some of the organizations I have listed are worthy. Some are not. What's extraordinary is that there are so many of them, with newsletters and contests, fellowships and committees and conferences. What's more extraordinary, these numerous organisations represent only the visible three percent—The Establishment, as people say who don't know what the metaphor comes from—the Archbishops of *poëbusiness*. The plupart of *poëbusiness* is disorganised loosely into an *underground*, as it calls itself—the metaphor of the Maquis makes the *New York Times Book Review* and its lackey *Atheneum* into Nazis. Its method of publication is *samizdat*, which turns Howard Moss of the *New Yorker* into Stalin, and the uncollected makers of Boston into Josef Brodsky.

But *poëbusiness* has its effect on poems, too.

Quantity becomes everything, in poetry as it is in business. One young poet sends out a flyer about himself, soliciting readings, in which he reveals that he has published four hundred and twenty-six poems in the last three years. Another person submitting to magazines sends as reference a mimeographed sheet which lists one hundred and four magazines in which his work has appeared recently. A poet just turned thirty, we learn in a biographical note, is author of twenty-three books and pamphlets of poems, 'with seven more due this year.' The same disease infects the middle-aged: the head of an MFA program casually mentions to the circuit poet visiting the campus that he has "averaged selling two poems a week over the last twenty-eight months." When he has concluded his boast, he blows on his fingernails and pretends to polish them against his blue work shirt, in the timeless, shameless gesture of pride.

There are hundreds of magazines, and hundreds of small presses. Anything can be printed. Cheapness of reproduction allows everyone to edit, everyone his own sad Maxwell Perkins, publishing books and magazines of no quality, no hope, and no readers. Of course there are good small presses producing beautiful books, and there are good magazines, and some people write good poems, and publish them in these magazines and pamphlets. *But that's enough qualification*: almost everything printed, in this gross barrage of print, is disgusting, untalented, narcissistic, worthless garbage. In *poëbusiness*, there is no discrimination at all. In one of the small magazines that monitors the flood, some idiot recently praised a young woman's book, but showed his *discrimination* by saying that she was not yet in the class of Sexton, Lifshin, or Plath.

Around this phenomenon of quantity without discrimination, *poëbusiness* flourishes. There are service organisations like *Poets and Writers*, which publishes the enormous catalogue *A Directory of American Poets*, containing "information about more than fifteen hundred living poets" arranged by states, with indexes of poets belonging to racial minorities.

Coda, a cheerful bimonthly featuring articles like "Vanity Press: Stigma or Sesame?," tips on new magazines, words on ripoffs like poetry who's whos, news notes, contests, changes of address. . . . And it discriminates not at all between poets of quality and poets of no quality. Admission to the sacred name of poet—for listing in the Directory—is qualified; you must have published in five *different* magazines: then a panel decides.

Fifteen hundred living American poets?

Poëbusiness sponsors as well a new bureaucracy, young men or women who oversee programs in the schools, whereby poets (and often ceramicists, dancers, painters) visit school systems on a regular basis, performing their art for the children, and encouraging the children to participate. The bureaucrats are often academic dropouts, eager to live in the real world. They hire poets to talk to the children; they themselves are poets; they get together to publish magazines, maybe of their own poems, maybe of the children's poems, maybe both together. It doesn't matter, because everybody is terrible.

The vast amount of children's poetry being published— usually accompanied by the adult's essay showing how resourceful and sensitive he was in soliciting the child's poem—provides a clue to the disease. Once you've read fifteen or twenty children's poems, you've read them all. But they keep getting published. They cannot be published because the people who publish them think that they're good; they cannot be published because the people who publish them think that they will be read. Reading poems, it seems, is not the point; publishing them is.

Or reading them aloud. I suspect that there really *are* five thousand poetry readings a year in the San Francisco Bay Area, the way people say. In Ann Arbor when I arrived in 1957, there was a poetry reading every year or so. As I was leaving the university last year, there was one reading a week sponsored by the English department; a local coffeehouse supplied one more a week; there were weekly readings in a park in the summer, that moved inside to a bar in the winter; and other local institutions had provided readings from time to time. I suppose there must be at least two hundred a year now.

I used to like poetry readings. I suppose I still do, when a good poet reads well. But in Ann Arbor (and everywhere) there has grown the notion of the "open reading," when after a few advertised readers, *anyone* in the audience may rise to read poems. It's all fine, democratic, and excruciating—as people monumentally stupid and colossally untalented read interminable hymns to their own intelligence and genius.

After a while, one catches on. One doesn't go, even when invited as bait for the other suckers.

These vast numbers—who write poems, and who attend poetry readings; not necessarily identical; well, almost identical, necessarily—do not buy books of poems. Some of them develop considerable expertise about contemporary poetry by attending poetry readings and by listening well. The young can listen better than their elders can. But they can't—or at any rate they don't—*read books.*

Street corner love poet doing a booming business, headlines the *Ann Arbor News*, and the story details how Allen Berg writes love poems for "donations humbly and gladly accepted," including one that says. "You are / Yes you are? Yes you definitely are a moon in the morning / and a sun in your smile. . . ." Allen Berg as far as I can determine is not yet in *A Directory of American Poets*. He is not yet reviewed in *Small Press Review* or joked about in *AWP Newsletter*. His work is not yet listed among the two hundred odd poetry titles in the *Semi-Annual Checklist of Poetry* put out by the *Academy of American Poets*.

Poëbusiness depends upon a debased version of the democratic creed which says that, in one way or another, everything is in the way you look at it, isn't it?, so really, it's all opinion, and if you don't like Milton but you do like Allen

Berg on moons in the morning, why, your opinion is as good as anybody else's. How *egalitarian*, when all opinions are equal. A young man wrote me recently that he had never read a poem he didn't like, and I realised that I had been *waiting* for someone to tell me that. America is forever the country of Will Rogers, who told us that he never met a man he didn't like.

But if you like *all* poems, you don't like *any* poems.

I think of Robert Graves's experience, when he was viva'd in the twenties, hearing his examiners snootily reprimand him for appearing to like some poems more than others. For the examiners, fifty odd years ago, it was vulgar to express preferences among the texts on the shelf. For American pseudo-egalitarians today, it is undemocratic to claim that some poems are better than others: *all poems are created equal!* If we insist that some poems are *terrible*, that they shouldn't be printed—then we are Fascists!

Poëbusiness invents the Church of St. Narcissus. Everyone in the congregation is a preacher, and he or she speaks one long poem all his life. No one need pause in the monologue except for the occasional ritual applause. Pause for applause. Poems are built to be spoken and forgotten, temporary creations like styrofoam cups. Poems are only an action or a doing; they are not objects which in any sense retain existence after they are uttered. No, for poet and for audience, the point is to continue the performance of self-worship, without looking back. Who would want to return to a past even like yesterday's lunch? A *poëbusiness* poem resembles yesterday's lunch considerably more than it resembles a mountain or a chateau. These poets speak McDonald lunches with assurance that they will not be found wanting, since no one is listening anyway.

Pseudo-egalitarianism is the theology of narcissism, which is the corporate soul of *poëbusiness*.

By the time I finish this letter, it is nearly March. The winter has been the coldest ever recorded. My grandmother who lived here ninety-seven years never knew so cold a winter. Like her we burn wood to stay warm. Like her we look out each morning at a mountain which stays the same, whatever the radio or the newspaper tells us of news. Some things endure. Most things pass. In the United States there are people writing poems outside the church of self-regard, lines which partake of the spirit of stone wall and mountain.

A Note on Innovation

(1981)

Every good poem is innovative. Some people would invert
the order: every innovative poem is good. I agree, so long as I
define innovation. There is gross innovation and there is
minute innovation. In *Lyrical Ballads* Wordsworth was grossly
innovative; so was Apollinaire in *Calligrammes*; and each poet
was minutely innovative as well, making not only obvious
breaks with convention but continually inventing on the
cellular level of language—sub-cellular, atomic, even partic-
ular. They combined what seemed impossible of combina-
tion; they resolved the unresolvable. On the other hand E. E.
Cummings's gross innovations, mostly typographical, were
genuine so long as they were obvious, but worked to disguise
stale romantic language, weary old metaphors and
symbols—goatfooted balloon men, for goodness sake—and
clichés of Victorian and Edwardian magazine verse. If we
take a cliché—"basic assumption" for example, or "Yankees
clash with archrival Red Sox," or "mud wonderful"—and
print it in red ink on blue paper in Germanic script with
perfume on it and project it from four projectors on four
walls at once, with four people speaking it at four levels of
pitch and volume—we still use a cliché; though we may have
a nice party going.

And on the other hand Robert Frost, with sonnets and
blank verse and quatrains, with conventional signs, with

familiar syntax, innovated minutely and genuinely in his particular syntax and diction, in the relationship of sentence and line structure. Or, say: Thomas Hardy's poetry is weird, innovative, unlike anyone's before him, and largely inimitable; the same is true of his contemporary Hopkins, with the difference that it is obvious in Hopkins.

Which does not make the one better than the other.

The Poetry Notebook: One

(1981)

I

The invitation arrived in mid-December in an envelope bearing as return address *The White House*. Under an engraved eagle the card read, "Mrs. Carter requests the pleasure of your company at a reception to be held at The White House on Thursday afternoon, January 3, 1980 at four o'clock," while another card specified "A Salute to Poetry and American Poets." At four o'clock on January third a taxi delivered us to the wrong place. As we walked in view of our proper gate I saw a long line, maybe two-hundred people, doubtless dropped by tourist buses. I joked, "Look at the line of poets trying to get in!" We walked closer and faces turned familiar: it was the line of poets trying to get in.

In the *Post* the next morning a writer explained the delay. Many poets had neglected to inform the Social Secretary that they were planning to attend; the White House had expected seventy poets and wound up with a hundred and twenty. The delay was considerable, and some of the poets groused about it. Myself, I had nothing to complain about, because as we walked to join the line of pedestrians a poet friend drove up in his car; he offered his back seat, we got in, showed drivers' licenses to a guard, and drove inside to park on the grounds.

At the back of the White House where we entered there was another line, as guards checked us again and collected our invitations. Over our heads sounded the amplified cries of birds screaming, and everyone in line speculated . . . Had Amy a new toy for Christmas? One of us remembered an old news story, how starlings could be frightened away by recordings of other starlings being strangled; someone else postulated the screech of a natural enemy, and speculation ceased. Directly in front of me in line was a familiar face. The *New York Times* story the next day reported rumors that Rod McKuen had been sighted at the party, but that the rumor was unconfirmed. I hereby confirm it. We chatted a bit but did not reveal our identities.

Of all the poets there, I suppose McKuen must have recognized the fewest faces. How strange. The most popular poet in the country—millions of copies in print, presumably as rich as a Shah—attends a gathering of America's poets—and no one knows him, and he knows no one. Henry James might have made a story out of it.

Inside we deposited our coats, and were offered white carnations to pin on our dresses and jackets. These carnations served to identify "published poets"—though not every published poet wore one—and to distinguish them from the other guests. For if there were a hundred and twenty poets at this reception, there were a hell of a lot of others; the papers claimed five hundred at the party. There were spouses, of course; there were critics—Hugh Kenner and Helen Vendler I can swear to—there were patrons of the arts, bless them. At first in the bustle of things I was confused, at a party for poets, by the mink and the perfume, the dark suits and the fifty dollar ties.

Near the flower-dispensary we were handed programs which included a welcome signed by Mrs. Carter and lists of rooms and readers. Twenty-one poets read their poems, three each in seven rooms at the same hour. In the Diplomatic Reception Room, there were David Ignatow, Ted Weiss, and Lawson Inada; in the China Room Philip Levine, Maxine Kumin, and Sterling Brown; in the Green Room

Jonathan Williams, Lucille Clifton, and John Nims; in the Red Room Louise Glück, Simon Ortiz, and James Dickey; in the Map Room Marvin Bell, Rudolfo Anaya, and Chaim Grande; in the East Room Stanley Kunitz, Josephine Jacobsen, and Robert Hayden; and in the Blue Room Gwendolyn Brooks, John Ciardi, and Richard Eberhart. John Frederick Nims had a lot to do with this occasion, and his generation was well represented.

We found ourselves in the China Room, standing next to George Washington's pattern, hearing Levine, Kumin, and Brown in an audience that included Sandra McPherson, Louis Simpson, Richard Hugo, W. D. Snodgrass, Robert Dana, Howard Moss, William Matthews . . . and I suppose eighty others. All three poets read well, which did not surprise anyone. Brown came last and was star of the show, with a dry delivery and a comedian's timing. He referred frequently to his antiquity, and once remarked that he had known Walt Whitman before Walt grew the beard. . . . One of America's leading poets, known for his gullibility as well as his narrative skills, whispered excitedly, "Did he *really* know Whitman?"

When we were let out we were shunted upstairs where Mrs. Carter had just ended a small speech to assembled guests. Then there was a half-hour's shoving as we gathered to file past the receiving line, one hundred and twenty of America's poets, compounded with critics and patrons, jammed like passengers on the 5:30 bus. Finally we met the President of the United States, Rosalynn Carter and Joan Mondale. "What State are you from?" said Mr. Carter. "New Hampshire," I replied. "Dartmouth?" said he, making an assumption about the employment of America's poets. "No," I replied with asperity. "Wilmot!"

From then on we partied. The White House was smaller and prettier than we had expected, and we wandered among the handsome rooms of the main floor. Wine was abundant, and hors d'oeuvres, and poets. All afternoon I encountered faces that I had not met for twenty years or longer—faces from college, teachers and students, faces from a poetry reading at Iowa City in 1956, and faces never before seen except on book jackets. Always the faces carried years added on to them like cracking varnish. The party was like nothing so much as a college reunion, and gathered to itself that frail gaiety familiar at reunions, frail because of the unspoken acknowledgment everywhere of aging.

I met a dozen people I had only corresponded with. I talked with Hugh Kenner who wanted to meet John Nims but did not know what he looked like; I found Nims and dragged him over to Kenner. I bumped into Karl Shapiro whom I had not seen for decades. "Ah, Don," he said cheerfully, "it's like a bad anthology." I found myself getting more and more excited, and not only because of the supplies. I would start talking with Dave Smith or John Ashbery or Robert Pinsky or Cynthia MacDonald and in five minutes we would be interrupted ten times. Consecutive conversation was impossible, and everything came to seem quite wonderful. There are so many poets, everyone says. I ricocheted around the room, shaking hands as if I were running for office. A wild benignity took over. By the end of the evening I was meeting—with genuine pleasure and warmth—poets whose work, whose opinions, and whose moral character I had loathed for decades.

Ah, what a roomful of divas, what a cage of egos, what a gathering of loners! Poetry begins in solitude, and for most people I think remains solitary. Not only for the poet. The *real reader* is one person mysteriously connected for a moment with another spirit. Yet here was solitude's opposite, a terminal gregariousness possessing a hundred and twenty living hermits. It was delirious and strange and unprecedented and brief.

And all over Washington, all night until early morning, the poets convened in smaller groups, progressively drunker, and argued about line breaks and reputations, over dinner and somebody's vodka. It was a happy time. Everyone was there—and when you started to count, everyone was absent. Many of the absences were voluntary, some of them scandals of non-invitation. On the whole, it was a happy communal crazy assemblage, which the *Post* said was the best White House party in years.

<h2 style="text-align:center">II</h2>

"There are so many poets, everyone says." Increasingly we hear this observation phrased as a complaint, which seems puzzling. People have always complained that bad stuff gets published; fair enough, though it is hard to prove that the bad drives out the good. But as the complaint is made these days, it seems that the object is number itself—as if there could be too many talented and accomplished poets. Doubtless some of the complaining comes from practitioners, only half-serious, wishing that there were fewer competitors. Even so, the numbers of magazines and small press publishers seems to have kept pace with the numbers of poets, so that while we have more poets than ever, we also have more publication than ever.

And there, perhaps, is the rub—because we have the same amount of time to read as we ever had, and there is more to be read. If you want to keep an eye on what is happening, your task gets harder. If you hang around a bookshop, or look at reviews in a few magazines, I suppose you cannot help but become aware of something like two hundred titles in a year. I look into more than four hundred books of poems every year. People who do regular reviews for magazines tell me that they receive upwards of nine hundred; no one can read nine hundred books a year.

So the response is fatigue—and a complaint that there are too many poets. For many people, the way out of this dilemma is to subscribe to the Star System, which declares that, although Poets and Writers certify two thousand American poets, and although three thousand more are pounding at its door, there are *really* only four or five decent poets writing in the United States. Or maybe seven or eight. This is the technique of the shortlist—and it is mere laziness. It is a way to take yourself off the hook, to excuse not reading widely, and to retreat into a complacent hole where you read only Ammons, Ashbery, Howard, Hollander, and Hine if you subscribe to one camp; or only Bly, Wright, Kinnell, and Simpson if you subscribe to another; or only Rich, Broumas, Fraser, Forché; or only Black Mountain; or whatever. . . . Geographical areas become regions of complacency; there are one or two eastern shortlists, others in the west and the south. . . .

Any shortlist which flatters itself for its high standards will come a cropper sooner or later. There are in fact numbers of good poets whose styles contrast and conflict: *only eclecticism can approach judgment.* Eclectic anthologies would seem to provide hope. I suppose they help, but they too provide problems. First, there are too many anthologies!—at least too many anthologies that are not eclectic enough, that restrict themselves geographically or stylistically. Second, it is difficult to make an anthology which includes poets of reputation, because of the intractability of publishers' reprint fees.

Possibly the way to deal with numbers is through criticism, through book reviews and articles that give samples of poets praised and blamed, and that attempt to argue for certain values. We need more responsible reviewing, not just journalism that lists names but judgmental criticism that raises standards, that praises and that blames—to reward virtue and punish vice, to make sense out of our welter, to make public our discoveries and our tastes.

III

Thirty years ago it was common to complain that American poets spent most of their time writing criticism. Fifteen years ago, in reaction I suppose, the poets seemed to be writing none. Now things have moved into balance, and a good number of American poets take stands in prose about poetry. I only want more to do it, to join Robert Bly, Robert Creeley, Adrienne Rich, Hayden Carruth, Denise Levertov, Louis Simpson; to join Robert Pinsky, Charles Molesworth, Dave Smith, Marvin Bell, Tess Gallagher. . . .

There are too many among us who never commit an opinion to a paragraph. Maybe if you never expose an opinion, no one will hate you for being wrong . . . but it is useless to denounce folks by supposing cowardly motives. Maybe most poets who do not print their opinions feel diffident about their ability to write critical prose. I want to assert: writing prose *is* difficult, but it is something which can be learned by diligence. The ability to break a line or coin an image does *not* mean that one can easily write sentences and paragraphs—but it suggests a capacity for language which can be encouraged into the forms of prose. Far too many American poets write nothing but poems. Essays, short stories, articles, biographies, and book reviews require a sensitivity to language—rhythm and nuance, analogy and transition—that poets employ in poems and can translate into the form of prose, if they will first admit that prose is a form.

Of all the prose writing I do, I find reviewing poetry the most frustrating. It is so difficult to explain judgment in short space. Often, it seems that to give the whole reason for judgment one should write a whole credo for poetry. My happiest experience as a reviewer, therefore, was a time when I was regular poetry reviewer for one magazine, where I felt that I could build from review to review, using my soapbox, and make a general case from an accumulation of particulars.

Reviewing is not easy, but it helps solve the chaos of numbers, for a corps of diligent reviewers will cover most of what is published. The more reviewers we have, the more diverse the range of opinion represented. And we need critical essays as well as book reviews, essays that return to past poetry and connect it with the present: W. D. Snodgrass, Louis Simpson, Adrienne Rich, and Galway Kinnell. *APR* columns have been useful.

In poets' critical writing at this moment I think that many people overstress the positive. Too many poet-reviewers might as well be members of the Boosters Club which Sinclair Lewis satirized, with its motto: "Boost, Don't Knock." Or I think of the cynical advice many of us received from our elders: "If you don't have anything good to say, don't say anything at all." Of course, denigration may be gratuitous. Some books are not worth condemning, but many books, I believe, are worth condemning indeed. Their worthiness arises especially under two circumstances: when inferior work receives general praise; and when a book exemplifies a common fault. If we are to have a critical climate which is useful to the future of poetry in this country, we must have courage to condemn as well as generosity to praise. Praise alone builds no cities of discourse: conflict makes energy; "Damn braces."

To Imitate Yeats

(1980)

I wrote my senior thesis at college on William Butler Yeats's revisions of early poems. Because the *Variorium* had not yet made these revisions public, I worked in a rare book room, comparing texts to find evidence of Yeats's indefatigable struggle to improve his work. Although I had loved his poems for years, and had chosen him for subject because of this love, it was this study which turned him into a model for me. I don't mean a stylistic model, for I never wanted to imitate him—I hope that the early traces of brogue have departed my poems—nor do I mean a model in his private life; no thorough biography exists, but I am confident that he was an imperfect model of the private life, combining affectation and honesty by turns, loyalty and disloyalty. Instead, I take him as a model for artistic morality.

When he was young he was literary-political, entrepreneurial, flattering important elders. Reading his letters to Katherine Tynan, or to Oscar Wilde, we find him a trimmer. But as we continue to read the letters—and heaven knows the poems—we watch his character alter profoundly. Gradually, slowly, decade by decade, he becomes more and more serious. Remember that Yeats turned fifty in 1915, and that if he had died at fifty we would not know him for "Sailing to Byzantium," "Leda and the Swan," "Byzantium," "Among School Children," neither the great work of *The Tower*, nor the amazing *Last Poems* written when he was dying. He was already middle aged when he announced that "I seek an image not a book." The younger man had sought a book indeed; now until the end of his life he sought an image or emblem or symbol which would tell or even discover *the truth*. No longer was he a poem-seeker, but a truth-seeker; however, it was by the poetic image that he sought it. In his pursuit he felt discouraged again and again. One can follow in the *Collected Poems*, and in the *Letters* the restless seeking, the sense that the image is there to be found, the triumphant energy of pursuit and apparent discovery—and then, every time, the disillusion and the sense of failure, the renunciation of past work done.

But when Yeats was discouraged about what he had accomplished, when Yeats renounced his old poetry as an embroidered coat or as mere circus animals, he renounced the old in order to try to make the new. He began the struggle all over again. It is this twin ability—first to see the failure of his work, then to use that failure as a starting point for new work—which makes Yeats the greatest model for another poet. Discouragement with old work drives some artists to despair and silence; complacency over former accomplishment is more pernicious still: we have the self-imitators. Yeats never suffered from complacency; and he was indomitable in surmounting his own discouragement.

When he was old and dying he wrote great poems. Early in January of 1939 he wrote his last poem. He did not know that he had written his last poem, and on January 4th he began a letter: ". . . I know for certain that my time will not be long. I have put away everything that can be put away that I may speak what I have to speak. . . . In two or three weeks—I am now idle that I may rest after writing much verse—I will begin to write my most fundamental thoughts. . . . It seems to me that I have found what I wanted. When I try to put it all into a phrase I say, 'Man can embody truth but he cannot know it.' . . . The abstract is not life and everywhere draws out its contradictions. You can refute Hegel but not the Saint or the Song of Sixpence. . . ."

Three weeks later Yeats died—instead of writing his "most fundamental thoughts." But he had done it all along, and he had done it because he never thought he had done it. It is the best possible death, still to pursue the desire of a life—into the grave.

Notes on the Image:
Body and Soul

(1981)

1. As W. J. T. Mitchell puts it, "To speak of 'imagery' . . . in temporal arts like . . . literature . . . is to commit a breach in decorum, or, to put it more positively, to make a metaphor." The poem's only genuine image is the squiggles of ink on paper which make letters and punctuation marks.

2. Sometimes people speak of the image as if it meant something else, and as if they knew what it meant. Here is a definition from a popular textbook: "Images are groups of words that give an impression to the senses. Most images are visual, but we can also make images of taste, touch, hearing, and smell . . ." A sensible definition, no doubt—but it has little to do with what we mean when we use the word "image" in connection with a poem. When we speak of images in poetry, we speak of four or five different things, some of which have nothing to do with making "an impression to the senses."

3. Literary terms, by appointment in Samarra, eventually contain not only what they started with but the opposite of what they started with. "Spirit and image" meant "soul and body." But image has come also to mean precisely not-body, not-X because an imitation or a copy of X. From a copy or representation of a thing, the word can then move to mean

the essence of a thing, therefore "image" comes to mean "spirit" which began by being its opposite.

As with literary terms so with literary movements. The manifestoes of the Imagist Movement praised the particular over the abstract, the local over the infinite; and we were enjoined not to speak of "dim lands of peace." When Pound reported in a metaphor taken from electricity that the image is language "charged with meaning," we no longer heard about description and detail; we heard about quality and value, about intensity and intelligence. Here was Imagism's appointment in Samarra: the movement which started as an assault on the symbol ended by requiring that symbolism house itself in the particular without an explanatory genitival conjunction linking it to an abstraction.

Two lines of Pound's are sometimes cited as the image's apogee: "The apparition of these faces in the crowd; / Petals on a wet, black bough." Like most of us, I enjoy this morsel; but it is not only "an impression to the senses." The word "apparition" introduces magic—how infinite, how *fin de siècle*—which by its connotation governs what follows. Pound the magician poet, as gifted as Ovid's deities, metamorphoses faces into petals; because the word "apparition" is poetic, the word "petals" takes on the association of beautiful flowers; and the word "bough" completes a natural scene. Thus the faces are by association pretty as they stand out against the dull crowd: bright petals torn by storm, blown by wind, stuck by rain to dark limbs. It is all accomplished by assertion.

4. We make poetry of our conflicts, our warring opposites, although we do not always pretend to; and we may not even know we do. When William Carlos Williams wrote "no ideas but in things," I suppose that he was aware of the paradox: the statement disexemplifies itself, an idea made of no things at all. And his famous image poem depends upon something besides an image: "so much depends / upon," claims W. C. W., with an imageless urgency that illuminates the

picture of a red wheelbarrow shiny with raindrops next to some white chickens.

5. Or take Ted Hughes, from a poem in *Moortown*: "The wind is oceanic in the elms. . . ." Is this an image? The wind which is invisible to the eyes becomes tangible and visible with the cooperation of the elms; the elms by responding make the wind visible—more, they make it audible: this image of course is a metaphor (airy wind compared to watery ocean) and the comparison takes place to the senses not visually but audibly. For the image to raise itself to sense-perception, the metaphor had to operate first.

"The wind is oceanic in the elms." . . . Beyond the audible comparison there is comparison of size. The wind is as vast as the ocean. And this is not a piece of sense data but an idea, a conceptual metaphor. But if it is imaginable we imagine it in terms of extent; I believe that "extent" is an abstraction of a visual experience.

6. ". . . Dim lands of peace" *does* seem like rotten language; we prefer this syntactical arrangement when it attaches particulars: "the camera of my eye." But this image is not visual or sensuous but conceptual, for an eye regarded as a camera looks no different from an eye regarded as an eye; the metaphor suggests not a datum of sense but an idea of function or utility. . . .

But if we despise "lands of peace," do we also despise "sea of trouble"? The man suggested that he might "take arms against a sea," which is surely an image, fantastic as Cuchulain—which becomes less image and more metaphor when we add the genitive.

7. Lautréamont's is probably the most famous surreal image: the chance meeting on a dissecting table of a sewing machine and an umbrella. Of course one can see it if one tries; it is not especially interesting to try: we don't imagine it, we illustrate it.

Surrealism is typically visual, perhaps excessively visual. If its pictures are literary, its narratives are pictorial. Many surrealist poems could be descriptions of a series of paintings. And the name of each of them is The Strange Encounter. It is always the umbrella and the sewing machine, even when the umbrella wears shark's teeth and the sewing machine has goat's ankles.

8. There is also the metaphor that is perfunctory as metaphor, and vivid as image. "That time of year thou mayst in me behold . . ." Obvious not because of overuse but because of natural symbolism, night as death and autumn as age . . . but: "When yellow leaves or none or few do hang . . ." becomes more interesting not because of the image of turned foliage but because of the rhythm of its syntax, hurtling and hesitate by turns. Then: "Bare ruin'd choirs, where late the sweet birds sang. . . ." The audacity is imagistic and metaphoric together; a comparison compared over again, a likeness distanced by a further likeness.

9. There are comparisons without images—"as futile as an old regret"—and of course there are images without metaphors: cold hands, sour cabbage, huge spider. . . .

On occasion we may use image as an honorific gesture like "nice" from which we would wish to withhold the cold shower of definition. Is it possible that when we enhance "image"—calling it charged, calling it deep; when we refuse to call it "an image" unless it is unreal—that we are saying something like "I only respect an image when it becomes a symbol"?

Anyone who considers the ambiguity of "image" a modern degeneration should consult the OED. If I suggested using "image" to mean a sense datum, often but not always part of metaphor or component of symbol, I would accomplish nothing, because metaphor and symbol, words which we use as if they describe things that happen in language, are as imperfectly defined as image is.

Poetry, Popularity, and the Golden Age[*]

(1982)

The man in the dentist's waiting room is friendly and tells us about his daughter. When he asks what I do, I reveal that I am a poet. *"Wow,"* he says; and because he is a man of feeling, he commiserates with me. "It must be tough," he says, "to practice a dying art." This man and Mr. Clausen have something in common. When I tell the man that this common knowledge is not wholly accurate, he thinks I am defending poetry. He tells me that poetry is really terrific, though he himself does not get time to read much of it.

I doubt that I shall convince Mr. Clausen, either, who tells us that "the poetic audience, even among intellectuals, has largely vanished," and "serious contemporary poetry has virtually no audience at all outside the English Departments." In these assertions there are no facts, no figures, no statistics—although if what he asserts is correct it should be easy enough to prove it. This view is so accepted that it requires no statistics. *Time* magazine knows that it is true: poetry has lost its audience. Corollary to this lamentation is faith in a past golden age when poetry was popular. Even the firm of Bouvard and Pecouchet, Publishers, which ought to know better, believes this received idea. A couple of years ago

---

[*] In these remarks I address myself to Christopher Clausen's *The Place of Poetry* (The University Press of Kentucky, 1981.)

313

the chief editor of a major firm asked me for a jacket blurb; when I turned him down saying that blurbs all sounded fatuous, he told me he agreed, that he deplored the necessity of this promotion, but that as I knew, the sales of poetry had declined steadily in modern times. I told him he was mistaken, and that his own firm published X's second book of poems in 1940, a moderate success of a moderately known young poet, in an edition of 750 hardbound copies; that by 1950 a poet of the same level was published in one thousand hardback copies, by 1960 1,500 . . . and the leap came in that decade, for by 1970 the same poet would appear in approximately 5,000 copies mixed hard and soft. (By 1980 the curve had flattened.) The editor wrote me that I was wrong but that he would look it up. He wrote me again, having looked it up; I was right.

I find it strange: there are three to four times as many books of poems published now as there were in 1940 (*Publishers' Weekly* estimates 1200 titles of poetry a year; of course this includes small editions and self-publication) and the print-orders of books published by major publishers is five to ten times greater than it was. Mr. Clausen gets other things askew; he says that the situation has never deteriorated so much in England. In fact, it has deteriorated in England and not in this country. One major English publisher has a standard print-order of four hundred and fifty hardcover copies of a book of poems; another prints six hundred. I find it strange that my man in the waiting room, my well-known publisher, and Professor Clausen all agree that the audience "for poetry has largely vanished," that "serious contemporary poetry has virtually no audience at all outside the English Departments . . ." when in fact the audience has increased in this country for forty years. I cannot pretend to understand but I will make five observations:

1) I think people need to believe in this loss whatever the facts are. Some of them must have read that Lawrence Ferlinghetti's *Coney Island of the Mind* has sold over a million copies; that other New Directions poets, like Denise Levertov and Gary Snyder, sell in the tens of thousands, that poets as

diverse as Robert Bly, Adrienne Rich, and Diane Wakoski sell books in numbers large enough to have made the fiction bestseller lists a few years back. Although the audience for poetry has increased decade by decade—as evidenced by magazines, by book publication, and above all by poetry readings—it remains *common knowledge* that "poetry has lost its audience." This knowledge has been common for as long as I have been alive—as it has been becoming less true. I wonder how long it has been common knowledge.

2) My second observation may be irrelevant. I observe it, and I intuit some connection with my first observation. The word "poetry" is held in awe, in high regard, by people who care nothing for poems. The exception to this generalization is intellectuals, who have not cared for it for some time ("the poetic audience, even among intellectuals, has largely vanished. . . ." Since when did intellectuals read poems?) Hardly a day passes when we do not find "poetry," used as an honorific dead metaphor—in newspapers, in magazines, on television, in news stories, features, ads. A recent *Inside Sports* printed the poems of a Georgia running back; more to the point, it included a baseball article by Thomas Boswell observing that there is a difference between the business and the game of baseball: "One is history, the other poetry." Because it is merely another trite comparison, this praise for "poetry" (not poems) would be uninteresting except for the common knowledge of poetry's downfall. The same people who nicknamed an orchestra-leader "The Poet of the Piano," or said that the point guard's play was "sheer poetry," or that the television series made "poetry out of the garment industry," will tell you with calm assurance that the art of poetry is dead. Maybe we derive some message like "poetry is wholly magnificent and it does not exist because I don't read it. . . ."

3) Concomitant to the universal dirge for poetry is the belief in a golden age of poetry and audience. Everyone speculates about the cause of humanity's general tendency to invent golden ages, to conjure disappeared Edens of sensibility, eras when we or our ancestors lived whole lives—

whether this place be an imagined rural arcadia, or the twelfth century, or playing high school basketball. (Some people suspect that this general golden age is memory of good times in the womb.) I wonder if the myth of poetry's golden age does not derive from a personal loss. Probably my theory does not apply to Mr. Clausen, but I think it applies to many teachers, publishers, and journalists who lament poetry's losses. These people, in my theory, were once an audience for poetry—in high school maybe, certainly in college—where they majored in English and listened to a silver-voiced Professor sing his Tennyson. They wrote a little themselves, if truth be known. They listened to visiting poets read on their campuses. They loved the latest poet—Dylan Thomas when I was in college, maybe Robert Bly or John Ashbery or Denise Levertov today—and bought the latest books. Maybe they even took a Ph.D. in English and learned all about Auden or Frost or Stevens.

We know what happened next; they entered the *real world*. For the English instructor with his fresh doctorate the real world was not James Merrill but freshman composition and committee meetings. For the journalist or the lawyer the real world was many things but it did not include James Wright nor Louis Simpson nor Gary Snyder nor Adrienne Rich. It is a human characteristic, when we abandon anything, to feel that we have been abandoned. So when the audience loses poetry it is natural that we hear complaints that poetry has lost touch with its audience. Maybe the golden age was sophomore lit.

4) My fourth observation is that poetry's popularity is wholly irrelevant to poetry's quality. Lawrence Ferlinghetti has sold a million copies, and he is a serious poet; I do not think that he is a very good poet. If we examine the nature of poems more or less popular, we may be able to generalize—but I think that we speak of society and education not of poetry. We will never derive a tool for evaluating poetry by looking at statistics. Yet implicit in the complaints that poetry has lost its audience is the notion that poetry has the duty to be popular—"as once it was"—which poets can fulfill or not

as they choose. I suggest that poets have a duty to write good poems and that their duty ends there.

Yes, Tennyson was popular and sold vast quantities and is a good poet. Martin Tupper outsold him which does not make Martin Tupper a better poet. Nor is the inverse argument defensible as a standard. If Tennyson outsold—oh, let us say the Doughty of "Dawn in Britain"—the information does not help us decide that Doughty is better than Tennyson. Frost and Stevens are both major American poets; it is interesting, perhaps, that the one grossly outsold the other; but does anyone claim that Frost's popularity and Stevens's obscurity measure quality? Frost was outsold at the beginning of his career by Edgar Guest and at the end of it by Rod McKuen.

For every example in one direction you can bring up a counter example. Popularity is irrelevant to quality. But if we are going to talk about poetry, popularity, and the public— why don't we get it straight?

5) Finally, let me say that I enjoy Mr. Clausen's literary history, or history of society's taste in poetry, when he writes about the nineteenth century—on Tennyson and Tennyson's Palgrave, on the ascendency of the lyric. I think he is weak on poetry and audience both before and after the nineteenth century. Mr. Clausen does not much *like* modern poetry. He prefers a poetry of statement, of ideas, a discursive poetry. (He should enjoy Robert Pinsky's *An Explanation of America* and James McMichael's *Four Good Things*; we witness some return to the discursive poem.) Therefore he praises eighteenth century poetry with excitement and enthusiasm. But poetry is a mansion with many rooms in it, and the style of its rooms depends not only on the volition of the artist but on the state of the language, on politics, economics, education, and technology. Because so many causes contribute, we cannot reproduce old modes exactly. The relationship between poetry and audience in the eighteenth century cannot be reproduced because the contemporary audience, real or potential, does not resemble the elite audience two hundred years ago. The contemporary audience

is more ignorant, less literate, and much larger.

But I mean to question *any* golden age of poetry and audience. Does it mean anything to say that Homer, or anonymous ballad-makers of the border, wrote for a large audience? For one thing, they didn't "write"; audience is not metaphor here. For us, a mass audience means network television or Harlequin Books, not a shaggy singer telling stories around a fire—an intimacy of "audience" no contemporary poetry reading can aspire to. Neither did Thomas Wyatt nor John Donne write for a large audience; in no sense were they popular, nor could they imagine such a thing. Neither did Traherne nor Vaughan, nor Shakespeare or Jonson in their poems. Somewhat later, an elite subscribed to translations by Pope and Cowper. Then larger numbers bought books by Byron, Moore, Tennyson. . . .

The golden age turns out to be a portion of the nineteenth century only—and only for a few poets. Think of Blake; think of Whitman and Wordsworth before they became venerable.

The Poetry Notebook: Two

(1981)

I

In the previous section, I complained about the Star System that picks out four or five contemporaries, declares that nobody else is worth reading, and proves it by reading nobody else.

Star System devotees tend to defend their prejudices by geographical fortification; I suppose the Eastern Consensus is worst because it is most complacent and governs most print; the East is a region that considers itself a universe. But other regions are just as provincial, and there are non-geographic oldboy subdivisions. I have heard graduates of the Writers' Workshop at Iowa speak of the number of living geniuses and then recite a list composed entirely of Writers' Workshop graduates.

All coterie associations—be they geographical, academic, sexual . . . —limit the possibilities of change and growth. Loyalty is handsome; poet-friends may help each other write better poems; one possible history of good poetry would be a history of competitive-cooperative friendships . . . but it is, alas, true that a history of bad poetry would also be a history of friendships—the kind we put down as mutual admiration societies. In order to be useful to us, our friends must be nasty to us. Most coteries encourage us to think well of ourselves, and to deplore the different. We despise the alien because it threatens our complacency. Coteries support the lazy reading of the Star System. There *are* other people out there whom we do not know, who went to different schools or did not go to schools, who make poems on premises different from ours. There is the East Village, there is Naropa, there is visual poetry, there is metrical poetry, there is sound-text poetry, there are the language poets. . . . We must not dismiss anything alien until we have lived with it enough to absorb its premises and judge from the familiarity of the atelier.

Thus, most of us will never know enough to make an honest judgment; nonetheless, most of us will pretend to judge.

If I suggest that there may be good poets out there whom no one reads, I do not go so far as some others go. When it comes to putative poetic multiplicity, I find myself flipping back and forth between populist and elitist notions. In *The Jewel Hinged Jaw*, Samuel Delany arrives at a populist supposition by algebra and multiplication.

In 1818 the population of England was near twenty million, eighty percent of whom were functionally illiterate. The literate field, then, was approximately four hundred thousand. This was not only the maximum poetry audience; more germane, it was the field from which the country's poets could come.

How many poets were there?

Coleridge-Wordsworth-Blake-Byron-Shelley-Keats. . . ? Certainly. But we can pull out over another dozen without even opening our *Palgrave:* Crabbe, Hunt, Reynolds, Campbell, Scott, Moore, Southey, Coleridge, Landor, Darley, Hood, Praed, Clare, and Beddoes were all writing that same year. And at this point we've pretty much scraped the bottom of the barrel for acceptable thesis topics in British poetry for that decade.

Twenty all together!

And if you can think of five more British poets of any merit what-so-ever who were writing in the year of Emily

Bronte's birth, good for you! Out of a field of four hundred thousand, that's six poets of major interest and fourteen of varying minor interest.

In the United States today we have nearly two hundred and twenty-five million people. Perhaps eighty percent are literate, which gives us a literate field of one hundred eighty million from which we can cull both our audience and our poets—a field fifty times as large as the field of Great Britain in 1818.

Forgive the litotes, but it is not unreasonable to suppose that where there were six major and fourteen minor poets in England in 1818, today there are fifty times six major poets (about three hundred) and fifty times fourteen (about seven hundred) of merit and interest in America today.

I don't see why Delany stops where he stops. If we applied the same demographics to the Elizabethan age, and made the reasonable claim that there was one Shakespeare alive in 1603, nine major poets, and fifteen poets of merit and interest—population about 4,100,000, literate population maybe 60,000—then in contemporary America by Delany's thinking we should have 3000 Shakespeares leading 27,000 major poets and 45,000 poets of merit and interest. . . . And America's population increases every two and one-half years by an increment equal to the population of Elizabethan England.

Reading Delany, of course I counter-leap; I seem to perceive an error in his assumption that population size relates to a culture's production of major poets; possibly one could look into language and its conditions, education, economics, politics, religion, the spirit of the age, and sun spots. . . . Delany's assumption about literacy is naive; many people assume that languages thrive when the population is illiterate.

But . . . suppose Delany were even *a little* right? . . . I swing myself back. . . .

There is not enough fame to go around, Delany tells us. "There are hundreds on hundreds on hundreds of American poets. Hundreds among them are good. One critic cannot even be *acquainted* with their complete work, much less have studied it thoroughly." Surely he is right to claim that there are hundreds who ought to be studied before they are dismissed. I suspect there are *not* hundreds who are good, but my suspicion is no better founded than Delany's counter-suggestion. Neither of us has studied enough to make a judgment. Suppose that Delany were even one-eighth right; immediately we understand that everyone (rebels, academics, bishops, anarchists, provincials) makes the typical error of using old tools to cope with new materials. Delany says: "Now the academic establishment, for years, has invested amazing energy, time, money, and (above all) mystification in perpetuating the view that, somehow, Eliot, Auden and Pound form some mysterious qualitative analog with Byron, Keats, Shelley. . . ." And he quotes, from a critical book a few years old, one of those ritual lists: "Berryman, Bishop, Jarrell, Lowell, Roethke, and Wilbur. . . ."

In 1888, Horace Traubel noted that "A couple of volumes of poetry by unknown writers reached (Whitman) by mail today"; and he noted Whitman's sputtering response: "Everybody is writing, writing—worst of all, writing poetry. It'd be better if the whole tribe of the scribblers—every damned one of us—were sent off somewhere with toolchests to do some honest work."

And on the other (elitist) hand: decades ago I remember settling into the notion that never, in the history of literature, had there been so many good poets alive at one time. . . . Even if giants no longer walk the earth (I liked to think) ours is an extraordinary time because of the numbers of poets of decent ability. . . .

Then I discovered that this vision of one's own time had become commonplace with the spread of literacy. For a hundred and fifty years, people have been making the same discovery. Whatever the real numbers, and whatever one's own time looks like from later vantage, good poets of one's own generation seem unusually numerous. Of course contemporaries *are* more numerous than the dead generations, because time (wearing the costume of indifference, diffidence, stupidity, or possibly intelligence) has culled the plupart. This vision is commonplace because it is comforting; if the elect are many we stand a greater chance of being elected. But Edward Marsh regularly announced that the Georgians were the most abundant of generations; and if you prowl among the special anthologies—*Greatest Poems of 1927, Major Figures of Southeastern Massachusetts, The Rhode Island Rennaisance, American-Italian Free Verse Love Ballads, Poetry from Princeton*—you will find the announcement made over and over again, always as if for the first time.

In Richard Kostelanetz's ninth edition of *Assembling*, a critical issue, that marvelous elitist Hugh Kenner makes himself the ultimate unDelany: "There have never been more than six writers who mattered alive at once." When I hear such exclusionary remarks my blood stirs to the blast of elitism's trumpet. But such remarks, alas, are calls to battle only; they refer to literary history as a Sousa march refers to slaughtered populations. In *The Pound Era*, Kenner attends to Pound, Eliot, Joyce, and Lewis; elsewhere, he has recorded his admiration for William Carlos Williams, Louis Zukofsky, Basil Bunting, and George Oppen; he has written a book on Beckett. If these overlapping writers number nine, which of them do not "matter"? We might add that Yeats was alive with these writers; without gross eccentricity, many of us would add the names of Stevens, Moore, Cummings, Aiken, Crane, Auden, Graves, Frost. . . .

II

After people complain that there are too many poets, the next thing they say is that everybody writes the same poem. Some complainants do not read what they criticize— ignorance discovers homogenity—but no reasonable observer can deny the prevalence of a new Magazine Verse. That term used to apply to the bland commercial product which occupied old monthlies, iambics written at a little distance from life and the idiom, stanzas gentle and formulaic; Magazine Verse lamented that leaves fell but held out hope that they might return. . . . The verses were optimistic, technically kempt, undistinguished, and indistinguishable.

The magazine poem of the present is different. It appears not only in the *Atlantic Monthly* but in the *Kenyon Review*, not only in the *New Yorker* but in *Poetry Now*. Possibly this makes the new Magazine Verse more dangerous than Richard Watson Gilder's.

Maybe there is always a Magazine Verse of some kind or other. Certainly in the late thirties and the forties there was a describable common style. Poems were iambic, mostly pentameter, rhymed in a stanza like ABABCC, and in content glorified an ordinary object not without irony—like John Frederick Nim's "Dollar Bill" and Karl Shapiro's "Buick." (Sometimes on the other hand it took a noble subject not without irony and domesticated it.) Practitioners included Nemerov, Ciardi, Brinnin, Moss—and twenty-five lesser sorts, and fifty younger sorts. When Wilbur and Lowell came along, they practiced their stanzas better than anyone else, and the young switched to follow Lowell and Wilbur, then later moved toward surrealism and free verse following Spanish models. Magazine Verse of our moment is written in imitation of these young, who are no longer young.

Our Magazine Verse is as formulaic as Richard Watson Gilder's and less aware of its own rigidity, because it is ignorant of literary history. To be rigid is to be self-limited by ignorance. Limitation by form, chosen and conscious—like J. V. Cunningham's or Richard Wilbur's—can create power. But today's magazine poem, like yesterday's, is limited not by choice but by fear. Once again, as with late eighteenth century practitioners of the heroic couplet, mediocre poets have made an extraordinary discovery: *the way to write poetry has been found.*

Two hundred years ago, "the way to write poetry" was in ten syllable lines with medial caesuras, end-pause, and end-rhyme; invert the first foot one line in twenty. Magazine Verse of the moment has vaguer boundaries: it is short, under two pages; its lines are short, around five to eight syllables; it is unaware of rhyme or assonance; its degree of enjambment is never extreme, running from pauses to run-ons between adjective and noun—the actor's one-beat pause-to-ponder; its diction is limited to simple nouns and adjectives, with a few verbs, and most of it dead metaphors; its syntax is Dick-and-Jane, simple sentences occasionally straying into compounds; punctuation marks extend as far as commas, periods, and dashes; each poem includes 1) description, 2) emotion, generally wistful, and 3) metamorphosis: an apple tree turns into the Iberian peninsula; a pen knife wriggles and becomes a snake. This mechanical fantasy is called "inwardness."

But I overstate my case. If there are a number of good poets now, and if some good work resembles other people's, good work becomes hard to distinguish. In a pine forest, who can with confidence pick the best pine tree? When I read manuscripts for the National Poetry Series a couple of years ago, I became aware that if there were a superb collection of poems which *looked like* other poems, I would be unable to find this book-needle in my haystack of manuscripts. My final few manuscripts were eccentric to this middle ground.

III

To concentrate on the prevalent ignores the unusual.

There is a lively avant-garde in the United States, which has flourished at least since the fifties, whose claims are rarely advanced in MFA places, whose work does not appear in the *New Yorker, Field, Poetry Now, APR, Kenyon Review, Iowa Review, Ohio Review, Ironwood, Kayak, Poetry Northwest. . . .* Nor do I blame the editors of these magazines. If it is hard to choose one tree in the forest, it is harder to choose among objects that look like coathangers, zeppelins, walruses, and pizzas—when you have grown up thinking that a tree looks like a tree.

When I speak of the avant garde as "lively," I use a term as evasive as "interesting"—because I must not put myself forward as capable of judgment. I cannot judge the success or failure of Jackson Mac Low, Bliem Kern, Dick Higgins, Ron Silliman, Susan Howe, or Curtis Favile. Yet as I hang around avant-garde street corners, I sense excitement and energy. If I remain incapable of judgment, I also remain curious. In a moment I will try making a sketchy, long distance report, but let me start by advocating mere curiosity.

When critics found Wordsworth obscure it was because it was "not poetry," because only an agreed-upon vocabulary in an agreed-upon meter made poetry. But then, critics have denounced every innovation for the past two-hundred-and-fifty years as "not poetry." Alas, the converse cannot be adduced: if everything new-and-good has been denounced as "not-poetry," everything new-and-bad has also been denounced as "not-poetry." Doubtless most innovative work, like more conventional work, will seem bad in fifty years. *But if we do not try to remain open to innovation, there is no chance that we will respond to excellence when it arrives in unexpected form.*

One need not look back to 1798 for examples of self-shut eyes. I remember when Prufrock was an obscure poem; in 1923 *Time* reported suggestions that "The Waste Land" was a hoax. . . . Cummings was a dangerous revolutionary as late as the forties. I dismissed "Howl" in 1957.

We refuse to acknowledge the existence of an avant-garde because it threatens our citadel. Really, the fear is silly: what is good will survive. The iambics of Yeats and Frost withstood the free verse dogmatists; the free verse of William Carlos Williams survived the iambic thirties and forties. Maybe our real fear is that we are no good at all. . . .

Everyone should read Dick Higgins's book of essays, *A Dialectic of Centuries*, published by Printed Editions. In his thinking, as in his artworks, Higgins is all over the place—with energy and vigor: he was a master of happenings, he writes visual poetry. Many avant-gardists hoe several gardens, like the *eminence grise* John Cage who is not only musician but poet and playwright. These terms lose definition—for it is definition that the avant-garde enjoys playing havoc with. Cage, Rauschenberg, Cunningham. One is drawn to such words as "mixed media," which I am almost as loathe to pronounce as "lifestyle."

If one notion ties much of the avant-garde together, over the past thirty years, it is concentration on construction rather than on feeling or idea. This construction may be aleatory, a concentration on the method of construction rather than on an intended shape. From time to time people have fiddled with dividing art into two camps called after the names of two movements: constructivism and expressionism. (I use small letters to indicate a usage more general than the movements named by capitalization.) Expressionist art expresses feeling (by distortion, exaggeration, fantasy); feeling is its end. Constructivism concentrates on form, be it structure improvised from the I Ching or be it a worked-out grid of shape and color: Malevich, Mondrian, and the minimalists; organization is its end. Obviously, Surrealism is devoted to expression; obviously, Russian Formalism and its derivative Structuralism finds all art constructivist whatever it considers itself to be, whatever its intention.

I should say that constructivist art is often conceptual art, the concept often a piece of wit or irony. I am thinking of things like—was it Yoko Ono's work?—the sculptured row of empty flower pots titled "Imagining Flowers." One characteristic of such work is its interchangeableness; describe it in words and you make a conceptual poem.

In avant-garde poetry I notice three points of reference: visual poetry, sound-text, and language-poetry. (Nobody agrees on these terms.) Visual poetry, which is sometimes called concrete, has been around longest and exists in many anthologies and in volumes by Mary Ellen Solt, Bliem Kern, Dick Higgins, Richard Kostelanetz and others. (Higgins has written a book about an early visual poet named George Herbert; of course everyone acknowledges the long history of visual poetry.) Sound-text is noises sometimes imitated graphically in print, sometimes only existent in performance or in sound-lab recording.

If visual poetry falls between poetry and painting, its technology is printing or graphics; pop art is uncle. If sound-text poetry falls between poetry and music, its technology is the tape recording; multi-channel rock recording is aunt.

Publicist and statesman of the new is Richard Kostelanetz— who is only forty, and who has published visual poetry, sound-text poetry, poetry in numbers—and at least seven thousand articles on all forms of art and all artists. He locates his attention especially on poetry that falls between genres, on "intermedia" as he calls it, like visual poetry and sound-text. His energy is vast, his output prolific. As editor of *Assembling* (the most remarkable magazine of its day, an invention of conceptual art); as Cicero to Jason Epstein's Cato; as tireless promoter of eccentric poets, unacceptable poets, outlandish poets, weird poets, and good poets—he is unlike anyone else in contemporary literature. If he reminds us frequently of the titles he has written and edited, he remains one of the most generous figures in contemporary poetry—endlessly publishing and promoting elders, peers, and juniors.

Newest of this trinity which I discern—and least interesting to Kostelanetz—is language-poetry. (The language-poet Bob Perelman tells me how much he *hates* this label— as if one might speak of sound-musicians or shape-sculptors. . . .) There is a New York magazine called $L = A = N = G = U = A = G = E$, edited by Bruce Andrews and Charles Bernstein, which gathers language-concerns. There is an active group in San Francisco, where the Tuumba Press publishes. Names that come to mind include Ron Silliman, Ray DiPalma, Fanny Howe, Steve McCaffrey, Clark Coolidge, Barrett Watten, Bill Berkson, Lyn Hejinian.

Coolidge and Berkson are old East Village poets; obviously Ted Berrigan, Ron Padgett, and Tom Clark—of the East Village/Bolinas axis—bear affinities; maybe Aram Saroyan was first of all. But . . . Robert Creeley is a language poet much of the time, and the minimalist wing of Black Mountain follows out of this side of Creeley; should one not mention Zukofsky? Jolas? Stein? Mayakovsky? The movement is international. . . . We go back to the egg.

But, you say, I have not said what language-poetry *is* . . . ? Ah, yes (*he clears his throat*) I am indeed glad that you asked that question . . . Well . . . well. . . .

Language-poetry attends to its medium, which it defines linguistically rather than visually or orally (visual poetry, sound-text poetry) or referentially/mimetically (as with expressionist, biomorphic poetry, including Magazine Verse). In general, it distrusts reference or mimesis. In essays by language-poets about their art, one hears about Russian Formalists and Jacobson, linguists and de Saussure, Structuralism, Derrida, Barthes. . . . As the other prongs of the avant garde seem outgrowths of the technology of electronic reproduction, language poetry responds to twentieth century linguistics.

To date I find it easier to appreciate the movement's ideas than its poems. I read Ron Silliman on "The New Sentence" and sense his excitement. If I read Barrett Watten's *1-10* with little comprehension, I sense his energy. $L=A=N=G=U=A=G=E$ is intriguing (available from Charles Bernstein, 464 Amsterdam Avenue, New York, New York), although it is sometimes hard to read, sounding as if it were ill-translated from French. I find the clearest discussions in *Talks*, which is number 6/7 of *Hills* (Spring 1980; available from 36 Clyde Street, San Francisco, California 94107 at $5) a magazine-anthology edited by Bob Perelman which collects eleven lectures and discussions. To read the poems and prose of the movement, look at the books published by Tuumba Press (2639 Russell Street, Berkeley, California 94705) or Barrett Watten's magazine *This* (1004 Hampshire Street, San Francisco, California 94110).

I will not quote. The poems are often long, and structure is of the essence: Snippets will never do.

Polonius's Advice to Poets

(1980)

When Polonius reached fifty, he looked at the poetry about him and he saw that it was not good. He saw more poets than ever before, more magazines, more books, more poetry readings, more audiences, and more dreck. Taking upon himself the burden of world-correction, he composed a series of rules, to which he attached parenthetic exclamations, explanations, anecdotes, and insults.

1. Do not live your life as if it were a fishing expedition, and poems were the fish.

(Some poets' greed is as boundless as Alexander's. "My sister's funeral was a drag," says one of them; "but I got a poem out of it.")

2. Read good poems at least two hours every day. Three-quarters of the poets read should be born before 1907 and outside Chile.

(Too many American poets read no poetry except translated poetry, which leads to wonderful images about "jaws of the melon seed" and "bamboo under the mountain-color mountain," but does little for one's ear, one's syntax, or one's shapeliness. Henry King, William Cowper, Ben Jonson, Emily Dickinson, and Alfred, Lord Tennyson may help.)

(Many American poets never read poetry at all, because books are expensive and you always need a new record; books are old-fashioned and out-loud is where-it's-at; if you read other poets it might spoil your original style because you would be influenced by them.)

(Poets who read no poetry tend to exhaust their resources rather *early*. . . .)

3. Revise everything you write over and over again.

(Although your first draft may be inspired, and you may not know what you are doing, before you publish the damned thing see that you know what you have done. In retrospect, intend every word and every piece of grammar.)

4. Do not show anyone the draft of a new poem until you have read it over, all by yourself, every day for six months.

(Do not show it to your husband, to your wife, to your roommate, to your student, to your teacher, to your friend's spouse, to your spouse's friend, to Howard Moss, to your Workshop Director, or to me.)

5. Do not publish a poem in a magazine until three years after you have first shown it to someone. Keep looking at it, and change it whenever you find something to change. If you get tired of it you can always throw it away.

(Horace said nine years; Pope said five; but the world has accelerated, as everyone knows.)

6. Try to remember that quantity is not quality.

(*Every* American knows that if the automobile industry sells eight million cars it is a wonderful year, and this wonderful year has "a ripple effect" throughout the economy. Six million car sales and we're sunk. Generally, farmers are happy to get more bushels of wheat from an acre this year than they did last year. Therefore our universities think that they have become better because they have become larger, and a Department of English which graduates twenty-seven Ph.D's who cannot find jobs feels superior to a Department of English which graduates twenty-one Ph.D's who cannot find jobs.

(Thus Polonius remembers sitting in John Berryman's living room to hear the poet, drinking coffee by the gallon, announce that he had just completed a collection of three hundred and eight Dream Songs, and Polonius's prophetic stomach sank. . . . And Robert Lowell, in mad Berryman-envy, rushed into mass-production of appalling unrhymed sonnets—and seven books in his last, disastrous nine years. And Polonius remembers the biographical note: "Ms. B____ published nine collections of poetry last year. . . ." And Polonius remembers the young poet who sent out a flier, advertising for readings, that bragged of four hundred and twenty-six poems published in a period of three years.)

7. Do not commit dead metaphors, clichés, or thievery from other poets; be as hard on yourself as you possibly can.

(But most people cannot do it alone, because most of us can fool ourselves even when we try hardest. Create for yourself a jury of tough readers, to go over your poems during the years between starting and finishing. Someone who hates everything you write is useless to you; so is someone who loves everything you write. Find people who agree with your ambitions but who notice discrepancies between ambition and achievement. If anyone starts praising more than half of your lines, let that member of the jury be dismissed and another added.

(If you live in Maine near the Canadian border, or on a Kansas farm, you may find it difficult to construct a jury from your immediate neighbors. You must do it by mail. Write fan letters to poets and critics you admire, and some will write you back. [Beware of letting pen-pals substitute for energy given to poems.] The best way to get good, harsh, useful criticism is to dish it out. To sharpen your ability to criticize other poets increase your observation of Rule Two.

(If you are of a certain age, you may find it difficult to retain the jury you have constructed. Old friends die, stay drunk, go crazy, become famous or obscure, wear out. You must continually reinvent the jury, but it is difficult to find good members among the young, if you are old and semi-famous. They are too impressed, and they praise bad work just because you wrote it. [As with most things in the world, there is a common converse—the young poet who wishes to convince himself of his incorruptibility, and therefore denounces every utterance that emerges from your pen or your mouth. Maim him.] You must search among old acquaintance, ex-jurors who have recovered their lost judgment, the rare young, the formerly young turned forty and no longer deferring to anybody.

(But as people have noticed in other connections one of the consequences of aging is narrowed acquaintance. And who is blind Homer's peer? Blind Homer, if he continues to take pleasure in composing verses, presumably learns to take the absent friends inside. The internal critic, harsh but fair, is known as the Muse.)

8. Be open to change, to other poetries, to poets you have disliked in the past.

(If you hate Shelley or Jarrell, be sure to reread them now and again, trying to see what others see. If you are Objective, read Fantastic. If you are Fantastic, read *Sulfur*. Polonius has been trying to get poets of his acquaintance, who love Pablo Neruda, to read Robert Pinsky's criticism, who does not. No growth without conflict!)

9. Do not date your poems. Do not submit multiply. Do not send the same poem twice to the same editor.

(It makes Polonius nervous to read a date on a poem—especially if it be a single day. He dreads the moment when he will read a poem dated "January 12, 1979, 8:02-8:17 p.m."

(It may come as a surprise, unless you have edited, that most editors *bother* over what they accept and reject. It annoys these editors when they discover that they have bothered to no avail. Therefore it is necessary to keep good records of where you have sent your poems. However, if you discover that you are devoting one-third of your time to postal flowcharts, revise your life. Marry the mailperson if you must, but remember what matters.)

10. Remember what matters.

(Remember that you love *poems*, those old stars burning in the sky forever: To His Coy Mistress, The Garden of Love, Lycidas, Ode to a Nightingale, The Return, During Wind and Rain. . . [Here let the reader supply a list.] Remember that you work not for publication, not for NEA grants, not for listing in *Poets and Writers*, not for praise, not for notoriety, not for money, not for Guggenheims, not for Pulitzers, not for Greek Islands, not for *APR*, not for Yaddo, not for tenure. Remember that you work to make a star that will burn—outside you and even for a while after you—high in the sky.

(Remember that love is serious, and death is serious, friendship, justice, and aging; remember that universities and magazines are not serious. Possibly you are serious, insofar as your poems are serious. Remember God and forget bibliographies.)

UNDER DISCUSSION
Donald Hall, General Editor

Volumes in the Under Discussion series collect reviews and essays about individual poets. The series is concerned with contemporary American and English poets about whom the consensus has not yet been formed and the final vote has not been taken. Among those to be considered are:

Elizabeth Bishop and Her Art
by Lloyd Schwartz and Sybil P. Estess

Adrienne Rich *by Jane Roberta Cooper*

Richard Wilbur *by Wendy Salinger*

Robert Bly *by Joyce Peseroff*

Allen Ginsberg *by Lewis Hyde*

Please write for further information on available editions and current prices.

Ann Arbor   **The University of Michigan Press**